Mornings with JESUS 2026

DAILY ENCOURAGEMENT *for Your* SOUL

365 DEVOTIONS

Guideposts

A Gift from Guideposts

Thank you for your purchase! We appreciate your support and want to express our gratitude with a special gift just for you.

Dive into *Spirit Lifters*, a complimentary booklet that will fortify your faith and offer solace during challenging moments. It contains 31 carefully selected verses from scripture that will soothe your soul and uplift your spirit.

Please use the QR code or go to guideposts.org/spiritlifters to download.

Mornings with Jesus 2026

Published by Guideposts
100 Reserve Road, Suite E200
Danbury, CT 06810
Guideposts.org

Copyright © 2025 by Guideposts. All rights reserved.

This book, or parts thereof, may not be reproduced, stored in a retrieval system, or transmitted in any form or by any means, electronic, mechanical, photocopying, recording, or otherwise, without the written permission of the publisher.

Cover design by Müllerhaus
Cover photo by Westend61, Getty Images
Indexed by Frances Lennie
Typeset by Aptara, Inc.

ISBN 978-1-961442-36-8 (softcover)
ISBN 978-1-961442-37-5 (epub)
ISBN 978-1-961442-38-2 (large print)

Printed and bound in the United States of America
10 9 8 7 6 5 4 3 2 1

Dear Friends,

Welcome to *Mornings with Jesus 2026*! We're excited about the 365 all-new, life-giving devotions in this year's volume. This year's writers were guided by the theme of kindness, as seen in Ephesians 4:32 (NIV): "Be kind and compassionate to one another, forgiving each other, just as in Christ God forgave you." Our beloved writers share how showing kindness and compassion to friends, family, neighbors, and strangers can lead to a life filled with love, joy, and peace. Kindness goes deeper than being nice; it stems from offering the love of Jesus to others in ways that are life changing and faith deepening.

We are grateful for the generosity of this year's contributors to *Mornings with Jesus:* Becky Alexander, Susanna Foth Aughtmon, Jeannie Blackmer, Isabella Campolattaro, Pat Butler Dyson, Gwen Ford Faulkenberry, Grace Fox, Heidi Gaul, Tricia Goyer, Pamela Toussaint Howard, Jeannie Hughes, Gloria Joyce, Jeanette Levellie, Ericka Loynes, Erin Keeley Marshall, Dianne Neal Matthews, Claire McGarry, Renee Mitchell, Cynthia Ruchti, Emily E. Ryan, Karen Sargent, Cassandra Tiersma, Barbranda Lumpkins Walls, Kristen West, and Brenda L. Yoder.

As you read each day's verse, followed by each writer's heartfelt devotion, we encourage you to consider how the ancient words of scripture and each writer's day-to-day experiences connect to your own life. We hope you will carry each day's "faith step" with you as a way to act out your faith and share Jesus's loving-kindness with the world.

Faithfully yours,
Editors of Guideposts

Especially for You!
If you would like to receive each day's *Mornings with Jesus* devotion straight to your email inbox, sign up at guideposts.org/newsletter/.

New Year's Day, Thursday, January 1

"Do not be like them, for your Father knows what you need before you ask Him." Matthew 6:8 (NIV)

New Year's Day typically is not one of reflection or planning for me. I get frustrated when I set goals that get derailed by stress or unplanned events. This past year was filled with such experiences. An automobile accident, broken relationships, and the deaths of close friends created ongoing challenges and losses. I awoke on January 1 feeling tired and ready for a new year to start.

I spent my devotional time thinking about the prior year's events. I had learned how much of life was out of my control. Could new beginnings with a fresh calendar reclaim anything? I wondered if goals for practical rhythms, including simple prayer practices, could help my overall well-being. I wrote down a few daily tasks that could sustain physical, emotional, and spiritual health no matter what the upcoming year held—exercising for five minutes each morning, taking vitamins, meeting a daily writing goal, and praying for three to five concerns. These felt achievable because they were small steps that could be built upon.

Posting the list on my bathroom mirror, I was reminded of hopeful beginnings and who gave them to me. I couldn't control my life, but there was Someone who did. Jesus already knew what the upcoming year held, including events I saw as unplanned. As I brought my needs to Him, while also caring for myself, He would meet those needs. New beginnings for a new year! —Brenda L. Yoder

Faith Step: *As you reflect on the past year, thank Jesus for always being in control. Whether you make resolutions or not, pray for Him to reveal the beginning you need.*

FRIDAY, JANUARY 2

Give thanks to the LORD, for he is good; his love endures forever.
1 Chronicles 16:34 (NIV)

NEW ENGLAND WINTERS ARE COLD, especially since we keep our thermostat on low in our house to combat the rising cost of propane. That means I'm eternally cold from October to May, even indoors. Knowing this, my husband gave me a heated vest for Christmas. It has a rechargeable battery pack that powers the coils sewn into the back of the garment, heating them up so they radiate warmth. It's an amazing invention and the perfect gift for me! Sometimes, I stop right in the middle of my busy day, close my eyes, and focus on the sensation. Taking the time to consciously bask in the warmth helps me appreciate how it envelops me with exactly what I need, protecting me from the cold.

Like all earthly things, however, it doesn't last for long. After four hours on the high setting, the battery pack becomes depleted. Because it takes a full eight hours to recharge, I have to layer up with more clothes to get through the day.

Unlike my vest, Jesus's love for me has no time limit. It endures forever. His grace is always radiating out from where He resides in my heart, spreading warmth and joy if I just stop long enough to close my eyes, focus on the sensation, and bask in the glow. No matter how much I call on Him, He never becomes depleted. Jesus constantly envelops me in the warmth of His love. —CLAIRE MCGARRY

FAITH STEP: *Put on a heated vest, get under an electric blanket, or put something on straight from the warm dryer. Close your eyes and feel Jesus's love radiate through you.*

SATURDAY, JANUARY 3

Why, my soul, are you downcast? Why so disturbed within me? Put your hope in God, for I will yet praise him, my Savior and my God. Psalm 43:5 (NIV)

WHEN I LISTED MY GOALS for the year, one was for healing of a skin condition called pityriasis rosea. But instead of writing the words out, I abbreviated my goal to "healed of pity." At first glance, I laughed at my silly sentence. On second thought, I'd created a perfect goal: to become free of feeling sorry for myself. And I know just the One who can empower me to do that: Jesus.

Jesus has many ways to heal a sickness, a situation, or a person. He also has unlimited grace for me to overcome the pity that threatens to steal my joy when things don't change as quickly or in the way I want.

When a sickness lingers, instead of questioning my worthiness to receive healing, I'd like to trust Jesus's perfect timing. When my plans fall through, I want to believe that Jesus will create better ones for me. When someone else is chosen to do the job I thought I deserved, I hope to rejoice with them and be content. My goal is to believe Jesus is at work to bring all sorts of good into my life, especially when I don't feel well.

Instead of getting a fresh sheet of paper to write my goals on, I left "healed of pity" just as it was. I think it's a worthy goal. Not only for this year but also for life. —JEANETTE LEVELLIE

FAITH STEP: *As you write out goals, make two columns. List those that only Jesus can resolve and ones you can work to achieve with Him.*

SUNDAY, JANUARY 4

If we claim to have fellowship with him and yet walk in the darkness, we lie and do not live out the truth. But if we walk in the light, as he is in the light, we have fellowship with one another, and the blood of Jesus, his Son, purifies us from all sin. 1 John 1:6–7 (NIV)

I LIVE IN A TWO-STORY townhouse, so it's a little short on sunlight on the ground floor. The builders compensated by installing many light fixtures, especially in the kitchen and connected foyer, for which there are seven light switches (I kid you not). As a matter of thrift and preference, I don't always keep all the lights blazing, which has some ramifications.

My downstairs floor is a variegated, sand-colored, textured ceramic that does an amazing job of concealing dirt. One fluorescent light is too bright for my everyday taste and reveals absolutely every smidgen of dirt. If that light isn't on—and especially if I'm not wearing my glasses—my floor looks perfectly clean. But if I really want a spotless floor, I must put on my glasses and turn on all the lights to see clearly.

God, Himself, is light. Just as my brilliant kitchen lights reveal the hidden dirt, in His light, I can see clearly how very much I need the purifying light of the world, Jesus. When I see my sin, I can gratefully repent and return to Jesus, who cleanses me from all unrighteousness (1 John 1:9). In Jesus's equalizing light, I can walk in right fellowship with God and others—and on a clean floor no less! —ISABELLA CAMPOLATTARO

FAITH STEP: *Pray for Jesus to illuminate any areas of unconfessed sin in your life. Then walk into your most brightly lit room and thank Him.*

Monday, January 5

He will cover you with his feathers, and under his wings you will find refuge; his faithfulness will be your shield and rampart. Psalm 91:4 (NIV)

You never know how you'll react in a crisis, but recently I found out. As my husband drove us to a homeschool conference in North Dakota, twelve hours into our eighteen-hour journey we hit black ice. The trailer we were pulling fishtailed violently and rolled into the ditch, threatening to pull over our truck with it.

"Hold on, everyone, we're going to roll!" he called out. Abruptly awakened from the passenger seat, I automatically shouted, "Jesus!"

Seconds later, the truck's wheels miraculously gripped the road, and the trailer astonishingly flipped back onto its wheels and jumped back onto the roadway.

I breathed a sigh of relief, glad that Jesus's attentiveness and mercy are not contingent upon the length or eloquence of my prayers but, instead, on His steadfast love and kindness.

You never know how you'll react in a crisis, but thankfully my first response was to cry out in prayer. I might have been sleeping, but Jesus wasn't. —Tricia Goyer

Faith Step: *Make an auto emergency kit. Include a flashlight, blanket, bottled water, and first-aid supplies. Include a piece of paper with Psalm 91:4 or a favorite verse written on it to calm you if you ever need to cry out to Jesus on the road.*

Tuesday, January 6

He who was seated on the throne said, "Behold, I am making all things new." Also he said, "Write this down, for these words are trustworthy and true." Revelation 21:5 (ESV)

EVERY YEAR, I SELECT A word to focus on, but this year I selected a phrase: all things new. We had lost our home and everything we owned to a wildfire that swept through our community. For almost three years, we worked through the insurance process to receive our payment to replace our contents and rebuild. It was a tedious and exhausting process where we had to create an extensive spreadsheet listing every item in our home that we could remember. My mind constantly focused on what we had lost.

Finally, we reached an agreement with our insurance company. I no longer had to add items to a seemingly endless inventory. This was a significant switch in my thought life. I could now put behind me trying to remember all we had lost and dream about our future.

As I was praying about my word for the year, I came across Jesus's promise to make all things new. Everything we will put in our home will be new to us. We will find a new couch, plates, linens, measuring cups, books, and more. This phrase seemed appropriate for me. Not just because of the new home and items that will fill it but because of the unique opportunity I have to allow Jesus to do new things in my life. The hopeful anticipation of newness was a needed shift in my daily outlook. Forgetting what was lost, I focused on the new things Jesus is doing. —JEANNIE BLACKMER

FAITH STEP: *Write in your journal about something new Jesus is doing in your life.*

WEDNESDAY, JANUARY 7

Saul's son Jonathan went to David at Horesh and helped him find strength in God. 1 Samuel 23:16 (NIV)

EVERY WEDNESDAY MORNING, A DOZEN friends and I meet on Zoom to discuss the Bible study we're doing. Afterward, the leader assigns partners with whom we share prayer requests and encourage in little ways until we meet again the following week.

I consider these women, whose age differences span thirty years, my sisters in faith. Our love for Jesus bonds us. Our Zoom room provides a safe place to be transparent without fear of being judged. We share our wins and losses, assured the others will celebrate our joys and feel our sorrows. Most of all, we commit to encouraging one another's relationship with Jesus so we can best flourish through thick and thin.

My sisters in faith demonstrated their commitment when a loved one's death left me feeling devastated. They listened with empathy as I processed my pain and then, one after another, spoke words of comfort before asking Jesus to hold me close to His heart.

They helped me find spiritual strength as I invested time and energy into the life of a local friend caught in a heartbreaking situation. They saw my emotional fatigue and asked Jesus to fill me with wisdom and discernment.

Jonathan did much the same for David. He knew David was scared for his life, so he went out of his way to find him in the wilderness. Then he spoke truth into David's life to help him regain a right perspective. By doing so, he helped David find strength in God.

That's what good friends do, right? —GRACE FOX

FAITH STEP: *Who, in Christ, is a sister in faith to you? Reach out and encourage her by Zoom or FaceTime today.*

Thursday, January 8

When pride comes, then comes disgrace, but with humility comes wisdom. Proverbs 11:2 (NIV)

WHO SAYS MULTITASKING IS A myth? I had it all figured out. Baking six dozen cookies to take to a church reception was time-consuming, but I could do other things while the cookies were in the oven. I read my devotions and ironed my jacket. I emptied the dishwasher and put a load of clothes in to wash. I answered some emails and wrote a get-well note to a friend. No matter where I was in the house, when I heard the timer go off, I'd remove the cookies and put in another sheet.

Feeling proud of my intricate timing, I decided to hop in the shower, wash my hair, towel-dry, and remove the last batch of cookies. Ten minutes. I had it down! Stepping out of the shower, I heard the timer blaring. *Perfect,* I congratulated myself. But the timer sounded odd somehow. I hustled into the kitchen, and I realized why. It was the smoke alarm!

The kitchen was filled with smoke, and my cookies were black. Something was horribly wrong with my oven. I jerked the smoking cookies out, thinking I'd need to call the repairman immediately. But then I noticed that right next to the button for bake was the button for broil. *Uh-oh. Wrong button, Pat.* In my desire to prove to myself I could do it all, I'd messed up. *Jesus, you're the only One who can do it all—that's no myth.* I had a dozen burned cookies to prove it. —PAT BUTLER DYSON

FAITH STEP: *Recall a time when your pride brought you down. Journal about it and put the page in your Bible next to Proverbs 11:2.*

FRIDAY, JANUARY 9

I praise the word of God; I trust in God, I do not fear. What can mere flesh do to me? Psalm 56:5 (NABRE)

Growing up in the northeastern part of the country, I had always loved winter. Sledding, hot cocoa, blanket snuggles, and chunky sweaters. A snow-covered town warmed my heart. However, after a diagnosis of moderate arthritis, winter was losing its charm. I quickly joined the ranks of those who could predict the weather by their joint pain. Amid a bitterly cold and icy winter, my bones and joints ached more than usual. I spent more time idly indoors, yearning for the coming of spring to ease my pain—warmer days, the vibrant colors of rebirth, happily chirping birds. My heart longed to run from the metaphorical abbey and spin in the open meadow like Fräulein Maria in *The Sound of Music*. If only my arthritic knees and seasonal allergies would cooperate.

Like Maria, I find consolation in Jesus and in song. Psalm 56 (my favorite) was both my lament and my praise to Him throughout the achy cold of winter. Unexpectedly resting with Jesus allowed Him to ease me into an unanticipated busy spring and summertime for my family. Jesus rejuvenated me. Despite my aches and pains, He sweetly prepared me with rest for the active seasons ahead. For Jesus pairs our sufferings and our joys to perfection, and He makes everything good in His time (Ecclesiastes 3:1). Spinning in the open meadow of His love, I will forever sing His praise! —Gloria Joyce

Faith Step: *Close your eyes and think of your favorite season. Imagine Jesus joining you in that beautiful place doing your favorite activity.*

SATURDAY, JANUARY 10

"Come now, let us settle the matter," says the LORD. *"Though your sins are like scarlet, they shall be as white as snow; though they are red as crimson, they shall be like wool." Isaiah 1:18 (NIV)*

THIS MORNING, I VENTURED OUT on our porch to see how much snow had fallen overnight. The once-bare tree branches were coated in sparkling frost. Every house was covered with a bright white layer of snow. Icicles hung off eaves. It looked magical.

My seven-year-old neighbor was perfecting snow angels in his front yard. "Do you want to come make some snow angels over here too?" I called. With a shout of laughter, he bounded across the street. Looking at the fluffy snow, I said, "I may need to make one with you." This made him laugh harder. We flopped down and began moving our arms and legs back and forth. He created a perfect snow angel and popped up to observe my attempt. "Your arms are too high." My snow angel looked like an overachiever with arms flung high above her head. We both laughed. Even with a funky snow angel, there was something beautiful and bright and joyful about the day.

It is amazing to know that when Jesus forgave me, He saw my heart as white as the pristine snow on my lawn. The dark blotches of sin and shame were wiped away with His willing sacrifice. When Jesus died, He made it possible for me to live a beautiful, bright, and joyful life. —SUSANNA FOTH AUGHTMON

FAITH STEP: *On white paper, write in pencil the sins that are burdening your heart. Ask Jesus to forgive you, then erase each one. Thank Jesus for making your sins as white as snow.*

Sunday, January 11

Let us keep our eyes fixed on Jesus, on whom our faith depends from beginning to end. Hebrews 12:2 (GNT)

The last time I played charades at my daughter's house, my four-year-old granddaughter stole the show. Each time Leo took a turn, which was frequently, her family knew what was coming. She would make the hand signal for movie, drop down on all fours, and start to look ferocious. One or more family members would shout, "*Lion King!*" and Leo would respond with an excited yes. A couple of times, Leo seemed about to imitate another animal, but when someone yelled "*Lion King*," she decided that was the correct answer. Even when someone guessed the answer before she made any movement, Leo couldn't resist saying yes. We all laughed and clapped as we enjoyed seeing Leo's excitement about one of her favorite movies.

That night as I went to bed, a thought played through my mind. It's not a bad idea to be fixated on a Lion King, not the Disney animated one but the One in the Bible. Jesus is called the Lion of Judah (Revelation 5:5) and King of kings (1 Timothy 6:15). What precious reminders that I always have a fierce Protector ready to battle for me, Someone who has power over anything that can touch my life. Having my thoughts fixed on Him is guaranteed to help me feel safe, secure, and loved.

The best part of having Jesus as my Lion King? There's never any charade involved, and He is always the right answer.
—Dianne Neal Matthews

Faith Step: *Jot down reasons why you love thinking about Jesus as your Lion King. Turn this activity into a prayer of praise and adoration.*

Monday, January 12

Do nothing out of selfish ambition or vain conceit. Rather, in humility value others above yourselves. Philippians 2:3 (NIV)

My son, Mason, auditioned for his high school's play, *Les Misérables*. He was elated when he landed a lead role. My daughter, Jocelyn, auditioned for her middle school's play, *Frozen*. She was heartbroken when she just got ensemble.

After Jocelyn's day of disappointment, she picked herself up, brushed herself off, committed to her part, and got excited for her brother. Hearing her brag to all her friends about his lead role and saying how proud she was of him filled me with joy.

I'm not one to verbalize my jealousy, but I sure do feel it. When wearing an old dress to a wedding, I resent the beautiful women in their fashionable clothes. As I drive by homes in my town that I know have amazing backyards with impeccable landscaping surrounding their built-in pools, envy washes over me.

Jesus never once expressed any desire for what others had. If anyone deserved better, it was Him. As King of kings, He had a right to live in a palace, draped in jewels, reigning over a kingdom that could have catered to His every whim. Yet He humbly valued others above Himself—even to Calvary (Ephesians 5:2).

Rather than listening to that voice of jealousy in my heart when others have what I want, I need to listen to the voice of Jesus speaking words of truth. When I think I deserve better, Jesus gives me the visual of my daughter valuing her brother above herself. How could I wish for anything more? —Claire McGarry

Faith Step: *Memorize Philippians 2:3 and recite it any time jealousy arises in your heart.*

Tuesday, January 13

A kind answer soothes angry feelings, but harsh words stir them up. Proverbs 15:1 (CEV)

I've never been one to jump out of bed at the first sound of the alarm. I need a slow start to my day. A morning that begins with an invitation rather than a command. This is why I used a snooze button and set my alarm for thirty minutes before I needed to wake up. The strategy was effective but not the most pleasant way to begin the day. Who wants to be jolted awake by a cacophony of alarms blaring into their ears every nine minutes? Not me—and certainly not my husband.

I finally found a better solution when I began experimenting with the alarm feature on my smartwatch. It doesn't use sound to wake me up but rather a subtle vibration on my wrist. The soft, gentle movement feels more like the wake-up taps of a loving grandmother than the harsh screams of a drill sergeant, and any negative or angry feelings I have about waking up have disappeared. My body responds, "I *get* to wake up now," rather than, "I *have* to wake up." Plus, I still get to snooze!

This shift in my morning ritual reminded me of how important it is to communicate with kindness rather than force. Jesus modeled this strategy often, speaking the truth in a firm but always gentle manner. This strategy draws me to Him even now, and it makes me want to communicate as He does—firm but kind. Even in alarming situations. —Emily E. Ryan

Faith Step: *Set an alarm for your busiest time of the day. When it chimes, let it remind you to be gentle and kind like Jesus.*

WEDNESDAY, JANUARY 14

All your robes are fragrant with myrrh and aloes and cassia; from palaces adorned with ivory the music of the strings makes you glad. Psalm 45:8 (NIV)

I SAT MOTIONLESS, STARING AT my son's silent guitar. The rich rosewood instrument seemed lost on its stand in the corner. I knew exactly how it felt. The pain of losing my son, Steven, in a car crash was more than I could bear. Tears dripped down my cheeks, knowing I would never hear him play again.

Steven had mastered almost every instrument, but the guitar was his passion. I remembered the last time our family was gathered. He played, while we belted out "Cheeseburger in Paradise." Even though the memory should have brought me happiness, the guitar only emphasized what I had lost.

Removing the instrument from its stand, I hugged it against my chest. I put it in its case and placed it in a closet. I figured if I couldn't see his guitar, I wouldn't be reminded of what would never be again.

Days later, I found myself humming one of the songs Steven had written. Then I thought about how the psalmist told us to make music to praise the LORD (Psalm 33:2). Isn't that exactly what Steven had done with his God-given musical talent?

I realized Steven's guitar was an instrument to show God glory. It didn't give me pain, nor could it take away my pain—only God could do that. I removed the guitar from the closet and strummed the strings. And for the first time in a long time when thinking about Steven, I smiled. —JEANNIE HUGHES

FAITH STEP: *Write down ways Jesus has taken away your suffering and replaced your sadness with the comfort of His love.*

Thursday, January 15

"Are not five sparrows sold for two pennies? Yet not one of them is forgotten by God. Indeed, the very hairs of your head are all numbered. Don't be afraid; you are worth more than many sparrows." Luke 12:6–7 (NIV)

STANDING AT THE WINDOW OF our cozy cottage, I stared out at the wintry scene. With temperatures well below freezing and the wind blowing amid an ice storm, no cars drove past, no delivery vans parked nearby. I saw zero activity, aside from the numerous birds gathered around our maple where the feeders hung empty. They looked hungry. And I worried—had my husband, David, and I stored enough provisions for ourselves to make it through until the weather cleared?

Getting seed out to the birds seemed daunting. A blanket of snow hid a thick layer of ice covering the walkways and road. The front and back stairs were too treacherous to consider. Then David mentioned the basement steps. Protected from the weather, they'd be the safest exit. We could help our feathered friends after all. As he made his way to the feeders, the birds scattered, then returned to feast on the nourishment they sorely needed.

I watched, giving thanks that we could take part in Jesus's safekeeping of this tiny part of His creation. As my husband stamped snow from his shoes in the mudroom, a sigh escaped my lips. I didn't need to spend my time fretting. Jesus's Word, emblazoned in my heart, reminded me I would not go hungry. To Him, I am worth many sparrows. A priceless promise, indeed. —HEIDI GAUL

FAITH STEP: *Do you know any sparrows, feathered or otherwise, in need? Set aside some time to fill your bird feeders, donate to a food pantry, or provide a meal for someone. Feed everyone with kindness as Jesus did.*

FRIDAY, JANUARY 16

*As for me, I look to the L*ORD *for help. I wait confidently for God to save me, and my God will certainly hear me.* Micah 7:7 (NLT)

MY SISTER, NAN, AND I decided to install cameras in the assisted living apartment of our ninety-year-old mother who has Alzheimer's disease. We were concerned about Mom falling and wanted to monitor her movements and the staff's care of her more closely. Mom often gets up in the middle of the night to walk aimlessly around the apartment for hours in the dark. Soon after we got the cameras, I saw Mom get up late one night and became worried that she was not safely in bed getting the rest that she needed. But then Jesus reminded me just to ask Him to leave my mother in His hands to watch over her. So I did, trusting Him to take good care of her.

Mom already knows she can trust Jesus. When she's alone and feels confused or needs assistance with a task, I frequently hear her say on camera, "Help me, Lord." And she randomly offers a "Thank you, Lord" for seemingly no particular reason throughout the day or night. I love to see and hear her do that. My mother was the one who taught me that Jesus tells us to call on Him at any time and always to give thanks. Even though Mom's memory may not be as sharp as it used to be, she remembers to call on Jesus and be grateful. I am inspired to follow her example. —BARBRANDA LUMPKINS WALLS

FAITH STEP: *What do you need Jesus to help you with today? Just say, "Help me, Jesus" and remember to tell Him, "Thank you, Lord!" when He comes through for you.*

Saturday, January 17

You have become weak, so make yourselves strong again.
Hebrews 12:12 (NCV)

As a fitness instructor, I'm always seeking new exercises for my students. Their physical challenges include back issues, heart problems, and joint replacements, so I'm constantly looking for beneficial, safe, but challenging exercises to help improve well-being and physical fitness.

Meanwhile, I'm torn between knowing I should exercise but preferring to sit and read my Bible instead during the cold winter months. Unless I'm teaching an indoor fitness program or aqua fitness at the pool, the only exercise I get is an occasional two-mile walk after church with a friend. Like most people, I'm too sedentary during the winter months. So, by the time all the winter holidays have passed, I'm ready to start moving again. Thankfully, my students are, too, and they make sure I know that they're ready to get going again ASAP. So, there's no avoiding it.

I want to be a better steward of my God-given body. Blessedly, Jesus provided a way to motivate me to get out and exercise by having me lead additional fitness classes at the community center. That way, I *have* to show up. And by creating an inspiring workout playlist composed of motivating, uplifting faith-based songs, I feel as though I'm flexing my spiritual muscles too. Plus, there's the added bonus of being able to share an encouraging message through music at the same time as we move our bodies. If I want to serve Jesus and the family of God, I need to be strong in body, mind, and spirit. —Cassandra Tiersma

Faith Step: *If you need inspiration or motivation to exercise your physical body, play some uplifting Christian music and move, praising the Lord Jesus for your God-given body.*

SUNDAY, JANUARY 18

Direct your children onto the right path, and when they are older, they will not leave it. Proverbs 22:6 (NLT)

FOR THE UMPTEENTH TIME, WE told our then-teenaged son AJ it was time to clean his bathroom. For the umpteenth time, he sighed and sing-songed, "Okaaaay." Eventually, it got done. Whenever my husband, the original Mr. Clean, supervised the operation, it got done very well. If he didn't, telltale signs of grime always remained. On one of those cleaning days, I noticed my hubby was watching television downstairs while I heard water running upstairs, the strong smell of bleach permeating the air. To my surprise, AJ was cleaning his bathroom—without supervision. "Dear, did you tell him to clean? Or did he do it on his own?" Andrew paused his program and answered, "Nope, he did it himself." We both exchanged a smirk and a raised eyebrow.

This started a pattern. AJ knew when to clean and didn't need prodding anymore. When it came to praying and reading the Bible, the same pattern emerged. At first, Andrew commanded the kids to come downstairs for Bible study. They dragged themselves to the dining room table, phones in hand (only to look up scriptures, of course), slumped into chairs, and mostly listened. Before long, when our study leader asked someone to open in prayer or read a scripture, they volunteered. Andrew and I exchanged another smirk, a raised eyebrow, and a smile. When we stuck to the process Jesus set in place for training our children in these ways, it *did* bear fruit. Now it is up to them as young adults to choose to stay on the path. —PAMELA TOUSSAINT HOWARD

FAITH STEP: *Thank Jesus that He is patient when He directs you again and again. Extend that patience to others.*

Martin Luther King Jr. Day, Monday, January 19

"Blessed are the peacemakers, for they will be called children of God."
Matthew 5:9 (NIV)

AMONG THE LONG LIST OF Martin Luther King Jr.'s accomplishments is his advocacy for the passing of the Civil Rights Act of 1964 and the Voting Rights Act of 1965. Both acts changed the course of US history forever. The only thing that eclipsed *what* MLK Jr. did is *how* he did it: peacefully. Despite being arrested twenty-nine times on charges ranging from civil disobedience to traffic violations—considered by many to be trumped-up charges—he never resorted to violence to defend himself. His constant message was this: "Hate cannot drive out hate, only love can do that." In fact, his stance of nonviolence won him the Nobel Peace Prize in 1964, making him the youngest recipient of his time, at the age of thirty-five.

As a minister, activist, and one of the most famous modern-day pacifists, Martin Luther King Jr. followed Jesus, the best example of all time. Jesus knew that physical confrontation and condemnation made others defensive and combative. Instead, He used love and tenderness.

Even when Christ was arrested on His own trumped-up charges, He never once fought back or uttered a word in His own defense (Isaiah 53:7), even when whipped and beaten.

To celebrate the legacy of Martin Luther King Jr., may we model his Christlike peacefulness and be an example of love in all situations. —CLAIRE MCGARRY

FAITH STEP: *If you're inclined to respond to someone with condemnation, try peace instead. Take note of the outcome.*

Tuesday, January 20

God has given both his promise and his oath. These two things are unchangeable because it is impossible for God to lie. Therefore, we who have fled to him for refuge can have great confidence as we hold to the hope that lies before us. This hope is a strong and trustworthy anchor for our souls. It leads us through the curtain into God's inner sanctuary. Hebrews 6:18–19 (NLT)

MY HUSBAND AND I HAVE a dream to cruise the Great Loop, a 6,000-mile yacht adventure through the eastern part of the United States.

When the time comes, we'll launch from Lake Michigan and make our way to the Mississippi River, then south to the Gulf of Mexico. We'll cross the Gulf to Florida, then navigate around it and back north up the Atlantic coast. Finally, we'll head west through the United States or Canada and back to the Great Lakes, where we'll complete the trip when we "cross our wake" where we began.

Along the way, we'll often anchor overnight to avoid higher dock fees. If done skillfully, anchoring can be safe and more economical. To anchor well, we'll need to master discerning whether the anchor takes hold deep on the seabed.

A lot of faith is involved in considering the Great Loop adventure. For now, we're anchoring our hopes in Jesus's provision and care for this dream we trust will happen someday.

The dream is already teaching me to anchor myself with Jesus and discern if my hold is truly on Him even when I can't see.
—ERIN KEELEY MARSHALL

FAITH STEP: *When it comes to a concern in your life, consider if you're anchoring yourself solidly on Jesus. Choose to believe He can keep you secure even when you can't see.*

WEDNESDAY, JANUARY 21

"If we let him go on like this, everyone will believe in him, and then the Romans will come and take away both our temple and our nation."
John 11:48 (NIV)

WE RECENTLY CELEBRATED A FAMILY anniversary—the day a match was found for a kidney transplant for my nephew. While he and his wife raced to the transplant hospital almost four hours away, the life-giving kidney donated by a grieving family began its almost 1,500-mile flight from the donor's hospital.

Any number of things could have delayed either the road trip or the flight. All had to happen precisely for the kidney to be viable when it reached the operating room. After waiting years for a rare match, how heartbreaking it would have been if it had been delayed too long!

We often wonder about Jesus's delay in responding to save Lazarus from death. In fact, His friend had been dead four days before Jesus reached him and called Lazarus out of his tomb (John 11:1–44). Verse 15 indicates Jesus let His disciples know He was glad for the delay, so they would finally believe.

But there's more to the story, as there always is with Jesus. Raising Lazarus was the inciting incident that pushed Jesus toward the cross. Those who witnessed the scene raced the two miles back to Jerusalem to report what had happened, what Jesus had done. The leaders were livid, fearful. "So from that day on they plotted to take his life" (John 11:53, NIV).

Christ's gift for Lazarus directly led to His ultimate sacrifice. We could say Jesus was the donor who gave us life. What response can we have but gratitude? —CYNTHIA RUCHTI

FAITH STEP: *Take a moment to thank Jesus for counting the cost and sacrificing His all for you.*

Thursday, January 22

> By wisdom a house is built, and through understanding it is established.
> Proverbs 24:3 (NIV)

"So much hard-earned, God-honoring wisdom," a friend messaged me after I was a guest on her podcast. I was the episode's expert as a therapist and someone with personal experience on a difficult parenting subject I rarely discussed in open forums. My expertise was professional and personal. Yet I felt vulnerable sharing personal struggles when I didn't know how they would be received. But the phrase in the text, "hard-earned wisdom," made me pause. Others rarely validated my most painful life experiences because few people were privy to them. The story I shared in the interview was one of the most challenging I had walked through. Had wisdom grown from that heartache? As a counselor, I knew it was important to share what I had learned so someone else would not feel alone as I had. As a parent, I worried about what others would think of me.

As I sat in silence that evening, I felt Jesus impress upon me that my pain had a purpose. Wisdom and encouragement evolved from the trial. As difficult as it was, my experience was a gift to be shared with others that could not be curated elsewhere. I felt gratitude as I accepted the gift of my friend's words that God never wastes difficult times. Being vulnerable and sharing problems are difficult, but hard-earned, God-honoring wisdom is Jesus's gift for life's sorrows. Wisdom from life's problems—a hard-earned treasure.
—Brenda L. Yoder

Faith Step: *Take a quiet moment to list the lessons you have learned from your difficult seasons, thanking Jesus for the wisdom you've gained. Be willing to share the gift of hard-earned, God-honoring wisdom when someone needs it.*

Friday, January 23

Therefore encourage one another and build each other up, just as in fact you are doing. 1 Thessalonians 5:11 (NIV)

HALFWAY THROUGH MY WORKDAY, I was feeling pretty weary. Not even a strong afternoon coffee provided the kind of pick-me-up I needed at that moment. Suddenly, a text flashed across my phone screen. *Cara!* "Prayed for you this morning." Five words strung together and accented with a heart emoji at the end. My spirit soared and a smile came across my face as I thought of this faithful friend I'd gotten to know so well over the last couple of months. My weariness melted away. How could Cara have known this was exactly the encouragement I needed at this moment?

People need encouragement. We need one another. It's easy for me to get distracted cycling through my daily to-do lists, laser focused on what I need to accomplish instead of being tuned in to who or what the Holy Spirit brings to mind. By encouraging others, I'm intentionally letting that person know I care and that they hold value and worth in my eyes. It probably didn't take Cara much time to type and send that text, but the benefit from it made all the difference for me. Her simple words pointed me back to Jesus because she had prayed for me. That text replaced my weariness with encouragement.

So how did Cara know just what I needed and when to give it? She didn't, of course, but Jesus did. Jesus is the ultimate pick-me-up. —KRISTEN WEST

FAITH STEP: *Ask God to show you someone who needs prayer and an encouraging text, then press* send.

SATURDAY, JANUARY 24

I will praise you, Lord my God, with all my heart; I will glorify your name forever. Psalm 86:12 (NIV)

DURING DINNER WITH SEVERAL FRIENDS from college, one of my classmates shared that his wife calls him "Mr. Wonderful." We all laughed and teased him about that. But later I thought that moniker was a great way for my classmate's spouse to affirm and express her love and appreciation for him and who he is to her.

In Psalm 86, King David does the same thing as my friend's wife. He gives honor and glory to the Lord for His wonderful works and for who He is. David says in verse 10 (NIV), "For you are great and do marvelous deeds; you alone are God." I, too, must praise Jesus for all He does for me. From waking me up each morning and protecting me as I go here and there throughout the day to providing everything I need and then some, Jesus deserves my constant thanks and gratitude. I know I often take so many things He does for granted, but I pray that the Lord will remind me that He isn't obligated to take care of me because I'm so wonderful. He does it because of His unfailing love, not just for me but for all His people. That's more than enough for Jesus to be my Mr. Wonderful, now and forever. —BARBRANDA LUMPKINS WALLS

FAITH STEP: *What wonderful things has Jesus done for you today? Write them down and praise Him for His loving-kindness.*

Sunday, January 25

For this is the love of God, that we keep His commandments.
1 John 5:3 (NKJV)

I PICKED UP MY COFFEE at the drive-through. As soon as the steaming cup contacted my palm, I knew my order was wrong. Again. A cup of half coffee and half cream should not be so hot—or so complicated. It's only two ingredients. The barista had steamed the cream, even though I'd asked her not to. I could drive away with my scalding drink, but it was late, I was two hours from home, and I needed a caffeine pick-me-up now, not after it cooled. With an apology, I asked the barista to remake my order. She explained so much cream would make my coffee cold and asked if I wanted an iced coffee. I smiled and sighed. "No. Just half coffee, half cream, please."

I get it. My drink is too simple. If I had ordered a venti iced skinny hazelnut macchiato with sugar-free syrup and an extra shot, light ice, and no whip, the drink would align with the intricate orders the barista was accustomed to.

How can something as simple as two ingredients be so complicated? I bet Jesus wonders the same thing—not about my coffee but about my walk with Him. Following Jesus requires two basic ingredients: to love and obey. But sometimes I add more and whip up a concoction I call "Good Christian Girl."

Study the Bible daily. Pray long prayers. Never miss church. Serve more. Don't watch that movie. Don't sin. All are good, but turning Jesus's simple order into a complicated checklist changes the flavor.

Love. Obey. That order is easier to swallow. —KAREN SARGENT

FAITH STEP: *Make a coffee date with a friend and share what Jesus has been teaching you lately.*

Monday, January 26

Timely advice is lovely, like golden apples in a silver basket. To one who listens, valid criticism is like a gold earring or other gold jewelry.
Proverbs 25:11–12 (NLT)

Within a few weeks of one another, three people gave me the same feedback: "You don't need to go into details and explain yourself." I was hurt because I listened to every single detail they shared whenever they talked to me. Yet they were quick to interrupt or hurry me along, signaling they got the gist of what I was saying. I'm sure they meant well by their comments, but I didn't agree with what they said.

It's not that I can't take feedback. I've received tough critiques before. Early in my career, one of my managers challenged my superfluous writing that produced multiple-page documents. She urged me to whittle down my text to one-page executive summaries. She clearly saw how much I loved words. That love earned me a playful nickname, "Wordy McWordy." Even though my writing style worked well in previous jobs, I embraced my manager's feedback and adjusted my style accordingly.

Feedback from other people may or may not be helpful, but the one person whose feedback is always true and edifying is Jesus. Whether I encounter rebuke or gain a new perspective from His Word, I hope to graciously accept His feedback and make whatever changes He says are needed in my life. Perhaps I could call myself "His Word McWordy" as a reminder. —Ericka Loynes

Faith Step: *Do you have a tough time hearing feedback from others or Jesus? Reflect on how you can embrace critiques to be your best self.*

TUESDAY, JANUARY 27

I will instruct you and teach you in the way you should go; I will counsel you with my loving eye on you. Psalm 32:8 (NIV)

MY DAUGHTER AND I OFTEN laugh about the Minecraft incident. Several years ago, my eight-year-old grandson decided to teach me to play his favorite video game during my upcoming visit. I thought that was sweet—but talk about pressure. Roman kept telling his mom beforehand that he just knew Nana would be a great player. After a brief session, however, he proclaimed me the world's worst Minecraft player. (I had chopped some leaves off a tree with my sword but didn't find any gold or weapons.) A couple of days later, Roman decided that his faulty teaching had been the problem, and he tried again. This time he instructed me simply to have my avatar follow his, but I couldn't even do that. And so ended his dream of transforming Nana into a worthy Minecraft opponent.

I'm thankful that Roman still loves me even though I'm pathetic at playing video games. I'm even more grateful that Jesus loves me even when I'm not as teachable as I could be. Jesus is transforming me to live a life worthy of my calling as His follower. He wants me to think, speak, and behave in a way that honors God, to bear fruit for His kingdom, and to grow in knowledge and understanding (Colossians 1:10). Some days I'm a poor student. But Jesus continues to instruct me and never gives up. —DIANNE NEAL MATTHEWS

FAITH STEP: *Have you ever felt as if you're not living up to Jesus's expectations? Don't play that game! Trust His unconditional love and His promise to lead and teach you day by day.*

WEDNESDAY, JANUARY 28

You thrill me, LORD, with all you have done for me! I sing for joy because of what you have done. Psalm 92:4 (NLT)

I LOVE RODEOS. I GREW up going to them, and every year we go to one in Denver. The wildness of the whole event thrills me. This year, I sat by a boy and his sister. His parents, juggling a baby, sat in front of them. When the lights went out and fifty women on horses, with saddles lit up, carrying flags galloped in and around the arena to loud music, he looked at me with his eyes wide open. Obviously, this was his first rodeo. Throughout the competition, his jaw would drop, and he would turn his face to me, shocked and delighted. I wish I had a picture of his face when the bull riding event started.

The day before the rodeo, I heard a podcast about the wildness of Jesus. His existence on earth didn't seem predictable and safe. He performed unbelievable miracles. Imagine Him, rubbing mud on the eyes of a blind man. When the man washed off the mud, he could see (John 9:6–7). I'd love to have a photo of that moment too. He must have been overjoyed about Jesus, the Son of God, who healed him.

The combination of the podcast and the wild rodeo that stunned and delighted the boy beside me challenged me to boldly share my faith with others. I truly do want to see the thrill on loved ones' faces when they realize what Jesus has done for them.

—JEANNIE BLACKMER

FAITH STEP: *Who could you talk to about Jesus? Take a risk, and start the conversation today.*

Thursday, January 29

When Jesus returned, a crowd welcomed him, for they were all expecting him. Luke 8:40 (NIV)

Our daughter Esther recently bought her first new home as a single mom. Rather, an old home. Super old. When the realtor showed the darling two-story Cape Cod to Esther, she said, "It's in good shape. It just needs some TLC." Of course, the realtor didn't mention that her definition of the word *some* was more than most people's.

The first time the heat went out in Esther's house, snow and ice were gusting southward from Lake Erie into our Illinois prairie. Schools were closed. Supermarket shelves boasted no milk, bread, or batteries. And White's Cooling & Heating repairmen had to work overtime.

"Can we stay with you guys for a day or two until our heater gets fixed?" Esther texted.

I knew she asked only out of politeness. Esther knows our home is always open to her and the grandkids.

"Of course you can!" I replied. I pulled a second pound of hamburger from the freezer for tacos, put sheets on the extra beds, and set the table with our special occasion goblets in each person's favorite color.

Similar to how our home is always open to our daughter, Jesus is always available to me. He's free to talk and listen 24/7 (Matthew 28:20). He shares divine wisdom through His Word (Psalm 119:105). He strengthens me through His Holy Spirit (Ephesians 3:16). And every time I ask for His help, I hear His sweet voice, "Of course I'll help you. You're family." —Jeanette Levellie

Faith Step: *Think of all the ways Jesus is available to you. In a prayer of commitment, make yourself available to Him.*

Friday, January 30

When Jesus spoke again to the people, he said, "I am the light of the world. Whoever follows me will never walk in darkness, but will have the light of life." John 8:12 (NIV)

I STRUGGLE WITH DEPRESSION AND anxiety. Someone once said this is like having Tigger and Eeyore living inside the same body, which is pretty accurate. This morning I woke up before it was daylight in the fetal position. As I tried to go back to sleep, my heart slammed against my chest and echoed in my ears. It seemed like ants were crawling through my veins. I wanted to jump out of my skin (anxiety), but inertia and exhaustion held me to the bed (depression). It's a hard place to rest. The worst of both worlds.

It was into this world of human misery that Jesus came. As God, He didn't have to take on flesh, but He did. Jesus willingly stepped inside our skin and walked around, experiencing the inner life we know with all its emotional complexity, as well as the tangible, physical limits of being human. Jesus became one of us to rescue us from these bodies of death (John 11:25–26).

As the sun started to peek over the horizon this morning, the light reminded me of Him, staring into the darkness, the howling void of our fallen world, and not turning away. With Jesus as my Light, it's an easy place to rest. The Light of life. The best of both worlds. Even Eeyore would agree. —GWEN FORD FAULKENBERRY

FAITH STEP: *Make a Pinterest board or a magazine/photo collage called "Light." Fill it with images that remind you of ways Jesus, our Light, overcomes the darkness.*

SATURDAY, JANUARY 31

Religion that God our Father accepts as pure and faultless is this: to look after orphans and widows in their distress and to keep oneself from being polluted by the world. James 1:27 (NIV)

"How was your chicken, Nannie?" I asked.

"That ole raw chicken was so burned you couldn't eat it," she mumbled, face scrunched in a scowl.

I chuckled. Only Nannie could use *raw* and *burned* in the same description.

Nannie lived in the nursing home where I worked as activity director throughout college. At eighty-nine, her body was spry, and her mind was sharp. Her spirit, however, seemed angry and troubled. The widow made negative comments about everything and everybody, pushing back potential friendships with other residents. Perhaps she had offended her family also. Her son lived five miles away but never visited once during my years there.

Even though Nannie scared me at first, my job description was to relate positively to all residents. I pushed my fear aside and reached out. Soon Nannie was helping me set up for activities. She fed the aquarium fish on my days off. She got up early, dressed, and waited for my arrival. We eventually became friends, and I took her negativity with a grain of salt.

Jesus looked after the widows while on earth. He defended them against the teachers of the law (Mark 12:40). He uplifted a widow for her generosity (Mark 12:42–43). He showed compassion by raising a widow's son back to life (Luke 7:12–15).

I'm glad I got to be like Jesus with Nannie. Our friendship blessed and enriched both of our lives. —BECKY ALEXANDER

FAITH STEP: *Look for an opportunity to be like Jesus as you reach out to a widow at work, at church, or in your family.*

Sunday, February 1

Older women ... admonish the young women ... Titus 2:3–4 (NKJV)

I ALWAYS LOVED MY GRANDMA'S hands. As a child, I remember crawling into her lap, holding her hands, and admiring them as I traced the wrinkles and veins with my fingers. Grandma's hands reflected a lifetime of wisdom, experience, and faithfulness. Years of loving her husband, raising her children, serving her community, and helping her neighbors. Her beautiful hands and her presence helped shape my life as she modeled the love of Jesus.

Now having crossed the threshold of middle age, I'm a grandma. I fall into that blessed bracket of older women that Paul mentioned in Titus. Those verses inspire me to let Jesus use me in unique and purposeful ways as I connect with younger women who need my voice, my experience, my stories, and my wisdom.

One of my greatest callings as an older woman is to invest in those coming behind me by authentically sharing my testimony and insights. How did I navigate sleepless nights with a colicky baby? How did I prioritize my time with Jesus when days were hectic and the calendar was full? What did I do to stay encouraged during "for better or worse" in my marriage? I don't need a stage or podium for this assignment, just a willingness to be used by Jesus—one conversation at a time.

How do you know if you're qualified to be an older woman? Just look at your hands! —KRISTEN WEST

FAITH STEP: *Trace your hand on a sheet of paper, and pray for Jesus to show you five younger women you can encourage. Write their names on the fingers, and reach out to each of them this week.*

Monday, February 2

Taste and see that the LORD is good; blessed is the one who takes refuge in him. Psalm 34:8 (NIV)

For Christmas I like to give experiences, so I gave my husband, Zane, a certificate for an adventure dinner. I made a reservation at a restaurant in Leadville, Colorado, called the Tennessee Pass Cookhouse. The dinner is in a yurt (a portable circular building) that you cross-country ski one mile up to at the top of a pass called Tennessee Pass. After dining, using a headlamp, you ski back down.

Neither of us is an experienced cross-country skier, but being comfortable on downhill skis, we quickly adapted to the skinny, wobbly equipment. We started the trek at dusk. The snow carpeted the ground, and a full moon slowly appeared. It was magical. The yurt was cozy, and dinner was delicious. I thanked God for giving us our senses because they can bring us such delight.

Jesus often performed miracles that impacted people's senses. He made the disciples breakfast on the beach (John 21:12–13). He allowed the blind to see (Matthew 9:27–29). He stopped the wind and calmed the waters (Matthew 8:23–27). Experiences that remind me He is good.

The ski down from the yurt was challenging. It had been a warm day, so the ski track had melted and then frozen with no new snow, making it an icy course. We slipped and slid, feeling awkward at times, but laughing together. That night we experienced all our God-given senses, gifting us with a memory for a lifetime.
—Jeannie Blackmer

Faith Step: *Go for an adventure walk with Jesus tonight with a flashlight or headlamp, and tune in to your different senses. What do you see, hear, feel, and smell that gives you delight?*

TUESDAY, FEBRUARY 3

Each of you should give what you have decided in your heart to give, not reluctantly or under compulsion, for God loves a cheerful giver.
2 Corinthians 9:7 (NIV)

MY FOUR-YEAR-OLD GRANDDAUGHTER, LEXI, AND her two-year-old brother, Josh, were playing with friends. I entered the room as the two youngest children began tussling over a stuffed dinosaur. Instinct told me to step in and fix it, but I stepped back instead when I saw Lexi approach the dueling duo. The words she spoke brought a mile-wide smile to my heart.

"Sharing is caring," said Lexi. "That's the emergency word when people aren't sharing." Wisdom spoken from the mouth of babes, right?

Sharing is caring. No matter the language we speak, these three words translate as kindness. Sharing our time with a friend who needs a listening ear or soft shoulder shows care about her emotional well-being. Sharing our hard-earned expertise with a younger person following a path like ours shows care about his future and success. Sharing finances or material resources with the disenfranchised shows care for their physical needs. But there's one caveat needed to convey the intended message: a cheerful heart.

If one toddler had shared the stuffie by heaving it at the other, I doubt the recipient would have interpreted his behavior as caring and kind. The same is true if I respond to someone's need with an inner eye-rolling or a sigh of resignation.

Sharing is caring, especially when done with a cheerful heart. Jesus modeled this well. And with Jesus's help, I can do likewise. —GRACE FOX

FAITH STEP: *Examine your attitude concerning sharing. Decorate a note card with the words "Sharing Is Caring" and place it where you will see it often to remind yourself to be a cheerful giver.*

WEDNESDAY, FEBRUARY 4

"Teacher, which is the greatest commandment in the Law?" Jesus replied: "'Love the Lord your God with all your heart and with all your soul and with all your mind.'... And the second is like it: 'Love your neighbor as yourself.'" Matthew 22:36–39 (NIV)

"HI, NEIGHBOR!" A LITTLE VOICE called out. Five-year-old Maddie waved furiously from the yard beside mine. I threw my hand high in the air and waved back with equal enthusiasm. Her sweet greeting always made me smile.

I am blessed with good neighbors on both sides—to the right, Maddie's family in a red brick house, and to the left, a man named Ben in a white wooden house. We don't see each other daily and only chat occasionally. But we know if help is needed, it's a few short steps away.

During a recent ice storm, that proved to be true. Maddie appeared at my front door one evening wearing a hat, gloves, snowsuit, and boots. She handed me a container of homemade chili for supper, which my husband and I ate gratefully. Then Ben slipped on his slick driveway, hit his head, and dislocated a finger. My husband and I called 911 and cared for him until the emergency vehicle arrived.

I encountered kindness in two directions that week. I received kindness from Maddie and extended kindness to Ben. Those interactions allowed me to experience Jesus's command to love my neighbor as myself on a local level. And through them, Jesus gave me a warm nudge to show kindness more often beyond my corner of the community. I'd just have to wait for the ice to melt.
—BECKY ALEXANDER

FAITH STEP: *No matter the weather today, pray for your neighbors and then do something nice to warm their hearts.*

Thursday, February 5

> Give all your worries and cares to God, for he cares about you.
> —1 Peter 5:7 (NLT)

When Ron and I married, I inherited my mother's piano, which she'd had since childhood. She, my sisters, and I played it in our youth. As a young bride, I imagined my future children carrying on the special tradition of playing the family piano.

Our four kids grew up. I didn't play the piano anymore, and only one of our children took piano lessons. The heirloom became a household nemesis instead. I kept the piano with respect for its family memories, hoping one of my kids would want it when they moved out, but none of them did.

Did I dare get rid of it? I felt guilty even thinking about it! Though it seemed like a trivial dilemma, I asked Jesus for the courage to sell our piano. After weeks on Facebook Marketplace, the Klein family purchased it.

When they picked it up, I was delighted as they carefully dismantled each piece. The Klein family sang gospel music and promised the piano would be well used. It seemed as though Jesus handpicked them to become our heirloom's new family. His kindness washed over me as they gingerly carried it out. Imagine Jesus caring about something as silly as an old piano!

Weeks later, Mr. Klein texted a photo of the piano, saying how much his family loved it. I smiled. Jesus released me from the guilt of letting go of my family heirloom. He replaced it with divine comfort, showing me He cared about those who treasured the piano, both past and present. —Brenda L. Yoder

Faith Step: *Is there something trivial you're hesitant to pray about? Bring it boldly to Jesus, knowing He cares about the request because He cares for you.*

Friday, February 6

Be merciful, even as your Father is merciful. Luke 6:36 (ESV)

GUILTY CONFESSION: I'VE BEEN KNOWN to check my phone when I'm sitting at a light in heavy traffic. I suspect that maybe, just maybe, I'm not alone (wink). Living on Florida's popular Suncoast, I'm sometimes caught in traffic backed up through a few light cycles, only creeping up slowly before we finally get through. I can get distracted by my phone in an attempt to pass time.

Usually, I'm very alert and scoot along as soon as the traffic moves. Sometimes, the person in the car behind me will angrily lean on the horn and glare. Other times, someone beeps gently to prompt me to go. Occasionally, I have been humbled and amazed to casually glance up to notice cars way ahead of me while cars behind me wait patiently for me to get a move on. No honking at all. I'm stunned by their patience at my pokiness.

I usually wave an enthusiastic apology with genuine gratitude. As sappy as it sounds, it touches my heart because it's so merciful and kind that it reminds me of Jesus. I want to believe that Jesus looks on my failures with the same kind of long-suffering tolerance.

The mercy these fellow motorists extend to me motivates me to be more patient with other pokey, distracted drivers. I pray Jesus will enable me to extend that same mercy in other more high-stakes situations too. —ISABELLA CAMPOLATTARO

FAITH STEP: *Think of a recent instance when someone showed you mercy. Are you extending that same mercy to others? Pray for Jesus to help you.*

SATURDAY, FEBRUARY 7

> *For physical training is of some value, but godliness has value for all things, holding promise for both the present life and the life to come.* 1 Timothy 4:8 (NIV)

I JUST DOWNLOADED A NEW fitness app on my phone. It has short workout demonstrations and encouraging instructors. I'm trying to rebuild my strength. I have been wrestling with an autoimmune disease that weakens my muscles. My muscles weren't that strong to begin with. Sometimes it feels easier just to lie on the couch. But I know strength is built gradually, and if I want to be strong in the future, I better keep working out.

My muscles aren't the only things that need exercise. My spirit needs a daily workout too. I want to work God's Word down into my spirit. I need to build my spiritual muscles with prayer and fasting. Fasting is a discipline that doesn't come easy to me. I really love snacks. But I know spiritual disciplines are built gradually. To be close to Jesus in the future, spending time with Him now is essential.

Jesus knows I'm weak both physically and spiritually. He understands the areas of my body, mind, and spirit that need work. The good news is that when I am weak, His strength shines through me (2 Corinthians 12:9–10). Even better, He promises to strengthen me and uphold me with His right hand (Isaiah 41:10). He wants me to grow in His strength and power (Colossians 2:6). Working out daily with Jesus, I will! —SUSANNA FOTH AUGHTMON

FAITH STEP: *Spend time today in spiritual exercise. Read 1 Timothy 4, and ask Jesus what disciplines you need to practice to grow stronger in Him.*

Sunday, February 8

I led them with cords of human kindness, with ties of love. To them I was like one who lifts a little child to the cheek, and I bent down to feed them. Hosea 11:4 (NIV)

A FEW YEARS AGO, MY friend Michelle and I embarked on a transformative journey by starting a daily podcast in which we read and discuss the Bible. We started this project with the hope of helping more people read and understand God's Word, but the personal growth within us has blossomed into something we hadn't fully anticipated.

As my friend and I daily read and discuss God's Word, my grasp of the Bible's overarching themes has become clearer, and my relationship with Jesus has also deepened. One joyful discovery has been that despite humanity's repeated sin and rebellion, God's unwavering kindness consistently shines through. This realization has reshaped how I view the Bible. What once seemed like burdensome laws are now understood as divine guidelines meant to sanctify and prepare believers for communion with a holy God.

Each passage and story we explore in our podcast continues to layer my appreciation for Jesus's enduring grace and mercy. It serves as a reminder that no matter how often I stray, His kindness remains a steadfast bridge, inviting me back into His loving embrace. By helping others understand God's Word and know Jesus better, I have been truly blessed. How marvelous! —TRICIA GOYER

FAITH STEP: *Take a moment to journal how you have experienced Jesus's gentle guidance through His Word. Let this understanding of divine kindness inspire you to extend a simple act of kindness to someone this week.*

Monday, February 9

> *The LORD their God will save his people on that day as a shepherd saves his flock. They will sparkle in his land like jewels in a crown.*
> Zechariah 9:16 (NIV)

ON A RARE SUNNY MORNING after many gray, rainy days, my husband, John, pointed out something sparkling in the distance. Looking out the window, I saw glistening in a tall tree about a block away from our house. Not just a single sparkle either. The towering evergreen shimmered in the breeze, glinting in the sun. What could be causing all that radiance?

Mesmerized, I had difficulty tearing my gaze away during our daily devotions that morning. Shiny object syndrome! I had to exert willpower to focus on our devotional lesson. When we finished, the investigative journalist in me embarked on an exploratory walk to solve the mystery of the sparkling tree. When I peered up into the grand evergreen, I discovered its branches were bedazzled with ribbons of iridescent, holographic, reflective tape. Aha! What had been intended to deter woodpeckers had attracted a human seeking answers.

What would it look like, I wondered, if my life reflected the light of the Son like that? Just as that tree captivated and drew my attention to it, I want to live a life that sparkles and draws people's attention to Jesus. My intent is to reflect Jesus's radiance to the world. I can't help but praise Him for showing me the lesson of a sparkling, shimmering tree. —CASSANDRA TIERSMA

FAITH STEP: *Put on something sparkly, perhaps some glitter nail polish. Every time it catches your eye, pray that Jesus will inspire you to reflect His radiance to the world.*

TUESDAY, FEBRUARY 10

Praise be to the God and Father of our Lord Jesus Christ, the Father of compassion and the God of all comfort, who comforts us in all our troubles, so that we can comfort those in any trouble with the comfort we ourselves receive from God. 2 Corinthians 1:3–4 (NIV)

"ARE YOU OK?" THOSE THREE simple words, texted during an ice storm, meant more than my close friend could guess. When loved ones reach out to me, I'm reassured and strengthened by their concern. It warms my heart, and I bask in the cozy hug of their kindness.

I adore historic architecture, so to maintain our old farmhouse's integrity, I've kept the original wavy-glass windows and resisted the temptation to install insulation. As a result, when winter offers up her bitterest days, my sweet cottage can turn quite chilly.

Thus, when power outages leave friends' homes without heat, I understand their helplessness and discomfort. I might not be able to restore their electricity, but just as Jesus comforts me through friends, I am blessed to offer my warmth and caring.

Jesus understands me and my varied trials. His empathy and compassion are boundless. Whether I face illness, loneliness, ice storms, or any other trouble, I can lean in to the warmth of His love and find comfort. And, yes, because of Him, I'm more than OK. —HEIDI GAUL

FAITH STEP: *Make a list with three columns. In the first, name some challenges you've encountered in recent years. In the next, record the ways Jesus offered you comfort. In the last, name people you know who are facing troubles and ways you can provide comfort.*

WEDNESDAY, FEBRUARY 11

No one has ever seen God; but if we love one another, God lives in us and his love is made complete in us. 1 John 4:12 (NIV)

EARLY IN HER FIRST TRIMESTER, while her pregnancy was still a secret, my daughter Kelli called to tell me she had received the best compliment of her life. An elderly woman sitting at a table in a coffee shop told her, "You're absolutely glowing." Kelli smiled and shared her secret with the perceptive stranger, who quickly responded, "Oh no, honey. You're glowing with the love of Jesus." What a compliment indeed!

I tried to imagine what the woman might have observed in Kelli that allowed her to see Jesus. Perhaps as the woman entered the coffee shop, Kelli held the door and let her go first. While standing in line, maybe Kelli struck up a conversation with someone behind her. As she placed her order, she probably said "please" and "thank you" and put money in the tip jar. Looking for a table, I can see her smiling and making eye contact with people she didn't know.

Kelli didn't walk into the shop with a Jesus girl T-shirt, Christian tattoos, a Bible, or other visible signs of her beliefs. Yet a stranger saw the love of Jesus in her. As her mom, that is the best compliment of my life too. —KAREN SARGENT

FAITH STEP: *Wherever your day takes you, look for Jesus in someone. Make it a point to stop and tell them so.*

Thursday, February 12

If we confess our sins, he is faithful and just and will forgive us our sins and purify us from all unrighteousness. 1 John 1:9 (NIV)

We have a designated kitchen drawer that holds seldom used items that my husband and I don't know where else to put. We toss paper clips, rubber bands, and birthday candles into what we call the "junk drawer." If one of us can't find something, the first question is, "Did you check the junk drawer?" When I opened it today, it was crammed so full, the contents were totally unmanageable. I immediately got busy cleaning it out one item at a time.

As I peered at that random, jumbled mess of useless and unneeded items, I couldn't help but imagine what a designated drawer for my spiritual sins might look like. My sins were also a jumbled mess. Sometimes I commit a sin without thinking about it. Perhaps something I should have done for someone but didn't. I'm bad about using excuses to justify my sins. "I'm too tired" or "There will be plenty of volunteers there." At times I'm not even out of the church parking lot before I've spoken ill about someone. And talk about the thoughts that run through my head!

Thank goodness for Jesus! By confession of my sins, I receive forgiveness. Because of Him, I'm able to keep the contents of my spiritual drawer manageable. —Jeannie Hughes

Faith Step: *Commit to cleaning a too-full drawer today. As you throw away items, confess every sin you can think of to Jesus, then thank Him for forgiving you and making you clean.*

Friday, February 13

Little children, let us stop just saying we love people; let us really love them, and show it by our actions. 1 John 3:18 (TLB)

I TURNED ONTO THE DRIVEWAY leading to my grandkids' school, and a man stepping from his car grabbed my attention. Wearing a coal black suit and a pristine white shirt, he carried a generous bouquet of red roses. My curiosity kicked into gear. Maybe his wife worked at the school, and he wanted to surprise her for Valentine's Day. Or maybe he planned to propose to one of the staff members. When I looked in my rearview mirror, I saw that instead of walking toward the school, he had turned into the adjacent small cemetery. Now I wondered even more about his story. Was he continuing an annual tradition of giving flowers to his loved one even though she had passed away? Or had he waited to start the practice until after she'd died?

The image of that sharply dressed man walking into a cemetery with a huge bouquet stayed imprinted on my mind. I couldn't see his face, so I can't help wondering if he wore an expression of regret that he had not expressed his love more often, before it was too late. I hope that was not the case. As in all things, Jesus is my ultimate role model. His loving words and actions impacted my life for eternity, so I want to intentionally share Him with others. On Valentine's Day and every day, I want to *really* love those Jesus has placed in my life while I can. —DIANNE NEAL MATTHEWS

FAITH STEP: *Who in your life needs to know they are loved? Ask Jesus to inspire you on how to do a loving gesture for that person this week.*

VALENTINE'S DAY, SATURDAY, FEBRUARY 14

See what great love the Father has lavished on us, that we should be called children of God! And that is what we are! 1 John 3:1 (NIV)

I SPECIFIED MY VALENTINE'S DAY preference early in my forty-four-year marriage. "Flowers are pretty, and jewelry is nice, but I love, love, love turtles." I was talking about those sweet treats made of crunchy pecans and creamy caramel, covered in milk chocolate.

So, for our first decade together, Tim gave me a big heart-shaped box of turtles each February 14. I could stretch the gift for several months if I rationed myself to one or two pieces per week. I looked forward to replenishing my stash when the final bite was gone.

One Valentine's Day, Tim handed me two rectangular boxes of my favorite candy. "These hold more turtles than the heart-shaped boxes," he said, with a wink. And from there the progression began. Three boxes . . . four boxes . . . last February, five generous boxes with a balloon tied around them from the loving man who calls me his wife.

Tim's extravagant, chocolatey surprises, in a small way, helped me understand the word *lavish* in John's description of God's love. God sent His Son, Jesus, to the cross as a payment for my sins. Because I believed and received that offer of forgiveness, I am now called a child of God. How extravagant a sacrifice, how generous a gift, how lavish a love.

Tim hasn't given me my Valentine's Day present yet. But I know it'll be chocolate turtles to show his lavish love for me. Could it possibly be six boxes? —BECKY ALEXANDER

FAITH STEP: *Give a heart-shaped box of candy to someone today. Attach a card with the words of 1 John 3:1.*

Sunday, February 15

The God of all grace, who called you to his eternal glory in Christ, after you have suffered a little while, will himself restore you and make you strong, firm and steadfast. 1 Peter 5:10 (NIV)

ONE OF THE HARDEST THINGS about losing all I owned in a fire was losing the items that had meaning attached, such as photos, journals, silver that belonged to my great-grandmother, and many handmade things my sons created in elementary school. For Valentine's Day, I remember getting a few of those handwoven hearts made of construction paper from the boys. All those special keepsakes filled with love are gone forever.

After mourning so much loss, I can confidently proclaim Jesus, in His grace, has restored my joy and made me stronger. When I feel sad about lost things, I change my thinking to what I've gained from the experience. One of the biggest lessons I've learned is to value relationships above everything. Relationships with God and others. They are truly what matter most in life.

Then Jesus showed me He can even creatively restore items we thought were lost forever. On Valentine's Day, my twenty-eight-year-old son, Jake, surprised me with a handwoven paper heart. "Remember these? We used to make them in school," he said. Tears came to my eyes as I held it in my hand. I may have lost the former handmade expressions of love, but I was delighted to begin my new keepsake collection. —JEANNIE BLACKMER

FAITH STEP: *What special keepsake reminds you of Jesus's ability to restore? Place it somewhere visible to remind you of His steadfast love for you.*

Presidents' Day, Monday, February 16

Trust in the LORD with all your heart; do not depend on your own understanding. Seek his will in all you do, and he will show you which path to take. Proverbs 3:5–6 (NLT)

"DO I FINAGLE?" I ASKED my husband, Kevin, after I'd shared my brainstorm on how we could afford a second car.

Kevin spoke slower than usual. "Sometimes you do, Jeanette." Was he using his best diplomatic skills gained from fifty years as a pastor or forty-nine years as a husband? "You like to arrange situations so they turn out the way you want." I laughed on the outside, but inside I cringed. Because as much as I hate to admit it, I am a champion manipulator and schemer.

I can't count the number of times I've finagled circumstances and people, I'm ashamed to say, to get my way. A hint here. A look or a sigh there. Very subtle, usually. But not very Christlike.

Lately, Jesus has shown me that finagling was not His best for me. That it's rooted in fear and worry. *Uh-oh.* Jesus wants me to acknowledge Him in all my ways and ask Him for what I need (Matthew 7:7), to trust that He will provide for me (Philippians 4:19), to not live by my own scheming but to rest in His plan for me—which, of course, always turns out for my best (Romans 8:28).

Weeks after my conversation with Kevin, some friends offered to sell us their extra car for next to nothing—not because of any finagling on my part but because of Jesus. —JEANETTE LEVELLIE

FAITH STEP: *Write down the situations you are trying to manipulate. Then trust the outcomes to Jesus.*

Tuesday, February 17

"Enter through the narrow gate. For wide is the gate and broad is the road that leads to destruction, and many enter through it. But small is the gate and narrow the road that leads to life, and only a few find it."
Matthew 7:13–14 (NIV)

THE DRIVEWAY AT OUR NEW home begins narrow at the street then widens at the garage, creating an abrupt curve that is hard to navigate. When we first moved, it became my job to manage the awkward turn every morning when I went to work. I used every mirror at every angle to avoid accidentally driving onto the grass beside the driveway as I backed up, and I thought I was doing a great job. Then my sons pointed out all the ruts I'd made in the grass. Soon the whole family was giving me, a woman with thirty years of driving experience, lessons in how to drive properly.

Just when I was ready to sell the house just to get rid of the troublesome driveway, I tried one last-ditch strategy. I stopped focusing on the grass I was trying to avoid and began looking at the small, thin line in the middle of the driveway where the two sections of concrete connected. Once I focused on that straight and narrow line, I made it through without any more problems.

The success made me think about Jesus's words in Matthew. It's hard to navigate this world and all its distractions. Only when I ignore the temptations and focus on Jesus can I find the narrow road that leads to life. —EMILY E. RYAN

FAITH STEP: *Today, respond to challenges and temptation by looking less at yourself and more to Jesus.*

ASH WEDNESDAY, FEBRUARY 18

I set my face unto the Lord God, to seek by prayer and supplications, with fasting, and sackcloth, and ashes. Daniel 9:3 (KJV)

ASH WEDNESDAY, THE BEGINNING OF the Lenten season for many Christians, is a representation of humility and mortality (ashes to ashes, dust to dust), of repentance and gratitude for Christ's suffering on the cross. This year, I'm being more intentional to give it the attention it deserves. The attention Jesus and soul-cleansing deserve.

I wanted to know more about traditions and ways Ash Wednesday is observed around the world. In Iceland, for example, children dress up in costumes and roam their towns and villages, asking for candy—almost like a version of Halloween. But one tradition speaks more significantly to my heart. For centuries, palm branches used on Palm Sunday are saved almost an entire year so they can be burned to create ashes for the following year's Ash Wednesday observations. I'm impressed that such care and intentionality is afforded to this holy tradition.

Less than a week after Jesus entered Jerusalem in triumph, with the crowd cheering and waving palm branches, that same crowd called for His crucifixion. When has that crowd been me?

What needs to burn up in my life? What fickle faithlessness or self-serving actions need to turn to ashes as a symbol of my commitment to my Savior? Will I allow Him to set fire to what I once held tightly—accomplishments, successes, even spiritual triumphs—so I can form a symbolic, ashy cross of soul-cleansing repentance and renewed faithfulness to Him? —CYNTHIA RUCHTI

FAITH STEP: *On this day of reflection, let a cross made of ashes, visible or invisible, adjust your perspective too.*

THURSDAY, FEBRUARY 19

"Now set your mind and heart to seek the LORD your God. Arise and build the sanctuary of the LORD God, so that the ark of the covenant of the LORD and the holy vessels of God may be brought into a house built for the name of the LORD." 1 Chronicles 22:19 (ESV)

ALMOST THREE YEARS AFTER WE lost our home and all of our possessions in a wildfire, we were finally building. I knew rebuilding and replacing everything would be a marathon, not a sprint, but it felt like a long slog. And I was tired of it. I began to doubt our decision to rebuild. *Is it worth the stress and effort?* I talked to Jesus about this, and then, as a sort of Bible roulette, I randomly opened my Bible to 1 Chronicles 22:19 and read the words, "Set your mind and heart to seek the LORD.... Arise and build..."

This was David's charge to Solomon, to build a house for the Lord. We were not building a temple, but it is our dream to use our home for the Lord's purposes. In our previous home, we had hosted rehearsal dinners, home concerts, and even a formal dance for a college student ministry. This verse encouraged me to persevere and to "arise and build."

I went to write this scripture down in my one-line-a-day journal that I had kept throughout the rebuilding process. On the exact same day, February 19, the year before I had written down this same Bible verse. A knowing came over me. Rebuilding was worth the stress and effort. —JEANNIE BLACKMER

FAITH STEP: *Randomly open your Bible now, and see what Jesus has to say to you through His Word. Consider writing today's date in the margin for future reference.*

Friday, February 20

As a prisoner for the Lord, then, I urge you to live a life worthy of the calling you have received. Be completely humble and gentle; be patient, bearing with one another in love. Ephesians 4:1–2 (NIV)

I EMPATHIZED WITH MY FRIEND Mike as he shared an incident when he was reprimanded at work. His words were fine, but the vocal tone he used when attempting to get his important point across was what got him into trouble.

For me, my voice changes to one of sternness, most times conveying a tone of anger and not one of caution or correction as I intended. As a rebellious teen, my words intentionally had a harsh or firm tone as I asserted my independence. But over time, I found that a more sensitive, gentle tone worked better if I wanted to gain cooperation or prompt action from my children and husband. When attempting to make a point, I remind myself to take a deep breath and clearly state my words so my tone does not interfere with the message I want to convey.

This was something Jesus did very well. He spoke a message drastically different from that which was prevalently being heard in His day. Not everybody wanted to hear His words, yet His calm, patient delivery prompted people to listen (Luke 5:1). Many chose to follow Him as a result (Matthew 4:25). Jesus's tone clearly delivered God's message with compassion and love. Following His example, I can too. —GLORIA JOYCE

FAITH STEP: *Is there something you are struggling to get across to a friend, loved one, or coworker? Pause and listen for Jesus. Ask Him to provide peaceful and loving clarity to your words.*

SATURDAY, FEBRUARY 21

The name of the LORD is a strong tower; The righteous run to it and are safe. Proverbs 18:10 (NKJV)

AS I PULLED MY TEEN son's long-legged jeans out of the dryer that morning, I felt a nudge. Something drew me to pray and hold those jeans tight. I giggled a little; what a strange thing to do. Aaron, a senior in high school, would surely get a kick out of it if he saw his mom holding onto his pants. I hung them up and went to work like any other day.

That afternoon, I received a message at my office. Aaron had packed his bag and gone to stay with my mom, who lived in another state. No notice, no discussion. He was seventeen and just gone! We'd been having some disagreements lately, but I hadn't realized how strongly he felt. I begged him to come home, but the three of us decided Aaron would live with my mom for the time being. I felt guilty, sad, and afraid.

On my way to work several days later, a song with the lyrics "the name of the Lord is a strong tower; the righteous run into it and they are saved" came on the radio. An image popped into my mind of Jesus with His arms opened wide and me running to Him and collapsing into His embrace. There was nothing I could do to change the situation, but the image of being in Jesus's arms sustained me.

Aaron eventually came home, and our relationship remained strained. But no matter what happens with Aaron or anything else in life, I know Jesus is waiting for me with open arms. —RENEE MITCHELL

FAITH STEP: *Think of a situation that has upset you. Picture Jesus with His arms wide. Run into His embrace.*

Sunday, February 22

"The grass withers, the flowers fade, but the word of our God shall stand forever." Isaiah 40:8 (TLB)

My church produces a devotional booklet for Lent each year that encourages everyone to spend sacred time in prayer and meditation daily during the forty days before Easter. I have collected these booklets over many years. Recently I saw a stack of them on a bookshelf at home and started to look through them, flipping the pages and taking note of the contributing writers.

As I began to read the meditations written by beloved church members, I realized that many of these fellow believers are now gone and resting in heaven with Jesus. While they are no longer here on earth physically, their words of wisdom live on and beckon me to look at myself and my relationship with Jesus.

Those old devotionals also pointed me to the ancient words of the Bible that still live on today to encourage and direct me. Words such as "If you believe, you will receive whatever you ask for in prayer" (Matthew 21:22, NIV). "Because of the Lord's great love we are not consumed, for his compassions never fail" (Lamentations 3:22, NIV). And "Seek first his kingdom and his righteousness, and all these things will be given to you as well" (Matthew 6:33, NIV).

I find it amazing that God's Word never grows old. This compilation of wisdom, thousands of years old, still guides Jesus's followers and me today. In future generations, I'm assured His Word is the one thing that will not change. —Barbranda Lumpkins Walls

Faith Step: *Look at one of your favorite Bible passages. How do those ancient words speak to your life now? Share them with someone today.*

Monday, February 23

"Love the Lord your God with all your heart and with all your soul and with all your mind and with all your strength." The second is this: "Love your neighbor as yourself." There is no commandment greater than these.
Mark 12:30–31 (NIV)

ONE OF THE FUN ASPECTS of being an empty nester is reliving the joy of parenthood through friends and family members who are just beginning their journey as parents. Recently, our neighbors shared with us that they were expecting their first child. Remembering those exciting—and scary—times, my husband and I decided we wanted to be as much of a blessing as possible.

Although it wasn't much, we volunteered to provide them with meals one of the first weeks after bringing their little one home. In addition to wanting to help them in a practical way, it was also our hope that this small act of kindness would reflect the love of Jesus in a big way.

This was not a foreign concept to me. Although it's been more than two decades, I still recall how blessed I was when family, friends, and coworkers showered us with furniture, supplies, and visits as we began our journey into parenthood.

Such generous actions may seem simple and mundane, but Jesus sees them differently. He gives us two important commands to prove it: Love God with all your being, and love your neighbor as yourself. In a world full of hurt and heartache, one of the best ways I can demonstrate the kindness and compassion of Jesus is by showing how much I love God by loving the people He has placed in my life. —ERICKA LOYNES

FAITH STEP: *Ask Jesus to inspire you to do something special for family or friends today.*

Tuesday, February 24

*Again Jesus said, "Simon son of John, do you love me?"
He answered, "Yes, Lord, you know that I love you." Jesus said,
"Take care of my sheep." John 21:16 (NIV)*

I RECENTLY DEVELOPED A PHOBIA of driving in wintry conditions. My biggest fear is the invisible menace of black ice. I've heard one too many stories of people hitting it, losing all control, crashing their cars, and suffering significant injuries.

These fears flashed through my mind when my husband, John, was at the wheel during a recent storm. To ratchet my anxiety up to a new level, he was driving with just one hand, relaxed as can be. I kept thinking how vulnerable we'd be if we hit black ice and he wasn't gripping the wheel with both hands. To further complicate the situation, my husband doesn't like to be told how to drive.

As I contemplated how to solve the problem, John 21:16 came to mind. Rather than reprimanding Peter for the three times he denied Jesus, Jesus chose to frame His questions with love. Doing so prevented Peter from feeling judged or rebuked. Instead, Peter was inspired to put the needs of "the sheep" before himself.

I decided to try the same approach and asked John if he loved me. When he answered, "Yes," I gently requested he drive with both hands for me. Looking at the situation through a lens of love, John put both hands on the wheel and my needs ahead of his.
—CLAIRE MCGARRY

FAITH STEP: *If someone asks you to do something from a perspective you don't quite understand, look through a lens of love. Place their needs before your own.*

WEDNESDAY, FEBRUARY 25

When I said, "My foot is slipping," your unfailing love, LORD, supported me. Psalm 94:18 (NIV)

ONE OF OUR DOGS WENT in for a teeth cleaning yesterday morning. I'd had little sleep because she awakened several times, thirsty from no food or water since midnight. I was ready for a nap before I dropped her off at the vet.

The procedure went fine, and I picked her up after lunch. But she has a sensitive stomach, so she struggled coming out of the anesthesia. I spent hours cleaning up after her, while trying to work and oversee my teenagers' activities after school.

Finally, by evening, I had a few minutes and some brain cells left to knock out a task at my desk. But before I could focus, my phone dinged with a text from my daughter, letting me know she was ready to be picked up from a music rehearsal.

I paused for a deep breath, let it out, and texted back: *Alright. I'm in my way.*

Immediately, I laughed. I'd done a pretty good job not getting in my own way in the chaos that day, which is not always the case. Many times I trip myself up by letting frustration take the lead over lightheartedness.

I backspaced and retyped: *Alright. I'm on my way.*

I thanked Jesus for His ability to help me avoid getting in my own way with a frazzled attitude.

My dog is doing well, I will sleep again, and I'm grateful for small victories that bring a smile. —ERIN KEELEY MARSHALL

FAITH STEP: *Memorize Psalm 94:18. Ask Jesus to bring it to mind the next time a chaotic day tempts you to join the fray and get in your own way. Remember you always have the support of His unfailing love.*

THURSDAY, FEBRUARY 26

Those who hope in the LORD will renew their strength. They will soar on wings like eagles; they will run and not grow weary, they will walk and not be faint. Isaiah 40:31 (NIV)

I WROTE A TO-DO LIST to keep myself focused amid a multitude of deadlines. I figured that tackling one or two tasks each day would soon bring me to the end of that list. The weight of my workload would lift, and I'd breathe easy, right? My plan sounded reasonable, but it didn't turn out as I hoped.

My pastor asked me to serve on a committee. My publisher asked me to record teaching videos for my soon-to-be-released book. As mission agency directors, my husband and I had to represent our organization at two weekend conferences within a month. And so it went. For every task I struck from my to-do list, I added two more. The weight of my workload grew heavier rather than lighter.

One morning, I took a walk along the Fraser River. An eagle's call drew my gaze upward to see the massive bird perched on a branch almost directly overhead. The words from Isaiah 40:31 came to mind, and I thanked God for reminding me that He would provide strength for the work He'd given me. I'd scarcely finished my prayer when two more bald eagles swooped in from opposite directions and landed near the first.

I stood in awe and stared at the trio. I'd often seen two eagles together, but three? Never. This was truly a God moment. I thanked Him again and headed home, ready to face my to-do list with renewed strength. —GRACE FOX

FAITH STEP: *Google the words "bald eagle interesting facts" to learn more about the bird mentioned in Isaiah 40:31.*

Friday, February 27

Do not conform to the pattern of this world, but be transformed by the renewing of your mind. Then you will be able to test and approve what God's will is—his good, pleasing and perfect will. Romans 12:2 (NIV)

EVEN THOUGH MY OLDER SON, Pierce, is a young adult, I still like to make him an Easter basket that truly pleases him—a cool, stylish athlete who isn't into sweets. I decided to shop at one of his favorite economical, youth-oriented online stores. The website had a dizzying array of options, and I wasn't at all sure what he would like most. I used the filter to search for "most popular" to tune in to the teen trends—and, boy, was that alarming!

The Holy Spirit inside my soul bristled a bit. Though I personally love fashion and feel taste *is* decidedly subjective, the proposed selections offered on this website were questionable by many standards, with vulgar sayings, garish colors, and odd designs. I scrolled through pages of tasteless options before abandoning the filter and searching based on my own judgment and knowledge of Pierce's aesthetic.

I found a handful of sporty and beachy options, including coordinating swim trunks with rubber duckies for both Pierce and Isaac. Not the height of good taste, I admit, but not shockingly offensive. After I gave my life to Christ, I no longer conformed to what was popular or fashionable if it didn't honor God. In Christ, I'm free to be me, but I want to consider Him in all I think, say, do, and wear.
—ISABELLA CAMPOLATTARO

FAITH STEP: *Take time today to go through your closet. Do your fashion selections conform more to Jesus's pattern or the world's?*

SATURDAY, FEBRUARY 28

"Forgive us as we forgive others." Matthew 6:12 (NOG)

ANNIVERSARIES CAN BE LOVELY CELEBRATIONS—beautiful remembrances of past events. Or anniversaries can be painful, as today is for me. Six years ago, a drunk driver smashed into my daughter Brooke's car, changing her life forever. I can still hear the emergency sirens and the shaky tone of Brooke's boyfriend when he called to say he didn't know if she was OK or not.

Jesus's grace was with us that night as Brooke was taken to a premier trauma center and given the best care. Nonetheless, her ankle was crushed, ligaments torn from her tibia, and after three surgeries, she endured extensive rehabilitation. She can't run, dance, or coach soccer as she did, but she lives her life with joy. Unlike her mother.

I try not to think of the man who did this to her, but when I do, I'm angry and bitter that he made the choice to drive drunk. I don't know what happened to him, except he was jailed that night. Maybe he's in prison. He should be. How unfair that through no fault of her own, a twenty-six-year-old teacher and soccer coach would have her life turned upside down. My brother was an alcoholic. He got a few DUIs, but he never physically injured anyone that I knew of. I had compassion for my brother and loved him despite his addiction. I feel Jesus whisper, *Isn't this man your brother as well?*

I've carried this unforgiveness long enough. Maybe next year, I'll commemorate a different anniversary—the anniversary of forgiving the man who hurt my daughter. —PAT BUTLER DYSON

FAITH STEP: *Implore Jesus to show you how to forgive a long-held hurt.*

SUNDAY, MARCH 1

Now people cannot look at the light when it is bright in the skies [without being blinded]. Job 37:21 (AMP)

THE DARK DAYS OF WINTER are nearly over. After a bleak run of gray, rainy days, the long-lost sun finally reappeared, shining through our little chapel's gothic windows. Bliss! What a welcome blessing was the dear lace curtain hanging across one particular window, which, if uncovered, casts a blinding glare into the eyes of those sitting in the pews.

But last Sunday, the curtain was missing. It wasn't the first time either. Previously, I'd discovered the wayward window cover in a utility room in the church basement. Relieved to have found it, I'd promptly restored it to its rightful home in the sanctuary. But a second time? This was too much. Frustrated, I texted a fellow church member who promised to search. Surprise! Found again, the curtain was returned to the window to resume its sun-filtering duties.

What lesson is Jesus teaching me through this frustrating pattern of events? He's showing me the importance of having a covering. Not only for a bright, sunny window during late Sunday morning services but also for God's children. Where would I be without His covering? Although I'd worn a lace chapel veil on my head to mass as a young girl, only now do I understand its significance. The Bible addresses having a symbol of being under authority (1 Corinthians 11:10). Ultimately, I'm under His authority. Whether a lace chapel veil or lace curtains, the covering that matters most is Jesus's covering over me. —CASSANDRA TIERSMA

FAITH STEP: *Wear a hat or a veil today as a symbol of being under Jesus's authority. Thank Him for covering you with His blood.*

Monday, March 2

Peter followed Him at a distance... to see the outcome.
Matthew 26:58 (NIV)

At age twenty, I joined a company near Kansas City. For a country girl from a small town, the experience was wonderful and overwhelming. My coworkers loved the company. I was certain I would too.

I first met the owner, who I knew was not a Christian, when I climbed into his car with coworkers he was treating to lunch. On the drive, I listened to the chitchat, quickly deciding he was a kind, thoughtful man. Then he asked, "Does anyone believe in Jesus?" Dead silence.

In the rearview mirror, his eyes looked directly at me. Heart pounding, I waited for someone else to respond. Finally, I said yes, much less boldly than I should have. When he asked why, his tone didn't carry curiosity but a challenge. I bumbled some generic response I don't even remember. But I do remember being caught between loving Jesus and loving my job, and I feared both were being threatened.

When I read Matthew 26 and see Peter follow at a distance as Jesus is arrested and taken to Caiaphas, I want to shame Peter for being a coward. But then I remember the times I followed Jesus at a distance because of something I might lose—or gain—if my light shines too brightly.

Thirty-something years later, I would welcome that conversation with the owner, who truly was a nice man. Today, my regret serves as a reminder to follow closely and boldly. —Karen Sargent

Faith Step: *Why do you believe in Jesus? Write down and memorize your answer so you are prepared when someone questions your faith.*

TUESDAY, MARCH 3

"At the time of the banquet he sent his servant to tell those who had been invited, 'Come, for everything is now ready.' But they all alike began to make excuses. The first said, 'I have just bought a field, and I must go and see it. Please excuse me.'" Luke 14:17–18 (NIV)

WHEN I ASKED MY ALMOST-ADULT grandson how his relationship with his girlfriend was going, he said, "I have no idea. She's ghosting me."

"Hip" Grammie that I am, I knew what he meant. He'd been texting her, maybe trying to call her, to set up a date or a time to talk, and she was not responding.

As the owner of a local business, my oldest son knows the feeling too. He often hires new employees, goes through the interview process, then tries to contact the person for a starting date. No response. Ghosted. Rather than making excuses as the characters in the story Jesus told in Luke 14, those invited these days might not respond at all. Or they work a week and then—without so much as a "Goodbye! No, thank you!"—don't show up. Their absence is apparently their unspoken notice.

Jesus has issued us love-engraved invitations to come to Him. He's invited us to accept the gift of a place at His table. He's established a recurring opportunity to talk with Him daily. Because of an evergrowing relationship with Him, I can't imagine intentionally ghosting Jesus. May my ears always be attuned for His voice and my lips always ready with a "Hello, Jesus! Yes, thank You!" —CYNTHIA RUCHTI

FAITH STEP: *Be still for a moment and ask Jesus to reveal ways you've ignored or ghosted Him. Ask forgiveness and move forward in your relationship.*

WEDNESDAY, MARCH 4

There is one God and one Mediator who can reconcile God and humanity—the man Christ Jesus. He gave his life to purchase freedom for everyone. 1 Timothy 2:5–6 (NLT)

COMBINE A LONG BRIDGE, A large body of water, and extreme height, and you get...one of my worst nightmares! For years, my husband and I lived in an area that had water in every direction. We drove over some of the longest, steepest, and oldest bridges in the country. Our new location doesn't have nearly as many bridges, but I do have to cross one when I visit my mom. It's short, level, and crosses a minor river. It shouldn't make my hands grip the steering wheel—except when I remember how the previous bridge collapsed in 1989.

I've decided that from now on, I will use any bridge I face to remind me of Jesus. His death on the cross made it possible for us to cross over the great gulf of sin that separated us from God. It bridged the gap between God's chosen people and the rest of the world (Ephesians 3:6). Jesus can still be a bridge that connects estranged people. He can also help me cross obstacles in the path He has chosen for me.

Physical bridges can erode and fall; many have posted weight limits that shouldn't be surpassed. But I know Jesus will never fail, has no load limits, and can bear any burden. —DIANNE NEAL MATTHEWS

FAITH STEP: *How do you need Jesus to be your bridge today: in a troubled relationship, in a difficult decision, or in a frightening situation? Remind yourself that He can safely get you to the other side.*

Thursday, March 5

Therefore if the Son makes you free, you shall be free indeed.
John 8:36 (NKJV)

Today I'm uploading a favorite photo to use as my computer's wallpaper. It depicts four sheep on a grassy hillside, with trees and a slow-moving river in the background. Three of them are facing the same direction, crowded together behind an ancient iron gate, as if willing it to open. The irony is that there is no fence on either side of the gate. It stands alone. There is nothing to stop the livestock from stepping past it.

The fourth sheep peeks out around the edge of the gate, its eyes wide.

Why does this photo resonate so strongly for me? Because I see myself in every one of those sheep. In the past, I've allowed barriers of my own making to bar my way forward. Insecurities and fears threatened my well-being. Unseen enemies lurked, ready to topple my dreams, leaving me frozen in place. It didn't matter that they resided solely in my imagination.

But Jesus, the Good Shepherd (John 10:11), reminds me to follow Him. When I maintain my trust in God, He leads me to rest in green pastures (Psalm 23:2). His rod and staff (Psalm 23:4) protect and comfort me. I am safe. I am loved. And, like the fourth sheep stepping past the closed gate, because of Jesus I am free indeed. —Heidi Gaul

---

Faith Step: *Make a list of the barriers you face, both real and self-created. In prayer, hand each one over to the Good Shepherd. Acknowledge your freedom in Him.*

Friday, March 6

"Which of you, if your son asks for bread, will give him a stone? Or if he asks for a fish, will give him a snake? If you, then, though you are evil, know how to give good gifts to your children, how much more will your Father in heaven give good gifts to those who ask him!" Matthew 7:9–11 (NIV)

MY MIDDLE SON, WILL, IS a junior in college. He attends a school more than 800 miles away in Southern California. Living on his own as a young adult can be challenging sometimes. He is responsible for making his own meals and buying his own groceries. I know figuring out how to make ends meet in college can be worrisome for him.

Last month, I had a business trip in Southern California. I flew in a day early to see Will. When I got to his apartment on campus, I offered to take him on a Trader Joe's run. (Trader Joe's is our family's favorite grocery store.) He was so excited. I filled up his fridge and freezer with all his favorite meals and snacks. I love being able to surprise Will with goodness.

Jesus loves surprising me with goodness too. I find that life as a not-so-young adult can be a challenge sometimes. Financial worries can creep in. Stress about steady work can cause me to be anxious. But Jesus knows what I need. He overwhelms me with His lovingkindness. He always provides for me. —SUSANNA FOTH AUGHTMON

FAITH STEP: *Turn on your favorite worship song about Jesus's wonderful provision. ("Great Is Thy Faithfulness" and "Jireh" by Elevation Worship & Maverick City Music are full of encouragement.) Sing along, praising Jesus for all He has given you.*

SATURDAY, MARCH 7

When Jesus saw him lying there, and knew that he already had been in that condition a long time, He said to him, "Do you want to be made well?" John 5:6 (NKJV)

MY HUSBAND, HAL, RECENTLY HAD a health scare that prompted his physicians to order some lifestyle changes. While the doctors had been telling Hal for a while that he needed to lose weight, improve his eating habits, and incorporate more exercise into his daily routine, Hal now had to take heed and follow instructions if he wanted a full recovery.

I made it my mission to remind my husband of what he needed to do. And whenever he started to make excuses, I'd simply ask, "Do you want to be made well?" It's the same question that Jesus asked the invalid man at the pool of Bethesda who had been waiting for 38 years to be healed. He told the Lord that he had been waiting for someone to help him into the water, which was believed to have healing power. But Jesus healed the man right on the spot—no water needed (John 5:2–9).

I know when I feel physically tired and out of sorts, I sometimes feel a weariness in my soul. Rest and sleep can help, but what I truly need is a rejuvenation of my spirit. I can be well again by seeking and spending extra time with the real Healer and lover of my soul.

While Hal and I are looking for a cure for our ailments, Jesus is always there to make us well, both physically and spiritually. He is the greatest Physician of all. —BARBRANDA LUMPKINS WALLS

FAITH STEP: *Do you want to be made well? Tell Jesus what you need and ask for His healing power.*

Sunday, March 8

Therefore, as we have opportunity, let us do good to all people, especially to those who belong to the family of believers. Galatians 6:10 (NIV)

Last year, the cable on my prosthetic elbow broke. The manufacturer insisted it could not be repaired and that I must purchase a new elbow. Terry, my local prosthetist, placed the order. Even with insurance, the specialty part carried a hefty price tag.

My arm was locked in a 90-degree angle for one long, difficult week before the new joint arrived and could be installed. I walked with Terry to the checkout desk happy to be fully functional again. He said, "If you leave the old elbow with me, I'll take it apart. The manufacturer positioned that cable initially. I don't see why I can't replace it."

I didn't think about the broken prosthesis until this week when the cable popped on my new one. I called Terry. "Do you remember that elbow I left with you?"

"It's right here on my desk. I was able to fix it. Come in, and we'll change it out. No charge."

Wow! Terry saw an opportunity to apply his unique training and skills to help another person. His good deed required valuable time and tedious effort, while offering him no financial gain. But what a gain it was for me. Jesus used Terry's act of kindness to bless me in a big way.

Now both of my arms are working wonderfully—the one with cables and mechanics and the one with skin and bones. And I'm hoping to embrace my own opportunities to do good, being the hands, arms, or elbows of Jesus to others. —Becky Alexander

Faith Step: *Wherever your day takes you, be watchful for opportunities to do good and help others in the name of Jesus.*

Monday, March 9

Love each other with genuine affection, and take delight in honoring each other. Romans 12:10 (NLT)

LORD, I'M TOO BUSY. MY *plate is so full, I feel like I'm at an all-you-can-eat buffet.* I felt overwhelmed by my job, deadlines, and household chores. I thought of all I did and what I could eliminate. Reading? No way. That nourished my soul. Gardening? Nope. That was stress relief. Finally, I hit on what seemed like the perfect activity to omit: sending greeting cards to loved ones and friends who needed encouragement.

Choosing the perfect card from the hundreds I'd collected, writing a note, and addressing the envelope took a good chunk of time. Even though this fun hobby gave me immense joy, it wasn't a necessity.

Girl, was I mistaken.

Weeks later, a second bout of shingles caused a painful rash on my back. When friends from a ladies group sent me a get-well card, I teared up. Just knowing they thought of me made me feel cherished. I kept that card on our microwave for months.

Then a friend's husband had a stroke and was dying. I decided to send Sadie a "thinking of you" card most weeks during those long months while she cared for him at home. After he passed, she told me at the funeral, "I really appreciated all the cards you sent me, Jeanette. They encouraged me so much."

That's when I realized my greeting card ministry was essential. I might feel overwhelmed, but I'll never be too busy to encourage others. A full plate satisfies everyone. —JEANETTE LEVELLIE

FAITH STEP: *Make a pie chart of your commitments on a paper plate. Designate one piece of the pie to feed others. Let Jesus inspire your ministry of encouragement and kindness.*

Tuesday, March 10

It's better to live alone in the corner of an attic than with a quarrelsome wife in a lovely home. Proverbs 21:9 (NLT)

Growing up, I lived with my family in a modest co-op apartment about 20 minutes from Manhattan. It was not a big house, but it was a good home (even though we had that ubiquitous 1970s plastic on the couches). Why was it good? Because my parents took pains to cultivate an atmosphere of peace that went far beyond the structure, the size, or the decor. There was love and acceptance there. For the most part, words were chosen carefully—used to edify, not to discourage.

Recently, Jesus showed me that my husband, Andrew, and I had not achieved the same level success in our own home. Yes, we live in a nice, spacious house. And I took great pride in furnishing it with love, creativity, and a little splurging too. Not every brown girl in America gets to experience these joys, so I savored every minute.

But for a while, peace was scarce in our household. Andrew and I began bickering about the smallest things. Our conversations were laced with sarcasm and unspoken expectations. Snarky comments, quarrels, and digs ruled the day. We laughed together less and less, and we spent more time apart. The peace and sanctity of our marriage was threatened.

It took a near-crisis for me to wake up and make a change. Where I lived wasn't as important as who I lived with. I chose to extend to my husband and family the same grace Jesus gave me, and they returned the favor. —Pamela Toussaint Howard

Faith Step: *House yourself in Jesus's grace the next time you are about to quarrel with someone, especially a loved one or spouse.*

WEDNESDAY, MARCH 11

Then shall they see the Son of man coming in the clouds with great power and glory. Mark 13:26 (KJV)

"Angelic vehicles!" exclaimed one of the worshipful onlookers with her neck craned upward. Everywhere I turned that day, I saw people stopped in their tracks, gazing heavenward with cell phones raised to capture snapshots of a massive, disc-shaped cloud in the sky. If I didn't know better, it would've seemed that such an awe-inspiring celestial event was none other than Our Lord Jesus coming in the clouds (Revelation 1:7).

Whenever these flying saucer–shaped clouds appear here in Northern California where I live, some people believe them to be UFO spaceship sightings. Some locals, as well as international visitors, are convinced that these strange, ethereal clouds are extraterrestrial spacecraft transporting otherworldly beings. In reality, we're all witnessing the same thing—none other than the heavenly handwork of our Creator. These rare cloud formations, called lenticular clouds, are unique to only a few places in the world. Often appearing as halo-like rings encircling the peak of a mountain or hovering just above, these clouds never fail to amaze me.

Though lenticular clouds may not be supernatural, they are, nevertheless, awe-inspiring. Earlier in my life, when I was searching for something more, I, too, might've been tempted to believe these clouds were mystical UFOs. But now I believe in Jesus. So, magical as some clouds might seem, the only "angelic vehicle" I'm interested in seeing is Our Lord Jesus coming in the clouds. —Cassandra Tiersma

Faith Step: *Search the Internet for lenticular cloud images. As you view His wondrous cloud creations, praise Jesus that He will one day come with great power and glory in the clouds!*

Thursday, March 12

Do you not know? Have you not heard? The LORD is the everlasting God, the Creator of the ends of the earth. He will not grow tired or weary, and his understanding no one can fathom. Isaiah 40:28 (NIV)

I WENT TO OUR LOCAL hardware store to purchase some picture-hanging hooks. The store was empty, so several employees asked if I needed help finding anything. One of the men started telling me jokes. He began with one about his neighbors who had just come home from the hospital with their identical twin girls. When he asked what they named them, the wife said, "Kate and Duplicate." I laughed. I noticed the other employees rolling their eyes. Apparently, they had heard his jokes. As a captive audience, he kept reciting jokes to me, and I kept giggling. Then he mentioned he was performing at a coffee shop soon. It would be his first show, so he was practicing. He just needed someone to listen.

I found the hooks I needed and said goodbye. On my drive home, I recalled his joke-telling. His coworkers were obviously tired of hearing his funny quips, but it was fresh content to me. I enjoyed it. Our interaction reminded me of how Jesus doesn't grow weary listening to us. We can pray the same things over and over again, and He is not annoyed. Thank goodness.

I think I'll start naming my persistent prayers Kate and Duplicate, knowing Jesus understands my need to be heard, even if I've prayed about the same thing a thousand times. —JEANNIE BLACKMER

FAITH STEP: *Write down on a note card something you consistently pray about. Now place it in your Bible near Isaiah 40:28 as a reminder that Jesus does not grow weary of hearing your prayer.*

Friday, March 13

Whether you turn to the right or to the left, your ears will hear a voice behind you, saying, "This is the way; walk in it." Isaiah 30:21 (NIV)

AGGHHH. THAT WAS MY REACTION after missing my exit on a stretch of road that had been rerouted. Someday I trust it will be wonderfully simple to navigate. These days, however, the GPS does not match the direction signs over the road or the painted markings on the pavement.

I was late for an appointment because I took a circuitous route twice before figuring out an alternate plan. I texted updates to the person I was meeting, and fortunately she was gracious and did not ask me to explain the whys of my tardiness. But the whole experience was highly frustrating.

Sometimes I wish God's signs were clearer too. A megaphone might be nice when I'd like crystal clarity from Him regarding decisions I'm weighing or issues I'm navigating.

Maybe, "Here's where you went wrong. Here's where you didn't."

Or how about, "Give this person another chance, but your best bet in that other situation is to walk away and trust Me to bring truth and justice."

And finally, "Your teen was quiet today because he needs to process on his own. Give him space, then check in tomorrow."

When I'm confused, I can count on God to help me understand His voice because He promises to show me His ways (Psalm 32:8). But I have to quiet myself inside so I can hear which way to go. Together with God, I can move with assurance to find my way and arrive right on time. —ERIN KEELEY MARSHALL

FAITH STEP: *Read Psalm 25:4–5, Psalm 32:8, and James 1:5 for truth about seeking God's guidance.*

SATURDAY, MARCH 14

When he had received the drink, Jesus said, "It is finished." With that, he bowed his head and gave up his spirit. John 19:30 (NIV)

EVERY WEEK WHEN A PAYCHECK is deposited directly into our family account, I feel relief that I once again can pay my bills. Despite the normal challenges that we all experience in our jobs, I am grateful to be gainfully employed. Nevertheless, I must admit I still fantasize about hearing my doorbell ring and opening the door to find someone holding an oversized check with several zeros made out to me. If this were to happen, I would not just pay my monthly bills; I would pay off all my debt.

I've had a taste of this in the past. Several years ago, a dear coworker, hearing about my credit card debt, graciously agreed to pay the balance. I still recall the feeling of seeing the debt paid in full after years of slowly paying it off.

Jesus extends a similar offer. In John 19, He states, "It is finished," bows His head, and dies. On the cross, Jesus paid the sin debts of all humankind. If the eradication of earthly debts brings me joy, then the cancellation of my eternal debts thrills my soul. Better than a gigantic paper check with several zeros in the payment column, my eternal paycheck has been directly deposited because Jesus paid it all—for me and for you. And there's no bigger relief than that.
—ERICKA LOYNES

FAITH STEP: *As you purchase things throughout the day, praise Jesus for paying off your spiritual debt.*

Sunday, March 15

"No longer will you be called Abram; your name will be Abraham."
Genesis 17:5 (NIV)

WE ARE CURRENTLY KNEE-DEEP IN college tours with my middle child, Mason. The recurring message at each school is that students will have the chance to reinvent themselves with the new transition. Working with a clean slate, they can shed the unwanted nicknames, bullying, and labels of their high school years. What isn't mentioned is that in giving up the old, one can sometimes lose what is familiar or what feels safe. Like crustaceans that molt, growing into new and bigger spaces can mean expelling the smaller shells we've grown accustomed to.

In the Bible, when God transforms people, He, too, asks them to shed the old to make space for the new. In extreme cases, like Abram to Abraham, He even changed his name, signifying the call to walk before Him faithfully and blamelessly (Genesis 17:1).

With every gift of grace I received from Jesus, I can recognize where I was asked to let go of what was comfortable, bad habits that weighed me down, and even things I enjoyed that didn't serve Him. The shedding process for me has never been easy—in fact, it's often very painful. But from the vantage point of time and distance, I now see how giving up who I was and what I thought I wanted brought me closer to Jesus and closer to becoming blameless in His sight. —CLAIRE MCGARRY

FAITH STEP: *Map out the major transitions in your life. See if you can identify where Jesus was asking you to shed your old ways to become a new person in Him.*

Monday, March 16

I am prompt, I do not hesitate in observing your commandments.
Psalm 119:60 (NABRE)

I WAS STARTLED AWAKE BY my phone shortly after I'd turned out the light, and I answered quickly. Hannah, a friend's daughter, said her dad was supposed to pick her up but had not arrived. She couldn't reach him or her mom by phone. Could I give her a ride? Of course!

Dressing in haste, I grabbed my keys just as another text came through halting my departure. Hannah's dad was there later than expected, and my pickup was no longer required. She apologized, and I texted her back that it was no bother. The important thing was that she was safe and would be home soon.

As I climbed back into bed, the adrenaline coursing through my veins from the startling call left me unable to sleep. Opening my Bible, my eyes fell on Psalm 119:60. I don't hesitate when a friend or one of my children needs me. I expect the same of Jesus when I frequently call upon Him. Yet I wondered how many times I have jumped for Jesus, as I did for Hannah. Do I course with cooperative adrenaline when He lights up the screen of my heart? Or does doubt cause me to ignore His call, roll over, and go back to sleep?

Speaking into the darkness, I asked Jesus to forgive me and recommitted myself to my most important relationship. Next time, I will not swipe Him away. —GLORIA JOYCE

FAITH STEP: *Has Jesus been calling you to action in some area of your life? Stop hesitating. Take a step forward today in faith, and answer His call.*

Tuesday, March 17

Now these three remain: faith, hope, and love. But the greatest of these is love. 1 Corinthians 13:13 (HCSB)

FOR TWO YEARS NOW, MOST of our possessions, including my seasonal decor, have been in a storage unit while my husband and I make decisions about housing for our post-retirement years. That's why I enjoy holiday visits to my daughter's house even more. I love seeing what she arranges on the three shelves on her living room wall. During a recent visit, I walked into the room on the evening of St. Patrick's Day to find the shelves stripped almost bare, awaiting Easter and spring decor. Only one object remained—a large wooden block inscribed with the words of 1 Corinthians 16:14 (ESV): "Let all that you do be done in love."

That wooden block with the scripture reminder is the one constant in my daughter's holiday decorating—just as Jesus's love is a constant in all seasons. Everything He did was motivated by love, whether teaching, healing, feeding crowds, speaking hard truths someone needed to hear, or dying on the cross. I want to be like Jesus and make love the foundation of all my attitudes, words, and actions toward Him and toward others. With His help, maybe I can learn to do even hard things in a loving way, such as being patient when it seems impossible or serving someone when I don't feel like it.

Circumstances and emotions can change like the seasons, but I want to decorate my life by doing everything in love. That way, I can reflect Jesus's love to everyone around me.
—DIANNE NEAL MATTHEWS

FAITH STEP: *Consider decorating your home with an object that reminds you to speak and act with love, as Jesus did.*

WEDNESDAY, MARCH 18

My sacrifice, O God, is a broken spirit; a broken and contrite heart you, God, will not despise. Psalm 51:17 (NIV)

MY HUSBAND AND I WALKED up the incline to our church sanctuary. As we made our way down the aisle, a small group huddled around a pew. "It needs to be fixed," someone said. As we came closer, I saw what they were talking about—the underside bench was broken, and the cushion sagged toward the floor.

I stared at the slumped seating. It looked so dejected compared to the other pews. I couldn't help but see the parallel. That broken church pew was me. Sometimes, I felt as if my emotional brokenness from depression leaked through so others could see me slump too. The church service had started, but I couldn't stop thinking about that bench. We were both in God's house, broken and useless.

After church, my husband hurried to Home Depot for supplies. As a member of the maintenance committee, Roger was a skilled carpenter who formerly owned a contracting business. I watched him easily make the repairs. Before long, my pew soulmate was useful again. Now it was my turn. I sent up a prayer to Jesus, the Master Carpenter. I knew it would take more than a few screws and nails to help me on my depression journey, but with skilled hands maybe I was on my way to being better too. —JEANNIE HUGHES

FAITH STEP: *Pray about a way you are broken, then take it to the Master Carpenter. Listen and allow Jesus to make the necessary repairs.*

Thursday, March 19

When the kindness and love of God our Savior appeared, he saved us, not because of righteous things we had done, but because of His mercy. Titus 3:4–5 (NIV)

The song "My Story" by Big Daddy Weave has a line about "the kindness of Jesus that draws me in." I identify with that. In this world of isolation and polarization, it is the kindness of Jesus that continually draws me in, closer to Him. And I believe His kindness is the secret weapon we have as Christians to draw in others.

It is easy for me to be critical of Christians I disagree with on politics or biblical interpretation. When I see them being too dogmatic, I worry about the lack of kindness Christians display in public that turns people off of Jesus. But what about how I treat people in the quieter corners of life? The telemarketer who annoys me with his intrusive call. The server who gets my order wrong, again. The driver who pulls out in front of me. My child who doesn't listen when I tell her the first time. My elderly mother who won't wear her hearing aids.

There's not a time Jesus acted without kindness, even when being firm, because He is kindness. And I want to use that secret weapon of Jesus's kindness to draw others in. Because the way I treat people with or without the kindness of Jesus shows them my story.
—Gwen Ford Faulkenberry

Faith Step: *Think about your story. Where/when/to whom could you be kinder? Pray that Jesus empowers you to use the secret weapon of His kindness to draw others in.*

Friday, March 20

"My son, do not make light of the Lord's discipline, and do not lose heart when he rebukes you, because the Lord disciplines the one he loves, and he chastens everyone he accepts as his son." Hebrews 12:5–6 (NIV)

My son Isaac has Down syndrome. He's wonderfully loving, endearingly fun, and unbelievably obstinate—especially when it comes to essential tasks that he doesn't want to do. I can often wait him out, induce him with rewards, or withhold a privilege until he caves in, but not always. It can be a real problem when it's time-sensitive or important like getting blood work, as was recently the case.

Of course, most people don't like needles, but when it's necessary, they give in, even if they are faint or fearful. Isaac doesn't much fear needles; it's the whole ordeal he dislikes. Unfortunately, kids with Down syndrome are more vulnerable to conditions like leukemia, thyroid issues, diabetes, and autoimmune disorders. Regular testing is vital.

At this last checkup, Isaac dug his heels in. After many failed attempts, with every conceivable strategy, I'd about given up. Exasperated, the kid gloves came off. Unused to me being so stern, Isaac soon sweetly complied. Once the blood was drawn, he apologized and thanked everyone profusely. Thankfully, his blood work was clear.

Jesus is compassionate and merciful about our sin, giving us many opportunities to course-correct with His help. If I insist on defying His ways and warnings, I may face increasingly severe consequences until I turn it around. This is loving discipline, not punishment. It's intended to help me stay safe, to live in community, and to be all He designed me to be. —Isabella Campolattaro

Faith Step: *Prayerfully consider times you missed Jesus's gentle prompts to course-correct. What happened? Are you on the right path again now?*

SATURDAY, MARCH 21

I will extol the LORD at all times; his praise will always be on my lips.
Psalm 34:1 (NIV)

ON A RECENT FAMILY CRUISE to Jamaica, we encountered kindness as warm as the tropical sun. Tour operators greeted us with radiant smiles as we disembarked, setting a joyful tone for the day. The vibrant Caribbean music and the laughter of the local people further uplifted our spirits.

While lining up for an excursion, a minor confusion arose when passengers needed to form a new line. A cheerful employee smiled and said, "It is not a problem. Two lines work just as well as one." Her demeanor transformed potential stress into a moment of joy. Later, when our bus took a wrong turn, her grin widened and she said, "Look at this. I was going to walk you to the bus, but now the bus comes to you!" Her humor and grace turned mishaps into laughter, reminding me how a positive outlook can ease difficult situations.

Discussing this with my daughter, she pointed out that every bus bore the tagline "My God is real." The consistent kindness was a testament to the faith that filled our guides' lives with peace and resilience. This faith shone through in how they treated one another and us, turning every interaction into an expression of God's love.

"It's not a problem" became our family's comforting refrain throughout the day, and it continues to remind us how to handle life's challenges with grace and kindness. —TRICIA GOYER

FAITH STEP: *Reflect today on how you can show kindness in unexpected situations. Pray for the grace to respond with a cheerful heart and a loving spirit, embracing each act of kindness as a reflection of God's love.*

Sunday, March 22

For from his fullness we have all received, grace upon grace. John 1:16 (ESV)

As I opened the door of my 4Runner, a gust of wind caught it and skinned the car next to me. Oh, no! *Jesus, please don't let anyone be in that car.* It wasn't that I was trying to get away with anything. The same thing had happened to me a few years back, and an angry woman had run out of her car, shrieking curses at me. I didn't want a replay of that, but despite my petition to Jesus, a young man emerged from the car.

"Is it bad?" he asked. His car was low-slung and shiny. No telling how many bags of groceries this kid had sacked and carried out to buy this car. And now I'd damaged it. Cringing, I found the spot and started to work on it with my fingernail. It didn't seem like a scratch but more like a paint deposit.

"I'm so sorry," I moaned. All the while, I was scraping, which seemed to do some good, and then I rubbed vigorously with my thumb. Wonder of wonders, there wasn't a trace of a mark. "All gone!" I sighed. "Please forgive me!"

"No worries," he said with a smile, "it could happen to anyone."

The grace he offered reminded me of the grace Jesus extends me. He gently erases my mistakes, forgives me, and gives me another chance. Grace upon grace. —Pat Butler Dyson

Faith Step: *Follow Jesus's example and offer grace to everyone you encounter today.*

MONDAY, MARCH 23

As for you, be strong and do not give up, for your work will be rewarded. 2 Chronicles 15:7 (NIV)

BUSYNESS KNOCKED EXERCISE OFF MY list of priorities, but the resulting aches and pains nudged me to make a necessary change. When I learned about an online forty-day challenge to track exercise, I immediately signed up.

In full transparency, I'm a fair-weather walker. If it rains, I'd rather wait for another day before donning my walking shoes and taking a hike. What on earth was I thinking when I registered for a forty-day challenge in early spring when the sky often leaks five or six days in a row?

Knowing I'd have to post my daily activity online for other participants to see provided motivation to walk regardless of the weather. One morning, I grabbed an umbrella and headed out despite the downpour. More than once, I felt like going home, but I rejected the temptation and kept moving until I knew my round trip would tally two miles.

When I finally turned around, I glanced at the ground and saw something that made me laugh aloud. There, in the middle of the street, lay a soggy $5 bill. I think Jesus chuckled too. I imagined him saying, "Grace, perseverance yields rewards."

I get it. I'll stick to my resolve to walk every day, even when it rains, because doing so will yield better health. And who knows? I might find another $5 bill. —GRACE FOX

FAITH STEP: *Write "Perseverance yields rewards" on a 3 × 5 card and post it on your fridge as a reminder to stick to a personal resolve, whatever it may be.*

Tuesday, March 24

The LORD appeared to Abraham near the great trees of Mamre while he was sitting at the entrance to his tent in the heat of the day. Genesis 18:1 (NIV)

I RECENTLY STARTED A NEW Bible reading plan in Genesis for my morning devotions. Many stories were familiar. I wondered if I'd learn anything new. I became curious when details about great trees caught my attention, particularly in Abraham's life. In recent months, I often marveled at the trees around me. *What was Jesus trying to teach me? What was the purpose of the mighty trees in Abraham's story?*

I thought about the trees in our backyard that border a creek and the cattle pasture. We have a swing underneath a tree that I often sit on and talk to Jesus. I feel protected and safe there. It's my hiding place when life is challenging. Jesus, through trees and nature, calms and sustains me. Did such trees shelter Abraham too?

My thoughts went from trees to people with whom I feel safe. Like trees, these people have a strong yet sheltering presence. Reading the Genesis passages, I noticed Abraham camped near these mighty trees. I wondered who might be "camping" near me because they, too, needed a gentle, sustaining presence—maybe Linda, who experienced multiple losses, or Amy, who went through a divorce. I often encouraged them or tried to have a listening ear. It wasn't much. But under the canopy of great trees, good friends, and Jesus, a safe shelter is always found. —BRENDA L. YODER

FAITH STEP: *Sit under a tree or look at trees through the window. As you feel Jesus's presence, pray for those who also need His shelter and reach out to them.*

WEDNESDAY, MARCH 25

For the LORD is good and his love endures forever; his faithfulness continues through all generations. Psalm 100:5 (NIV)

I INSPECTED THE TWO RED Haven peach trees that frame our backyard firepit. It is early spring, and they are right on the brink of flowering. I love them so much. They remind me of the deep goodness of my childhood. I have named them Roy and Opal, after my grandparents Roy and Opal Blakeley. Their love anchored my formative years. It was foundational and far-reaching.

My family spent chunks of time with my grandparents every summer in their ranch house surrounded by almond and peach orchards. They welcomed us into their home with great joy. Grandpa, a pastor and farmer, would wake us up early in the morning to pick peaches. Then when the house was full of cousins, Grandma would make homemade peach ice cream with heavy cream. It was a little piece of heaven. They nurtured us with their love, surrounded us with their generosity, and taught us what following Jesus looked like. The goodness of being loved by them is buried deep within my bones.

Jesus's care for me began generations ago. His never-ending faithfulness in my life continues on and on. His generosity surrounds me. His mercy and forgiveness never fail. Day after day, year after year, He fills me with His hope and grace. Jesus's love for me is foundational and far-reaching. And the goodness of being loved by my Savior is buried deep within my bones. —SUSANNA FOTH AUGHTMON

FAITH STEP: *Make a family tree, then reflect on ways your ancestors led you to know Jesus's love for you.*

Thursday, March 26

"You are the light of the world. A city that is set on a hill cannot be hidden. Nor do they light a lamp and put it under a basket, but on a lampstand, and it gives light to all who are in the house. Let your light so shine before men, that they may see your good works and glorify your Father in heaven."
—Matthew 5:14–16 (NKJV)

Sunshine streams through the bathroom window where I prepare my morning bath. Steam rises from the water's surface as a candle flickers at the foot of the tub. Many people indulge in a candlelit soak in the evening, to help them relax. I light a candle as the day begins, to remember that, like Jesus, the Light of the world, I need to burn brightly.

Sometimes, as the wax melts, it threatens to flood the wick and drown the flame. The very fuel that feeds it can also endanger it. Similarly, at times life's challenges can seem overwhelming to me. Thankfully, my light isn't fed by things of this world but by Jesus. As a believer, my fire cannot be put out. The passion that defines and guides my soul—my wick, if you will—cannot be extinguished. I want to use my light to warm hearts and soften what can seem like an otherwise hard world. I choose to reveal the one true Light to those struggling in the dark.

I recently saw a quote that inspired me: "Light yourself on fire with passion and people will come from miles to watch you burn." I'm ready. —Heidi Gaul

Faith Step: *Light a candle for your morning prayers, and notice how it softens and steadies your thoughts. Reflect on ways you can be the light of Jesus and do the same for those you know.*

Friday, March 27

They went to a place called Gethsemane, and Jesus said to his disciples, "Sit here while I pray." Mark 14:32 (NIV)

I NO LONGER FIND IT startling when I open a familiar passage of scripture and discover something I hadn't noticed before. It happens all the time. In some ways, it reflects that Jesus is the Living Word, and His Word is alive, sharp, and powerful (Hebrews 4:12).

While reading the Gospel of Mark, I skimmed over what I thought I well knew. Jesus goes to Gethsemane. He prays in the Garden. He's grieved. Disciples fall asleep. Three times. Boom! He's arrested and on His way to an unfair trial and horrific execution.

Today, I read again, slowly, and caught nuances that had eluded me before. The disciples Jesus chose to go deeper into the Garden with Him—Peter, James, and John—weren't asked at first to pray. They were asked to "stay here and keep watch" while Jesus went to pray (Mark 14:34, NIV).

Later, Jesus returns and finds them sleeping (the part I remember) and says, "Couldn't you keep watch for one hour? Watch and pray so that you will not fall into temptation" (Mark 14:37–38, NIV). He now specifically asks them to pray, in addition to keeping watch.

It wasn't for Jesus's sake but for their own that He instructed them to pray.

At His most vulnerable and heavy-hearted, Jesus was still thinking of the humans who followed Him. Two thousand years later, I'm taking His advice to remain faithful to both pray and keep watch. Good advice then. Great advice now. —CYNTHIA RUCHTI

FAITH STEP: *Do you have a place or time you usually pray? Post a note there that reminds you to both watch and pray.*

SATURDAY, MARCH 28

Let us not become weary in doing good, for at the proper time we will reap a harvest if we do not give up. Galatians 6:9 (NIV)

FROM OUR KITCHEN WINDOWS, WE watch the trees on Buford Mountain usher in the seasons—new buds in spring, dark greens in summer, a fiery display in autumn, and winter's barren gray.

While nature's seasons are often a metaphor for life, sometimes identifying life's seasons is not as simple as observing the colors carpeting a mountain. My emotions tend to be my indicators. Do I feel the anticipation of something new? Am I growing? Are my efforts paying off? Or does life feel cold and hard?

Rather than ask how I feel during a season, I'm trying to ask new, more important questions. What does Jesus want me to do during each season? Am I doing it at the right time? Living in an agricultural area, I recognize the answers to these questions are vital. A farmer doesn't harvest in the spring.

Except, I try to harvest in all seasons. In fact, I'm in a growing season right now. I should be nurturing and weeding, but this is taking too long. I'm ready to harvest, but that season seems so far away. Sometimes frustration makes me feel as though I'm in a cold, barren winter. Oh, the joy I'm robbing from myself because I want to do the right thing at the wrong time!

I've done the planting. I see growth. Now I need to nurture what Jesus is producing so I can experience the harvest He has planned, which will be so much more abundant than I could ever imagine.
—KAREN SARGENT

FAITH STEP: *Plant flower seeds. As they sprout, grow, and bloom, remember to do the right thing in the right season.*

Palm Sunday, March 29

My soul, wait in silence for God alone, for my hope is from Him.
Psalm 62:5 (NASB)

I ONCE ATTENDED A CONFERENCE over Palm Sunday weekend, and the church service on campus was unlike any I'd ever experienced. Before entering, we were given an order of service with explicit instructions to "enter in silence and expectation." I'm used to a lively, boisterous beginning to my Sunday morning worship time, with plenty of opportunities for handshakes, hugs, conversation, and laughter. This, I quickly realized, was the opposite of that. Instead of fellowship and connection, the silence created an atmosphere of reverence and solitude that allowed me to acknowledge the significance of the beginning of Holy Week.

I thought about Jesus's triumphal entry into Jerusalem and how the crowd welcomed Him with palm branches, shouting, "Hosanna!" and blessing Him as the King of Israel (John 12:12–13). I remembered how my own heart swelled with excitement the first time I entered the holy city of Jerusalem several years ago and experienced the joy of walking in the footsteps of Jesus.

But I also thought about the speed with which everything shifted for Him during Holy Week. In just a few days, the same crowd that welcomed Jesus into their city turned on Him and condemned Him to death. I know I can be just as fickle in my own thoughts and actions. The extended time of silence allowed me to talk to Jesus about the inconsistent nature of my soul. What a blessing that He is consistent even when I am not. —EMILY E. RYAN

FAITH STEP: *Take time to sit in silence and think about the ups and downs of your walk with Jesus. Thank Him for His unchanging nature.*

Monday, March 30

"I, when I am lifted up from the earth, will draw all people to myself." John 12:32 (NIV)

Almost twenty years ago, our founding pastor shared an idea one Sunday morning. Our church was in the middle of a building project, and we were committed to open a new debt-free worship facility within the next few years. But that morning, he had a divine notion from Jesus to pause the project and shift to a different focus. He proposed erecting a large cross on the edge of our campus with the hope of drawing the community to Jesus through the symbolic representation of the Gospel. With a cross that big, he explained, people will have a choice. "They can reject it or be blessed by it, but they certainly won't be able to ignore it," he said.

I'm reminded of that choice when I see Easter decorations in stores. Bunnies and eggs are everywhere, while reminders of the true meaning of Easter have become a little harder to find. At times, I can feel discouraged that our culture decorates with few Christian symbols of Easter. But when I remember Jesus's promise in John 12:32, I feel peace and hope instead. I don't need to stage a coup against the Easter Bunny or initiate a boycott against plastic eggs. I can simply lift the name of Jesus and point to the cross of Calvary in everything I say and do. Jesus, as He promised, will draw others to himself. —Emily E. Ryan

Faith Step: *Make a bold move to ensure others don't miss the true meaning of Easter this week. Lift up the name of Jesus and point everyone to the cross using Christian Easter decorations.*

Tuesday, March 31

By the grace God has given me, I laid a foundation as a wise builder, and someone else is building on it. But each one should build with care. For no one can lay any foundation other than the one already laid, which is Jesus Christ. 1 Corinthians 3:10–11 (NIV)

When the church approved the building of a 170-foot-tall cross, my father's construction company was asked to oversee the project. I watched as church leaders ceremonially broke ground by thrusting clean shovels into hard earth, smiled for a camera, then moved aside so the real work could begin. For weeks, men in hard hats maneuvered heavy equipment to prepare the site and lay a foundation for the cross. They poured a slab and built a thick base of steel that would eventually secure and support the cross with a series of large anchor bolts. "All of this," my dad said with a nonchalant wave of his hand, "will be underground. You'll only be able to see the cross."

With the time and care that was going into the foundation, it seemed a shame that no one would ever be able to see it. It was a lot of work to go unnoticed and unappreciated. Later, however, when I stood at the base of the ninety-seven-ton completed cross, confident in its ability to withstand any storm, I was grateful for the strong foundation.

I thought about how my daily time with Jesus is the foundation for my faith. The minutes may go unnoticed by others, but the importance of that time is evident when others see Jesus in me.
—Emily E. Ryan

Faith Step: *Strengthen the foundation of your faith by praying, reading the Bible, and spending time with Jesus. Construct a special place to meet Him daily.*

WEDNESDAY, APRIL 1

*We all, like sheep, have gone astray, each of us has turned to our own way; and the L*ORD *has laid on him the iniquity of us all. Isaiah 53:6 (NIV)*

ONCE CONSTRUCTION WAS COMPLETE ON the ninety-seven-ton, 170-foot-tall cross, my father, the project manager, had to conduct a series of final inspections. One required him to inspect the cross from the inside, which meant entering a secure door at the base and climbing up the industrial ladder all the way to the top. He invited my husband to join him, and with harnesses secured and fastened, they began their ascent one rung at a time. When they reached the horizontal crossbeam and exited the ladder to walk along the base of the steel rectangle suspended dozens of feet in the air, they could still hear the buzz of freeway traffic below them. Each car that whipped past represented another soul our church was praying would meet Jesus through the cross.

Before they began their descent, my father wrote the words of Isaiah 53:6 in black marker along the inside wall of the horizontal crossbeam. He knew no one would ever see it, but that didn't matter. To him, it was a permanent, ongoing prayer that everyone who sees the cross will eventually come to understand that it represents Jesus, our Savior, who sacrificed His life for ours and paid the ultimate penalty for our sins. Now, when I see the cross, I'm reminded of that sacrifice and committed to pray for those who do not yet know Jesus. —EMILY E. RYAN

FAITH STEP: *Draw a cross on a sheet of paper and write the words of Isaiah 53:6 on it. Ask Jesus to bring to mind someone to give it to this week.*

Maundy Thursday, April 2

"Say to the owner of the house he enters, 'The Teacher asks: Where is my guest room, where I may eat the Passover with my disciples?' He will show you a large room upstairs, furnished and ready. Make preparations for us there." Mark 14:14–15 (NIV)

PREPARATIONS HAVE BEGUN TO HOST my family for Easter this year, and it's an all-hands-on-deck endeavor. Everyone has a job to do—cleaning, mowing, shopping, cooking—but it will still take several days to make our home ready for guests. As we scurry about, I think about the Last Supper Jesus had with His disciples. The Bible says the group met in an unnamed man's upper guest room that was "furnished and ready" for them. No last-minute scrambling necessary.

I can't help but notice how that Passover meal in Jerusalem stands in stark contrast to Jesus's birth in Bethlehem. In each case, Jesus needed available space. In Bethlehem, He needed a place to have His first meal. In Jerusalem, He needed a place to have His last meal. One moment shows Jesus being turned away because there was "no room for them in the inn" (Luke 2:7). The other shows a man laying out the welcome mat and inviting Jesus into his home.

I want my home—and my heart—to be ready for Jesus, just as the upper room in Jerusalem was. As I work to prepare my home for guests, I also work to prepare my heart for Jesus—so no last-minute scrambling is necessary for either. —EMILY E. RYAN

FAITH STEP: *Prepare your heart for Jesus by reading John's account of the Last Supper in John 13–17.*

Good Friday, April 3

> *"Crucify him!" they shouted. "Why? What crime has he committed?" asked Pilate. But they shouted all the louder, "Crucify him!"* Mark 15:13–14 (NIV)

MANY YEARS AGO, MY HUSBAND and I wrote a pageant for church that recounted the story of Jesus from birth to resurrection. To help the audience experience the truth of the Gospel without getting lost in cultural confusion, we traded first-century Jerusalem for a modern setting instead and allowed actors to wear jeans and tennis shoes instead of robes and sandals. A few of our scenes were prerecorded off-site and incorporated into the story through video.

To depict the trial of Jesus, a local judge allowed us to film in her courtroom. The plan was to have the actor who played Jesus face a group of citizens in the jury box to receive his sentence. Even though I had not written myself into the script, something compelled me to step into the jury box and participate in that one scene. The cameras began rolling, and when it came time to deliver our lines, I shouted with the rest of the jury, "Crucify him! Crucify him!"

Even though it was just a play, that was one of the most humbling moments I've ever had in my walk with Jesus. It broke my heart to realize it was me and my sin that sent Jesus to the cross. But what joy and love I felt knowing He went there willingly. The weight of His sacrifice brings me to my knees. I don't always feel worthy of—but am so grateful for—such abundant love. —EMILY E. RYAN

FAITH STEP: *Spend time in humble silence on this Good Friday. Imagine yourself in the crowd of mockers and haters, then thank Jesus for His love and sacrifice on the cross.*

SATURDAY, APRIL 4

Jesus replied, "You do not realize now what I am doing, but later you will understand." John 13:7 (NIV)

When I taught at a private school, the curriculum included a unit on Corrie ten Boom's famous Holocaust memoir, *The Hiding Place*. It was a challenging but rewarding study and provided many opportunities to discuss how we can still trust Jesus through times of darkness, evil, and uncertainty. At the end of the unit, students were required to memorize and recite a poem that Corrie shared with audiences as she reflected on her time in a Nazi concentration camp. The poem is often called "The Tapestry Poem," and it introduces the idea that life is like a tapestry woven by the Lord. The problem is that we can only see the underside of His weaving, which appears chaotic and confusing, as if nothing good could ever come from such ugliness.

There were many times when Corrie could not imagine how Jesus could bring anything good from her time of persecution. I have had similar doubts during dark seasons of my own life, and I imagine Jesus's disciples felt the same way the day after His crucifixion. What good could come from their Savior dying on a cross?

The poem ends with the promise that a time will come when our Lord will flip over the tapestry and reveal the beauty He was weaving the whole time. We'll see how the darker threads of sorrow worked together with the threads of gold and silver to create a beautiful masterpiece. Although Saturday was full of sorrow for the disciples, Easter morning revealed a beautiful tapestry of understanding. —Emily E. Ryan

Faith Step: *Watch Corrie ten Boom share "The Tapestry Poem" on YouTube as you reflect on the anticipation of Jesus's resurrection.*

Easter Sunday, April 5

"Where, O death, is your victory? Where, O death, is your sting?"
1 Corinthians 15:55 (NIV)

Years ago, my husband and I met a video crew from church at a local cemetery to film an Easter sunrise scene. We arrived in the wee hours of the morning as the groundskeeper unlocked the massive gate that granted us access through the main entrance, then followed the crew down the narrow road that meandered through the property. The men began unloading at one of the oldest sections of the cemetery where rows of elaborate, fading headstones rested under a canopy of mature trees. Their goal was to artistically illustrate the resurrection of Jesus by shooting indirect glimpses of an actor walking through the cemetery at sunrise.

While the team set up their camera equipment and tested lighting and angles, I wandered through the rows of gravesites in the darkness. Every headstone seemed to shout a victory for death. Every name etched in stone, another casualty of sin. It was sobering.

But then the sunlight began peaking over the horizon. It bounced softly onto the morning dew, creating a thin layer of fog that hovered just above the earth. On cue, the actor walked slowly through the misty morning, away from the headstones, as the camera captured his footsteps. The wet grass absorbed the imprint of his bare feet like a sponge, and I couldn't help but stare at the trail of footprints that lingered long after the fog began to lift. My heart swelled with gratitude as I imagined Jesus's footprints as He walked out of the grave on the first Easter morning and conquered death for good. —Emily E. Ryan

Faith Step: *As you celebrate Easter today, thank Jesus for His victory over death and for new life in Him.*

Easter Monday, April 6

A merry heart does good, like medicine, but a broken spirit dries the bones. Proverbs 17:22 (NKJV)

ONE MORNING MY HUSBAND, ZANE, woke up feeling awful. He had been struggling with high blood pressure that caused fatigue and headaches, but this morning he was worse. He took his blood pressure, and it was dangerously high. He called his primary care doctor, and she advised him to go to the emergency room immediately. At the hospital, Zane's blood pressure was even higher. Concerned, the ER doctor wanted to monitor him for a while. While we waited, we pulled out our cell phones to read the news. *This can't be good*, I thought, as the headlines were mostly about war, severe storms, and rising inflation. I knew Zane was already stressed and so was I. So, I suggested we watch something lighthearted. I searched for a show on Netflix and found an hour-long special with a wholesome comedian.

As we laughed out loud at the jokes on birth order, marriage, communication, and other relatable topics, I watched Zane's blood pressure drastically drop. The proverb that laughter is like medicine proved to be true. I know Jesus is the ultimate Healer. I know He is always with us, but times of waiting can be hard. Thankfully, He has given us the gift of laughter, creating in us a merry heart even while we wait.

After a couple of hours and a stable blood pressure, the doctor said we could go home but to follow up with a cardiologist. We didn't have all the answers, but we did leave with a biblical prescription: Find ways to laugh and live with a cheerful heart.
—JEANNIE BLACKMER

FAITH STEP: *Add playfulness to your time with Jesus today, and find something funny to watch or read.*

Tuesday, April 7

Your word is a lamp for my feet, a light on my path. Psalm 119:105 (NIV)

I've found a new gardening nursery that I love to visit. It offers a wide selection of perennial bushes, spring flowers, and fruit trees. Even better, it has a supercute coffee shop close by. If I time it right, I can swing by for a cup of delicious coffee before I head to the nursery. It's a double whammy of joy.

The problem is that this delightful nursery is about half an hour away from my house. It is not in the normal parameters of where I usually drive. I tend to forget how to get there. I find myself getting turned around, wandering streets that look familiar but are nowhere near the actual nursery.

Luckily for me, I have my phone's trusty map app. When I lose my way, I can punch in the address and listen to the reassuring voice tell me where to go. This last week, I arrived at the nursery with a steaming cup of coffee in hand, just in time to view the new shipment of dwarf willow trees. (Double whammy of joy indeed.)

Jesus has given me a spiritual map so I don't lose my way: His Word. I gain wisdom and insight each time I turn to it. His reassuring Word helps me navigate the stresses of life. His directions are clear. When I follow His Word, I end up right where He wants me to be. Following Jesus is a double whammy of joy.
—Susanna Foth Aughtmon

Faith Step: *Memorize Psalm 119:105, and repeat it aloud throughout this week. Remind yourself that Jesus wants you to rely on His Word as a map to direct you throughout your day.*

WEDNESDAY, APRIL 8

"There will be signs in the sun, moon and stars. On the earth, nations will be in anguish and perplexity at the roaring and tossing of the sea. People will faint from terror, apprehensive of what is coming on the world, for the heavenly bodies will be shaken. At that time they will see the Son of Man coming in a cloud with power and great glory." Luke 21:25–27 (NIV)

MY INDIANA HOME WAS IN the path of totality for the April 8, 2024, solar eclipse. For four minutes in midafternoon, we stood outside while the temperature dropped, the sky darkened, and an otherworldly calm transformed the landscape. It was the first total solar eclipse my state had experienced in 819 years, a once-in-a-lifetime marvel. Some Indiana interstates were clogged with vehicles as visitors sought a better view.

In the weeks preceding it, the hype reminded me of the leadup to another phenomenon the world anticipated at the turn of the century. Several years before 1999 rolled into 2000, businesses prepared for Y2K, a computer programming issue related to calendar data that was anticipated to wreak havoc around the world.

Both of those events—one natural and the other man-made—reminded me how little I can control. Life is bigger, greater, more awesome than I can imagine. I can't control the weather or know all the ways of Jesus or the timeline of His return to earth.

My smallness in Jesus's kingdom is both awe-inspiring and comforting. Nothing ever takes Him by surprise, and nothing is too great for Him. I can only marvel at the totality of His sufficiency. Nothing eclipses Jesus, the Son. —ERIN KEELEY MARSHALL

FAITH STEP: *Go outside and sit in the sun. Praise the Son for His power throughout creation.*

Thursday, April 9

Let each of you look out not only for his own interests, but also for the interests of others. Philippians 2:4 (NKJV)

I DIRECT A NONPROFIT WITH a simple purpose: to encourage people. I call it "The Inspire Channel." Most donations come from family and friends who want to join me in uplifting others and meeting immediate needs. A few years ago, a man in our community experienced a terrible fall from a tree. David survived the accident but lost the use of his lower limbs. A church gathered a work crew to build a wheelchair ramp for his house, and The Inspire Channel bought the wood and supplies.

Another man in our town is struggling to fight off a devastating infection. He's been confined in a hospital bed for eighty days. This week, his family received a generous check for help with the massive medical bills. The gift was delivered by David in his wheelchair on behalf of his church.

I immediately recognized the beauty in the situation—the circle of kindness. Many neighbors showed compassion for David in his darkest hours, and now he has passed that compassion on to a family in their time of darkness. Though David's struggles haven't diminished, he's chosen to look out for the needs of someone else.

In a world that suggests I should satisfy myself, the teachings of Jesus direct me to live differently. My focus should be outward, not inward. Giving, not receiving. Caring for others instead of being overly concerned with myself. As a Christian, Jesus inspires me and equips me to inspire others. So does David. —BECKY ALEXANDER

FAITH STEP: *Pray that Jesus inspires you with someone who could use a bit of encouragement. Take action, and help them.*

Friday, April 10

My soul thirsts for God, for the living God. When can I go and meet with God? Psalm 42:2 (NIV)

My grandmother has been a vibrant part of our family as she's lived with us for more than two decades. This past year, she faced a significant challenge when a medical emergency led to a rush to the hospital and urgent surgery. Her recovery in the intensive care unit was filled with uncertainty, and for a while, we weren't sure if she'd be able to return home.

When Grandma came home, she could no longer perform many tasks she once could, like getting out of bed unassisted. Despite these physical setbacks, her spiritual devotion remained strong. Grandma might sometimes forget my name, but she always remembers Jesus and still prays with deep faith. Her memory of movie stars has faded, but she can still recite and sing hymns with ease and devotion. Her songs, full of love and faith, prove how Jesus has transformed her life in beautiful ways. Our current season with Grandma highlights a crucial lesson for our family: The Lord's kindness transcends our physical abilities and memories. No matter what we can or can't do for Jesus, His steadfast presence offers strength and comfort, guiding us through challenges with unending love and grace. I'm not sure how long Grandma will be able to remain with us, but I'm assured that wherever she goes, Jesus will be there. —Tricia Goyer

Faith Step: *Reflect on Jesus's enduring kindness in your life. Think about how you can show this kindness to others, bringing light and hope to those around you through your actions.*

SATURDAY, APRIL 11

My whole being, praise the LORD and do not forget all his kindnesses.
Psalm 103:2 (NCV)

"FOR YOU, NANA!" LILAH HELD out a teeny-tiny purple flower she'd found in her yard. I pulled out my phone, and we snapped photos of the precious gift, some with the flower in her hand and others with it lying on different surfaces. As we looked at the pictures, we zoomed in and marveled over the bloom's intense color, its graceful, curved edges, and the intricate structures in the center. The little flower wilted quickly, but I still treasure those photos.

I have a tendency to sometimes get so caught up in the big picture of life that I miss out on little details that would encourage or inspire me. A daily goal or lifelong dream may seem too lofty to achieve unless I notice the baby steps I'm taking that gradually move me closer to achieving it. A problem may look too big to solve until I pay attention to the small signs of improvement.

I know Jesus is working in my life and in the world around me every day. Sometimes His presence and intervention are obvious, but He also shows Himself in subtle ways that might go unnoticed. If I train myself to focus on the little things that bring joy, comfort, or a glimpse of beauty, my life is sure to be richer and filled with praise. Zooming in on the smaller blessings Jesus pours out every single day is the picture-perfect way to live. —DIANNE NEAL MATTHEWS

FAITH STEP: *Walk around your yard or your favorite spot to observe nature. Zoom in on little details you might not normally notice. Thank Jesus for surrounding you with small blessings along with the big ones.*

SUNDAY, APRIL 12

*Out of the ground the L*ORD *God made every tree grow that is pleasant to the sight and good for food.* Genesis 2:9 (NKJV)

I USED TO SIT AT my desk in our apartment in Queens and look out at the one skinny tree that stood right outside my bedroom window. It was basically dead, except for one or two branches that spit out a few leaves every spring. I appreciated that hint of green so close to me, but one year I prayed, "Jesus, when you see fit, take me to live in a place where there are more trees close by, please." As the years went on, I forgot about that prayer, as I tend to do when I don't see things changing, and I pressed on living in my beloved concrete jungle.

Then I moved down south to Atlanta, Georgia. I was flabbergasted by the different species of trees that lined the roads: magnolias, dogwoods, southern pines. It was shockingly lush for the nation's ninth-largest metro area! Outside my new bedroom window were so many mature trees that they were impossible to count. They were "pleasant to the sight," and some branches hung so low I could almost reach them. It was then that I remembered the little request I made back in Queens, the prayer for more trees. Jesus remembered too. And He supplied, abundantly. —PAMELA TOUSSAINT HOWARD

FAITH STEP: *Talk to Jesus about everything you love and don't love in your life right now. Share your godly desires with Him and wait to see how He provides you with all that is pleasant and good.*

Monday, April 13

Do not love the world or the things in the world. If anyone loves the world, the love of the Father is not in him. 1 John 2:15 (NKJV)

I've noticed a repeated word in many televised and online ads. The influencer (aka, influence-to-purchase) begins their pitch with, "I'm absolutely (or totally) obsessed with _____." It could be a solar-powered camping light, a last-all-day lip stain, or a green smoothie formula for instant health/weight loss/energy/clarity of mind forever and ever, amen.

When watching those ads, I get stuck on the word *obsessed*. Is that what they really intend to say? Preoccupied with, controlled by, consumed by, dominated by a kitchen scrubber? A shade of blush? A wrinkle minimizer? A flavor of herbal tea? That last one hit too close to home. I adore peach tea!

It's easy to criticize the casual use of *obsession* to describe how much the influencer likes the product they're using and selling. But am I any wiser? I can become obsessed with, fascinated by, preoccupied with so many things that are worthless compared to knowing Christ.

First John 2:15 spells it out clearly. Loving—putting my affections on, becoming obsessed with—the things of the world can hamper my ability to reveal the love of Jesus in my life. Obsession with anything other than Him can overshadow my relationship with Him. If I love worldly things, the love of God is not in me.

Jesus pierces my heart with the reminder to guard my compulsions and what consumes me. I enjoy peach tea. But I adore Jesus only. —Cynthia Ruchti

Faith Step: *If casual use of the word* obsessed *makes you uncomfortable, ask someone to hold you accountable until it becomes a habit to use the word in a Jesus-honoring way.*

Tuesday, April 14

"I say to you, love your enemies, bless those who curse you, do good to those who hate you, and pray for those who spitefully use you and persecute you." Matthew 5:44 (NKJV)

MY HUSBAND AND I HAD been members of a community group, where our friendship with a woman blossomed. Then one day, I realized that when I waved hello or spoke to the woman, whom I considered a friend, something had changed. I had no idea what I'd done or said to anger her, and when I tried to ask, she walked away. My emotions moved from confusion to hurt to indignation. I lay awake at night, assuring myself I had every right to be miffed.

Then Jesus gently reminded me it's better to respond with love, trusting God to work things through in His timing and to His glory. After that, whenever thoughts of my past friend crossed my mind, I prayed—both for her well-being and for my spirit of forgiveness. It proved difficult at first, but over time, those prayers flowed with genuine caring. Jesus had healed my hurt.

This week while out running errands, I noticed her and called out a quick hello. As I searched the shelves for an item, she approached me, behaving as if there'd never been a problem. We chatted for a few minutes, then went our separate ways, smiling. None of the past troubles seemed to remain.

I don't pretend to understand the whys and hows behind what happened. Like a child, I choose to leave those burdens to a bigger heart and greater wisdom—Jesus. I'm satisfied to simply walk lightly where Jesus led me, on the path of forgiveness. —HEIDI GAUL

FAITH STEP: *Consider a relationship you struggle with. Pray daily for that person's well-being, and trust Jesus for healing as you accept and forgive.*

WEDNESDAY, APRIL 15

May you be completely faithful to the LORD our God. May you always obey his decrees and commands, just as you are doing today. 1 Kings 8:61 (NLT)

I RECENTLY OVERHEARD AN ANIMATED conversation between two young women about going to the movies. One lamented the cost of a movie ticket and the popcorn and beverage that she just couldn't do without. "Yeah, you have to commit to it," her friend responded.

Well, I certainly don't feel obligated to make popcorn and a Coke a part of my moviegoing experience. But the conversation made me think about what it means to commit to something or someone. A commitment can involve giving my time, money, and/or energy. I am committed to my husband and family, serving in my church, and maintaining relationships with friends. But my biggest commitment is to Jesus. He calls me to be faithful to Him, follow His teachings, and stay close to Him. I can only do that with the help of the Holy Spirit, who leads and guides me every day. And while I sometimes fall short of keeping my commitment to the Savior, He always forgives and beckons me to return when I stray from Him. Jesus is the ultimate commitment keeper.
—BARBRANDA LUMPKINS WALLS

FAITH STEP: *As you ponder your list of commitments, consider where time with Jesus ranks. If He's not at the top of your list, make a plan to better commit to Him.*

Thursday, April 16

"Come to Me, all you who labor and are heavy laden, and I will give you rest." Matthew 11:28 (NKJV)

I LOVE DRIVING BY MYSELF, with time void of demands and responsibilities. It's just me, my favorite music, and the cross-country scenery. So I wasn't bothered driving ten hours to Kansas City for board meetings.

This trip, though, could have been more carefree. More than one of my four children were going through difficult circumstances. I carried their hurts in my heart, which felt heavy and broken. Parenting was difficult when they were small, and I often had my hands full. I thought the job would get easier once the kids grew up, but adult kids have adult problems.

I wasn't driving long before my sadness spilled out in tears. I verbalized to God the grief and longings for each of my children's situations. I continued to do so during the drive as songs I listened to expressed feelings about things I couldn't control. I wanted to release these worries and be present and attentive to my professional responsibilities, which would soon be upon me.

As I neared my destination, Jesus gently reminded me that the burdens I carried weren't mine. They belonged to Him. *Would I let Him carry their troubles?* He wanted to care for me as I supported my children.

I imagined each child's situation and pictured it being placed in Jesus's hands. My heart lightened. Jesus helped me separate what was mine to carry from what was His. I might have my hands full with four kids, but Jesus could more than handle it. —BRENDA L. YODER

FAITH STEP: *What burdens do you need to place into Jesus's hands? Envision yourself giving each care to Him. Trust Jesus to handle them.*

Friday, April 17

"See, I will create new heavens and a new earth. The former things will not be remembered, nor will they come to mind." Isaiah 65:17 (NIV)

My daughter, Ana, and I enjoy the show *Flea Market Flip* on HGTV. During the competition-style series, two pairs of bargain hunters search their local flea market to find three items to update and repurpose. The team with the highest resale value for their pieces at the end wins. Watching together, Ana and I discuss how we would have recreated the projects differently.

A handful of times over the years, we have upcycled worn pieces for our home. Seeing a pair of chairs abandoned on the roadside last spring, we hopped out of the car and loaded them into our SUV. However, they sat in our basement gathering dust until we eventually cast the unfinished pieces out to the curb ourselves.

But Jesus never discards us. In fact, He came to this world specifically to save us. By His death and resurrection on the cross, we were cleaned of our sins and flipped into a new creation. Using tools of forgiveness, grace, love, and mercy, He continues to reshape us to be more like Him every day.

Weathered like those chairs, I sometimes lean into discouragement, forgetting that Jesus has not abandoned me on the curb. Jesus loves me, and I'm being remade and repurposed—not because of my skill but His. I believe the finished product will be amazing!
—Gloria Joyce

Faith Step: *Make a list of circumstances in your life you want Jesus to flip. Wait for Him to create something beautiful.*

SATURDAY, APRIL 18

Just as Christ was raised from the dead by the glory of the Father, even so we also should walk in newness of life. Romans 6:4 (NKJV)

LAST NIGHT WE ATTENDED AN annual gala sponsored by the cancer center that treated my husband's leukemia. One thousand people crowded into a ballroom at the Hyatt in St. Louis. Doctors said the gala is their favorite night of the year. Seeing healthy patients all dressed up was something to celebrate. One oncologist added, "With hair," drawing laughter from the crowd. Russ looked around the room and whispered, "We're the ones who made it. I wonder how many didn't."

My husband is approaching his fifth "new birthday," as the doctors refer to the transplant date, since bone marrow literally gives the patient a second life. Aggressive chemotherapy removes the diseased bone marrow. Then new marrow is infused and begins producing healthy cells. I still can't grasp how our daughter's bone marrow transplanted into her dad's body gave him new life.

Kind of like Nicodemus, who didn't understand when Jesus said he must be born again (John 3:3). Literally, the concept is impossible to grasp. Yet, I know the sin that flows through my veins. Bitterness and unforgiveness from the past are my disease of choice. They rob my life. I cannot fight sin with my own strength. Opening my heart and inviting Jesus to infuse His love in me and through me, overflowing, heals me to walk in new life with Him. Something to celebrate, indeed. —KAREN SARGENT

FAITH STEP: *Send a word of encouragement to someone who is fighting cancer and remember to pray for them.*

Sunday, April 19

"The King will reply, 'Truly I tell you, whatever you did for one of the least of these brothers and sisters of mine, you did for me.'" Matthew 25:40 (NIV)

As I drove down the interstate off-ramp, my mind swirled with my to-do list. At the stop light, my attention was drawn to a woman with a sign that read "Need gas money to get home." A harsh thought crossed my mind that she should get a job like everyone else and maybe she'd have money for gas.

Immediately I felt a nudge—honestly, it was more like a punch in my heart. *What if that were me?* I shifted uncomfortably as the light turned green, and I drove toward my destination. Again came the nudge. *What if I were holding a sign on the side of the road?*

As I pulled into a drive-through, I had another thought: *What if that were Jesus?* I am certain I'd give Him whatever He asked for.

As I placed my order, I reordered my heart and my mind. I drove back to the woman and gave her the cash I had with me, a warm sandwich, and a drink too. It wasn't my place to judge her, but as a Jesus follower I was called to show compassion and kindness and be helpful. Being the hands and feet of Jesus should always be on the top of my to-do list. —Renee Mitchell

Faith Step: *Wait for Jesus to nudge you when you see someone in need. Then be willing to be His hands and feet in that moment.*

MONDAY, APRIL 20

Jesus looked at him and loved him. Mark 10:21 (NIV)

I COULDN'T HELP BUT WONDER about the cashier as I stood in the checkout line. Her clothing was disheveled, she had bags under her eyes, and her hair was pulled up in a messy bun. This young woman didn't smile or make eye contact with the customers as she mechanically scanned their purchases.

I loaded my groceries onto the conveyor belt, pushed my buggy out of the way, and stepped up to the checkout counter. I bid her hello and began to gently engage her in conversation.

In doing so, I learned that this young lady was navigating a divorce, trying to raise a young son, caring for an aging mother, and holding down this stressful, customer-service, minimum-wage job to pay the bills. Sleep was a luxury at the moment. As someone who had personally navigated all those seasons in my own life at one time or another, my heart went out to her. I looked at her and discerned the Holy Spirit nudging me to show her some love.

"Could I buy you a coffee and bring it back to you?" I asked, as she held my receipt. She lifted her head and met my gaze. "You would do that for me?" she exclaimed and smiled broadly.

A small gesture, but a beautiful reminder that something as small as a cup of coffee could make all the difference. I couldn't have known how much it would mean to this woman, but Jesus sure did.
—KRISTEN WEST

FAITH STEP: *Is there someone the Holy Spirit is nudging you to look at and love? Ask Jesus how you can make a difference.*

Tuesday, April 21

Do to others as you would have them do to you. Luke 6:31 (NIV)

My nephew and his wife joined us for dinner on our sailboat one evening. After the meal, my husband suggested taking a little cruise in our dinghy. We donned life vests, climbed into the inflatable boat, and off we went.

Along the way, we noticed a power yacht anchored in a random place near the shoreline. Seeing no one on deck, we supposed its passengers might be relaxing inside. Our suspicions proved wrong when, on our return trip, we saw a man on deck waving his arms to attract our attention.

My husband turned our dinghy toward the yacht. As we drew closer, we saw something most unusual: The boat's anchor dangled about five feet above the water's surface, caught in a second anchor that was attached to a heavy chain.

Unbeknownst to the captain, he'd anchored his vessel above a sunken boat. When he raised his anchor to leave, it snagged the unseen boat's anchor and dragged it to the surface. The captain—the sole occupant—could not untangle them, and their combined weight made it impossible for the boat to move. The men quickly devised a plan: The captain would inch the boat forward until my husband and nephew could muscle the anchors apart. The plan worked, and the grateful captain was on his way within minutes.

Most mariners treat other mariners as they want to be treated because they know they, too, will need help sooner or later. They live by the Golden Rule as Jesus taught, a worthy principle that applies to landlubbers as well. —Grace Fox

Faith Step: *What kindness do you wish someone would show you? Do that same kind action for someone today.*

WEDNESDAY, APRIL 22

For we do not have a high priest who is unable to sympathize with our weaknesses, but one who in every respect has been tempted as we are, yet without sin. Hebrews 4:15 (ESV)

THE NEW TESTAMENT CONTAINS MANY lists that sometimes leave me feeling like a total failure. Take the fruit of the Spirit in Galatians 5:22–23: love, joy, peace, patience, kindness, goodness, faithfulness, gentleness, and self-control. Some days, I can barely muster a grape, much less that fruitful bounty of virtues.

Sometimes, I just wake up on the wrong side of the bed for no apparent reason. Everything is the same as yesterday, but today the glass seems half empty to me. I'm spiritually mature enough that I can act right when I'm not feeling right, but I still feel rotten.

I can't always pray or act my way to a better frame of mind. I just soldier through the day as best I can, trusting it will pass. *Sigh*. If I were keeping score on quantity or quality of Christian virtues, I'd definitely lose.

Thankfully, it's not up to me, and Jesus isn't keeping score. He already won the game. Jesus was in every way human and all too familiar with my weaknesses. He looks on me with compassion. I have His grace for bad days, giving me the strength to behave well when I'm not feeling it. On the days I can't seem to harvest those fruit of the Spirit, Jesus, my high priest, stands in the gap. Because He lived a perfect life, I don't have to. —ISABELLA CAMPOLATTARO

FAITH STEP: *The next time you have a rough day, talk to Jesus as a sympathetic counselor. Know that Jesus comforts, guides, and advocates for you.*

Thursday, April 23

"We will turn this responsibility over to them and will give our attention to prayer and the ministry of the word." Acts 6:3–4 (NIV)

When I volunteered for my daughter's play, *Frozen*, I was assigned to solve a problem with the traditional village dress Elsa wears for all of Act I. In Act II, she tears it away while singing "Let It Go," revealing the iconic teal gown underneath. But the magnets that kept the traditional dress together weren't strong enough to hold for the entirety of Act I. The director had already spent countless hours trying to troubleshoot the issue, but it was taking away from her ability to direct the show. When she gave me full responsibility to solve the problem, it inspired me to take complete ownership. I not only gave it my all but also confirmed before every performance that the Velcro I added was still working.

That's what asking others for help does: It empowers and encourages them to take full ownership. The Apostles in Acts 6 knew this when they made a select group of men responsible for distributing food to the widows. Doing so elevated a whole new group of people and freed up the Apostles so they could focus on spreading the Word to grow the church.

Letting it go and empowering others allows everyone to use their God-given gifts to shine, whether on the stage or for Jesus's kingdom. —Claire McGarry

Faith Step: *Are you frozen by trying to do everything yourself? Ask someone in your sphere to share the spotlight. Watch them shine the more you empower them.*

Friday, April 24

Because of his grace he made us right in his sight and gave us confidence that we will inherit eternal life. Titus 3:7 (NLT)

"Attention Beneficiary" states the email notifications I receive nearly daily. Apparently, I'm the beloved beneficiary of an unknown relative. It's true, people are trying to give me money. Obscenely large sums of money. It looks official, usually sent from an important-sounding barrister somewhere far away. All they need for me to claim my inheritance is my full name, address, phone number...and sometimes my bank account and routing number.

Scam letters like these are easily spotted and deleted. But it's understandable how they might tempt trusting, unsuspecting, or financially hurting souls into believing such auspicious news of promised riches. Regardless of how good they sound, they remind me of a more valuable inheritance. Whenever I see "Attention Beneficiary" or "Dear Beloved" in my email box, I remember whose beneficiary I *truly* am. Rather than wish these faux legal letters were true, I thank the Lord Jesus that He's my inheritance.

Through Jesus, I'm a fellow heir of God's glory (Romans 8:16–17), so I'm confident in my eternal inheritance. It won't require an officious directive from some online barrister because the Lord already has all my contact information. Moreover, He won't be needing my bank routing number for me to receive my divine inheritance—eternal life with Jesus—because that is already secured.
—Cassandra Tiersma

Faith Step: *Read these Bible verses about your eternal inheritance: Romans 8:16–17, Galatians 4:7, Colossians 1:12, Titus 3:7, and 1 Peter 1:3–4. In the margin, write, "I'm His Beloved Beneficiary." And if you get one of those emails promising you an unexpected inheritance, delete it!*

SATURDAY, APRIL 25

The third time he said to him, "Simon son of John, do you love me?" Peter was hurt because Jesus asked him the third time, "Do you love me?" He said, "Lord, you know all things; you know that I love you." Jesus said, "Feed my sheep." John 21:17 (NIV)

WHEN I TURNED FIFTY YEARS old, I started thinking even more about the goals I've achieved and the blessings I've received. I have a lot to celebrate and to be thankful for, yet there's this dark, shadowy corner in the crevice of my mind. It's a very unkind place with mental records of regrets, misunderstood moments, and missed opportunities that are hard to forget.

One of those misses was in my early thirties. A coworker who knew I was a Christian asked me about the origin story of Jesus. She was skeptical about Christianity because she heard older ancient cultures had stories that were very similar to biblical accounts. I didn't know much about other religions or their history, but I believed she was eager to get satisfactory answers. Although I intended to answer her questions, I never did.

I'm sure Jesus's disciple Peter could have related to my feelings. He had three opportunities when he could have acknowledged Jesus, but he didn't. Yet forgiveness is shown when Jesus tells him to feed His sheep.

In moments of failure, I can feel like Peter. But in the same way that Jesus extends forgiveness to Peter, He also extends it to me.
—ERICKA LOYNES

FAITH STEP: *Do regrets linger in your memory? Ask Jesus to forgive your past denials and pray for an opportunity to share His good news with someone today.*

SUNDAY, APRIL 26

"Let us know; let us press on to know the LORD; his going out is sure as the dawn; he will come to us as the showers, as the spring rains that water the earth." Hosea 6:3 (ESV)

THE DEVOTIONALS I WRITE ARE dirt-road dispatches from a ranch in rural Arkansas. No one comes to my house unless it's intentional, and even then the driveway is not for the faint of heart. I once had a friend visit from another country, and she told me my road was terrifying. "I was afraid tigers were going to jump out at me," she said. I nearly died laughing before explaining there are no tigers here. "Only bears and mountain lions." She was not comforted.

We keep gravel on the road, but what's under it is a mixture of clay soil. When it rains it becomes slippery, which is worse than just steep and stony. This spring we had so much rain that it washed all the gravel away. We had to keep driving on it to get back and forth to school and our jobs, and the road totally transformed into specific paths carved out by the water.

When Jesus rains so thoroughly into our lives, we come to know Him intimately. He transforms us much like my driveway. He washes away everything but the specific path He has for us to travel. And while it may not be the easiest route, it is the only way forward. I'm so thankful Jesus travels with me. —GWEN FORD FAULKENBERRY

FAITH STEP: *Put your hand under a faucet, and let the water wash over your skin. Thank Jesus for traveling with you in all kinds of weather.*

Monday, April 27

I will give you the treasures of darkness and the hoards in secret places, that you may know that it is I, the Lord, the God of Israel, who call you by your name. Isaiah 45:3 (ESV)

I DECIDED IT WAS TIME to replace my worn tan carpeting. I must have shopped at seven different stores, as I didn't know exactly what I wanted. I finally settled on a green shade. "It will save you money if you take up the existing carpeting yourself," the sales clerk suggested.

"That's a great idea! Hold off on coming to measure until I've done that," I said.

I started in one corner of the room. The old carpet easily released its grip and revealed something unexpected. *Oh my gosh!* There, beneath the drab carpeting, was the most beautiful hardwood floor. The oak boards had been hidden for decades.

I was amazed. I couldn't believe the wood floors had been there all along. It was just what I was looking for, and I didn't even know it. I loved it better than the carpeting I had chosen. The wooden treasure would never be covered again.

I couldn't help but wonder what other imperfect exteriors in my life were hiding beautiful surprises. —JEANNIE HUGHES

FAITH STEP: *Look around your house for objects with hidden beauty. Pray that Jesus will reveal the beauty hidden inside of you too.*

Tuesday, April 28

Care about them as much as you care about yourselves. Philippians 2:4 (CEV)

I HOPPED ON MY BIKE earlier than usual that morning for my seven-mile ride through the neighborhood. With this early start, maybe I could avoid the annoying people who got in my way and impeded my ride daily, slowing me down and making me swerve around them. The man with the cane who never failed to holler, "Good morning!" The woman in the hot pink tennis shoes, yakking on her phone. The thin guy being yanked along by his two large Labradors. The young mom who jogged behind the stroller with the crying baby. Miraculously, I didn't encounter one of these irritating strangers on my route.

Back home with my water bottle in hand, I marveled at how smoothly my ride had gone without having to go around the pesky strangers. I'd beaten my best time! Why, then, did I have this empty feeling?

Are they really strangers, Pat? I felt Jesus whisper. I saw these people every day. I didn't know their names, nor they mine. But we traveled the road of life together. I wondered if Young Mom was getting any sleep; the baby sounded colicky. Could I have a decent day without my greeting from Good Morning Man? Didn't Pink Tennis Shoes know it was dangerous to be on her phone when she was on the street? And what would Thin Guy do if his dogs got away from him?

No, I didn't know these people, but they had become part of my daily life, and I cared about them. Just as Jesus wants me to do.
—PAT BUTLER DYSON

FAITH STEP: *As you encounter familiar strangers today (neighbors, delivery people, mail carriers, etc.), ask Jesus how you might pray for them.*

WEDNESDAY, APRIL 29

We know that all that happens to us is working for our good if we love God and are fitting into his plans. Romans 8:28 (TLB)

I RECENTLY HAD SURGERY TO replace three bulging discs in my neck that caused pain and numbness to jolt down my shoulder, arm, and hand. Unfortunately, the operation had to be rescheduled twice, and it took place eight months after the original date. I was frustrated with the delays.

Thankfully the surgery was successful, and I came home the following morning. But I didn't receive the long list of restrictions until the hospital discharged me. No bending, twisting, looking down, lifting, or strenuous exercise. I prepared myself for a long, boring recovery.

On my fourth day home, my husband spotted a rose-breasted grosbeak at the feeder outside our dining room. Rosies migrate through our area in the spring and usually stay only a couple days. This handsome boy and his family hung around for more than a week. A few days later, orioles, with their bright orange bellies and black wings, arrived for their yearly vacation in our elm tree. They circled and soared, giving me a daily bird ballet of spectacular color. My flowerbed burst with irises like ladies dancing at a party, in gowns of deep purple, warm peach, and butter yellow.

I knew Jesus had arranged the perfect timing for my surgery, when the arrival of springtime birds and blooms would make a long, boring recovery more joyful. Of course, He didn't cause the delays to frustrate me, but He worked them out for my good.
—JEANETTE LEVELLIE

FAITH STEP: *Look at a calendar or clock, and tell Jesus that you trust His perfect timing no matter what delays you encounter in your life.*

Thursday, April 30

To be made new in the attitude of your minds; and to put on the new self, created to be like God in true righteousness and holiness.
Ephesians 4:23–24 (NIV)

AFTER EIGHTEEN YEARS, OUR HOME needed a fresh coat of paint and new flooring. Although we hired professionals, I wasn't fully prepared for the hard labor that clearing the rooms required. Boxing loose items and lifting furniture felt a lot like moving.

As I handled each item, I wondered, *Do I need this? Do I even like it?* The result was a massive purge. Some objects were easy to donate. Others weren't, even though I no longer wanted them.

Did I fear I might need that thing someday, like the old video camera my smartphone replaced years ago? Some items I'd hung on to simply because of who gave them to me, even if I didn't really like them. Other possessions I'd had forever. Wasn't that a good reason to keep possessing them? No. Into the donation box they went.

As I purged, I couldn't help but think about the clutter my heart had collected. Could I put it to the same test? I recognized my emotional attachment to the rejection from my deceased stepfather. I'm trying to let it go. Do I really think someday I might need that old guilt I keep hanging on to? And that fear of failure I've carried forever, isn't it time to drop it?

Decluttering my heart is not as easy as placing an item into a donation box, so I'm calling in Jesus and trusting His ability to renew my interior. —KAREN SARGENT

FAITH STEP: *Identify why your heart hangs on to physical or emotional clutter. Assign Jesus the task to renew your mind and help you purge both.*

Friday, May 1

Therefore, as we have opportunity, let us do good to all people, especially to those who belong to the family of believers. Galatians 6:10 (NIV)

This morning, I spent time in my kitchen making my favorite recipe: scones. In my old Pyrex bowl, I mixed two cups of flour, one-fourth cup of sugar, and one tablespoon of baking powder. I cut in one-fourth pound of butter and stirred in one cup of buttermilk. Patting them into a round on a cookie sheet, I cut and separated twelve wedges, sprinkled them lightly with sugar, and baked them for twelve to fifteen minutes at 400 degrees Fahrenheit. They were light, fluffy handfuls of deliciousness.

My friend Elizabeth shared the recipe with me more than twenty years ago, along with French roast coffee and a side of homemade blackberry jam. Best. Scone. Ever. Since then, I have shared them with many dear friends. These delectable treats are expected on family holidays. I've taken them to teacher appreciation days. I love sharing them with the people in my life.

Today, I'm baking celebratory scones because my parents are visiting from Colorado. As the smell of their warm goodness fills the air, I'm reminded this isn't the only goodness that needs to be shared.

Jesus is the embodiment of goodness. I can't keep the beauty of who He is and what He has done for me to myself. His faithfulness needs to be shared with every friend. His peace and hope with each neighbor. As I share the goodness of Jesus's love, maybe I'll bring some delicious scones too. Goodness upon goodness. One thing is for sure, Jesus is too good not to share. —Susanna Foth Aughtmon

Faith Step: *Take a sweet treat to someone in your life who needs to experience the goodness of Jesus.*

SATURDAY, MAY 2

When I discovered your words, I devoured them. They are my joy and my heart's delight. Jeremiah 15:16 (NLT)

I CHECKED THE EMAIL FROM the post office showing what mail to expect that day. I smiled when I saw the card from my mom. For the first time in forty years, I now live close enough that I can visit her at least once a week. She could have handed me the anniversary card, but she loves mailing notes to people. Mom wrote me a letter every week during my college years, even if it was just before a break. She continued to write weekly letters filled with news from home after I married and moved several hundred miles away. No matter how uprooted I felt during our relocations or how difficult life seemed to be, I always found comfort in my mom's letters.

I've also learned to depend on what my heavenly Father has written. The best part about reading the Bible is that Jesus is the Living Word (John 1:14). So whether I'm reading the history, poetry, prophecies, and wisdom books in the Old Testament or the gospel narratives and letters to individuals and churches in the New Testament, I'm getting to know Jesus more deeply. I grow in my understanding of who He is and how He works. I learn how He wants me to live to honor Him. My soul is nourished by the expressions of love I find there. It's like getting news from home, and it's available to read any time I need comfort. —DIANNE NEAL MATTHEWS

FAITH STEP: *Before opening your Bible today, sit quietly and ask Jesus, the Living Word, to direct you to the message you most need to read. Find comfort in His letter to you.*

Sunday, May 3

Since they could not get him to Jesus because of the crowd, they made an opening in the roof above Jesus by digging through it and then lowered the mat the man was lying on. Mark 2:4 (NIV)

From the balcony at church, I watched a family arrive several minutes after the service began. An elderly woman was lying in a cross between a wheelchair and a hospital bed and was being wheeled in by a younger woman who looked to be her daughter. The cumbersome contraption seemed hard to maneuver, but the younger woman navigated the aisles like an expert while the rest of the family trailed behind them. She parked the elevated bed in the small opening between seats and immediately began attending to the needs of the bedridden woman. She adjusted the angle of the seat, fluffed her pillow, offered a sip of water, and tilted her head so the stage was within her line of sight. Even after she joined the congregation in singing, she still paused every few minutes to look at the woman and care for her as needed.

I thought about the amount of effort it must have taken to get the elderly woman to church that day. The preparations. The supplies. The time. The determination. How many hands had been involved in bringing one person to Jesus? It reminded me of the men in the Bible who cut a hole in a roof so they could help their paralyzed friend get to Jesus. Sometimes, it takes more than an invitation to bring someone to Jesus. Sometimes, it takes hard work.
—Emily E. Ryan

Faith Step: *How can you help friends meet Jesus today? If they need a ride to church or a hot meal afterward, give it freely.*

MONDAY, MAY 4

Rather, it should be that of your inner self, the unfading beauty of a gentle and quiet spirit, which is of great worth in God's sight. 1 Peter 3:4 (NIV)

AFTER DECADES IN THE OPTICAL field as an optician, I'm naturally drawn to people's eyes. Color, form, obvious health concerns—all cross my mind in a flash. But faith has taught me to take a slower inventory, to see beyond the surface.

Entering the checkout line, I scrutinized the checker's stance and appearance: slump-shouldered, face downcast. After her monotone greeting, I waited before answering, pushing her to make eye contact.

William Shakespeare is credited with saying the eyes are the window to the soul. If that's true, then this woman's windows were shut, curtains drawn.

When she finally met my gaze, I answered her perfunctory greeting very specifically, "You have beautiful eyes." At once, her posture corrected, her expression changed, a smile flitted across her lips, and she thanked me. I'd glimpsed inside her soul and confirmed that what I saw was good. Though I'm unaware what challenges she battles, I believe my simple act of kindness, one soul to another, brightened her morning.

Jesus does this for me daily. Beyond simply reminding me that my eyes are lovely, I know I'm precious to Him. His loving eyes look at what lies deep inside my soul, a place only He can see. I don't have to be an optician to see how cherished I am in Jesus's sight.
—HEIDI GAUL

FAITH STEP: *Make it a point to truly look into the eyes of people you encounter this week. Be bold and mention something beautiful you see within each person.*

TUESDAY, MAY 5

If then you have been raised with Christ, seek the things that are above, where Christ is, seated at the right hand of God. Colossians 3:1 (ESV)

As my husband and I waited at the airport to board an early morning flight, I noticed a woman in a corner away from the crowd. She was in full workout gear, exercising with barbells and resistance bands. I watched her stretch, jump, and squat for at least 30 minutes. This sister was serious about getting in her workout that day! It was evident that she wasn't going to let the time or place stop her.

As much as I'd like to be, I'm not always as devoted to getting in my daily spiritual workout, which includes prayer, reading scripture, journaling, and sitting quietly listening for God. Some mornings I let my list of to-do items—errands, chores, salon appointments, doctor appointments, meetings, and more—take precedence over spending time with Jesus. There also have been times when I hit the snooze button instead of rolling out of bed to meet my Savior, even after I hear Him clearly telling me to rise and shine. I've found that when I fail to seek the things above and don't exercise the spiritual disciplines I know to follow, I suffer for it.

When I do fall off the wagon, I seek Jesus's forgiveness and get back on track to build my spiritual muscles and resistance to wrongdoing. Like that woman in the airport dedicated to her exercise routine, I, too, must be dedicated to my workout with Jesus, no matter what happens or where I am. —Barbranda Lumpkins Walls

Faith Step: *Make a list of what distracts you from spending time with Jesus. Write ways you can remove those distractions.*

WEDNESDAY, MAY 6

"Give careful thought to your ways. You have planted much, but harvested little." Haggai 1:5–6 (NIV)

WHEN MY DAUGHTER, JOCELYN, ASKED if she could take private violin lessons again this summer, I said she had to back up her request with action. She rarely practiced when I paid for lessons last summer. I can tell she has a natural talent; her teacher even emailed me about it. He was also impressed by her enthusiasm. What he didn't know is she's also enthusiastic about robotics, theater, volunteering, cross country, track, and many other activities. In fact, my 13-year-old plants her gifts in so many fields, she never has time to go back and harvest them. As I explained this to Jocelyn, my words echoed in my head, as if Jesus were saying them to me.

Perhaps the apple didn't fall too far from the tree. I never do my homework for drawing class. I've had to bow out of my conversational Spanish dinner more times than I can count. Let's not talk about my intentions to volunteer weekly at the shelter or the next book I keep vowing to write.

In His kindness, Jesus is always prompting me to remove the log from my own eye before I help my kids remove the splinter from theirs. First, I need to sit down in prayer, "give careful thought to [my] ways," set some priorities, and then use self-discipline to carry them out. Afterward, I can help Jocelyn do the same. —CLAIRE MCGARRY

FAITH STEP: *"Give careful thought"* to whether there are unfinished projects or incomplete actions in your life. Pray for Jesus to help you prioritize them, use self-discipline, and take action.

THURSDAY, MAY 7

Do not forget to do good and to share with others, for with such sacrifices God is pleased. Hebrews 13:16 (NIV)

LAST WEEK, MY YOUNGEST DAUGHTER and her husband came over to drop something off. I anticipated their visit would be brief; however, after arriving, they seemed to be in no hurry to leave. We sat and chatted, catching up on life. Before we realized it, an hour had elapsed. We didn't do anything special. Nothing eventful happened. From an outside perspective, it could have appeared totally boring. But after they left, it dawned on me what a precious gift they had just given me. Sharing their presence and their time made me know I was loved.

One of my favorite chapters in the Bible is Hebrews 13. Everything from showing hospitality to sharing with others is packed within its twenty-five verses. *Sharing*—when I see that word, I normally don't apply it to time. But I think Jesus did. Why else would He choose to put on flesh and spend thirty-three years among us? Jesus could have comfortably continued enjoying His eternal, time-free existence in Heaven, but He willingly stepped into a structured and finite time frame with humanity on earth. What would motivate Jesus to share His presence and time with the world? Love. Jesus came so we could know we are loved and experience a personal relationship with Him forever. —KRISTEN WEST

FAITH STEP: *Ask Jesus to show you three people to spend time with. Over the next couple of weeks, visit them and enjoy each other's company.*

Friday, May 8

> *That person is like a tree planted by streams of water, which yields its fruit in season and whose leaf does not wither—whatever they do prospers.* Psalm 1:3 (NIV)

MAY IS A BUSY MONTH for families with school-age children and those of us who work in education. It's often called "Maycember" because of the stress induced by end-of-year activities and responsibilities packed into an already full schedule. Like December, the month of May can feel overwhelming.

This May brought extra responsibilities for me as I filled in for a coworker, cared for my mom, and planned a goodbye celebration for our beloved principal, who was retiring. A plethora of details in each role belonged only to me. I was more stressed than usual. I wondered if I was doing any good in each responsibility as I hastily went from one activity to another.

Thinking ahead, I purchased a flowering tree three weeks early as a gift for my principal. The day before her party, I looked at the plant with horror. Though it bloomed with bright pink flowers, most leaves had fallen off. The weather during the last three weeks had been warmer than usual. The tree was clearly distressed. Once planted, it would survive—but it was not in the condition I wanted to give as a beautiful gift!

That scrawny tree mirrored how I felt. I, too, was very distressed this Maycember, but with Jesus's strength, I trusted my efforts were good enough. Thanks to Jesus, I'd survive—and, eventually, things would look beautiful again. —BRENDA L. YODER

FAITH STEP: *Place a plant, picture, or meaningful object somewhere to remind you that Jesus is working in your life, even when you feel stressed or overwhelmed.*

Saturday, May 9

Dear children, let us not love with words or speech but with actions and in truth. 1 John 3:18 (NIV)

WILLY WORE HIGHWATERS. THAT'S WHAT the kids who teased him called his pants because they only reached his ankles. Tall and lanky, he'd shuffle past me on the school bus and plop down in an empty row. He always sat alone.

One morning, I asked Willy to join me. He smiled and accepted. We talked nonstop until the big yellow bus rolled into the middle school parking lot. In the afternoon, Willy sat with me again. He seemed hungry for a friend, and I enjoyed his happy spirit. From that day on, we were bus buddies. We rode side by side, to and from school, for the next several years.

I saw Willy at my twentieth class reunion. We chatted for a while and laughed like middle schoolers. Then, out of nowhere, he leaned close and whispered, "Becky, you were my friend, and that meant so much to me. You have no idea what was happening to me during those years. Our friendship helped me through it."

Childhood Sunday school lessons had taught me about the kindness of Jesus. At a young age, my heart adored Him, and I desired to follow His example. Perhaps that's why I noticed a lonely boy and invited him to share my seat. Jesus knew Willy's pain and may have prompted me to love him—not with words but with actions. I'm thankful I was there to encourage him, though I didn't realize it at the time. —BECKY ALEXANDER

FAITH STEP: *The next time you see someone sitting alone, extend friendship and ask if the two of you might sit together.*

Mother's Day, Sunday, May 10

The LORD is near to all who call on him, to all who call on him in truth. Psalm 145:18 (NIV)

I SAW A VIDEO OF a news conference with a famous basketball player. Lights flashed from cameras, and journalists shouted questions. In the midst of everything going on around him, he looked down at his phone, picked it up, and said, "Hi, Mommy." The room went silent as he took several minutes to chat with her. This was so precious to me. I forwarded the video to my boys with a message that said, "Never decline a call from your mom."

That same day, while I was in a board meeting, my eighty-nine-year-old mom called. I hit the decline call button and continued with the meeting. Later, I received a text from my sister letting me know my mom was sick with worry because I hadn't answered. As my mother has aged, she worries incessantly. I felt awful to have caused her concern. I hadn't taken my own advice.

Thankfully, Jesus doesn't decline my call to Him when I pray. Jesus set the example of the importance of answering when called upon, and I should too.

After receiving my sister's text, I called my mom. I could hear relief in her voice. From that day on, I haven't declined a call from her no matter what I'm doing or who I'm with. I do feel loved knowing Jesus hears me, so I'll always answer my mom's calls because I want to assure her she is loved and a priority to me. —JEANNIE BLACKMER

FAITH STEP: *Today, give your most valuable gift to your mother or a mother figure—the gift of your uninterrupted time. Consider making this a common practice.*

MONDAY, MAY 11

When the kindness and love of God our Savior appeared, he saved us, not because of righteous things we had done, but because of his mercy. Titus 3:4–5 (NIV)

A FEW YEARS AGO, MY husband and son bought me a standing desk as a Mother's Day/birthday gift. What I had before was an old table that sagged in the middle from years of use. The promise of a new standing desk was an unexpected treat. I felt so special, and I was excited to receive the gift.

I haven't always accepted gifts so freely. My first birthday gift from my husband is a prime example. When I arrived home after work, I was greeted by a brand-new PalmPilot. It was beautiful and already charged and programmed by my tech-savvy husband. I was delighted as he had remembered that I wanted to buy myself one to celebrate my promotion, but feelings of unworthiness had slipped in. Instead of graciously accepting what I really wanted, I got overwhelmed thinking about how much the gift cost and how I didn't deserve it. In just minutes, I soured my celebration and trampled over my husband's kindness.

It's still hard for me to receive gifts, sometimes, if I don't feel worthy. Ironically, Jesus's gift of salvation is given to me because I am unworthy. I've done nothing in my past to deserve His kindness, and there's nothing I can do now or in the future to deserve it.

Yes, I am totally unworthy. Nevertheless, every day, Jesus deems me worthy—not because of my worthiness but because of His.
—ERICKA LOYNES

FAITH STEP: *On a sheet of paper, write or type the words "You are worthy" and then sign it "From: Jesus."*

Tuesday, May 12

By one sacrifice he has made perfect forever those who are being made holy. . . . Then he adds: "Their sins and lawless acts I will remember no more." And where these have been forgiven, sacrifice for sin is no longer necessary. Hebrews 10:14, 17–18 (NIV)

I ENDED THE CALL WITH our insurance agent and grimaced again over our new auto insurance rate. I'd heard that adding a teenage driver would be pricey but wowza. And we have a second one coming along in the next year.

Such is life. I will get over the rate hikes. But I had to bring a little humor to the situation by thanking Jesus for never raising my rate on salvation. I'm His, price paid and settled by Him. He will never require me to pay more than what He already gave to ensure my place with Him for eternity. His underwriting on this eternal insurance policy is solid as the Rock He is.

As I travel the roads of life with Him, I'll have mishaps along the way, from my own or someone else's errors. I'll never be a perfect human being or a perfect Christ follower, yet I can count on Him to keep me secure. My relationship with Jesus and my willingness to let Him develop His heart in me involve so much more than a get-out-of-hell insurance card.

As I accept my hiked-up auto insurance rates, I find refreshing peace in the blessing of Jesus's eternal assurance of salvation, knowing He paid the price for me. —ERIN KEELEY MARSHALL

FAITH STEP: *Create a calendar reminder for paying your insurance premium. When that day comes, thank Jesus for never raising your rate on receiving His salvation.*

WEDNESDAY, MAY 13

The Holy Spirit produces this kind of fruit in our lives: love, joy, peace, patience, kindness, goodness, faithfulness. Galatians 5:22 (NLT)

I'M ASHAMED TO ADMIT THAT occasionally I'm less than a holy participant when I'm in a church service or on a Zoom Bible study. If there's a lull in the teaching or a biblical point that's being overstated, I'm given to a secret eye roll or side whisper. Maybe I am just getting old, but if the service goes more than ten minutes overtime, sometimes I get irritated or might log off before the end.

In Bible college, it was drilled into us simply to give the message God gave and then sit down. We were often given impromptu sermon topics to practice-preach in front of our classmates and had a strict timer to follow. Our instructors believed it was vanity—and a sin—to stay in a pulpit longer than necessary. But that didn't give me the right to judge others.

As I continued in my ungodly attitude, Jesus gently interrupted my inner dialogue. *The people in the pulpit may not have perfect technique, but they are faithful.* He kindly reminded me that while I teach only occasionally, these folks were grinding it out every Sunday, Tuesday, and Thursday evening. Some were up at dawn interceding when I was still asleep. Being critical wasn't edifying or encouraging to the body of Christ who faithfully served every week. I checked my heart and self-corrected. Jesus rewards faithfulness over perfection, and I will too! —PAMELA TOUSSAINT HOWARD

FAITH STEP: *Keep a humble attitude when participating in church services or Bible studies. Pray for the person teaching; be patient and kind.*

Thursday, May 14

Good will come to those who are generous and lend freely, who conduct their affairs with justice. Psalm 112:5 (NIV)

THE BUDS OF OUR MINIATURE azalea have opened, drenching the breakfast nook in color. Just outside, our climber thrives. When in bloom, it's stunning. The softest shade of pink imaginable and as thickly petaled as an English rose, its fragrance both sweet and musky. Beside it rests my gravity chair, which distributes body weight evenly, easing the backache I often battle. Like the plates of cookies and the decorative bowl I use when entertaining, these items are gifts from my friend Clara. Things she claimed she'd bought by accident. "I didn't realize it was a climber until I'd thrown out the receipt, and then it was too late." Sometimes she said she didn't like the color, shape, flavor, or size of an item. I'd have believed her, but I knew her taste.

Every one of these non-gift/gifts was handpicked perfectly for my husband and me. Clara understands our financial situation and that we focused strictly on our needs. She made it her job to tackle our wants.

Through Clara's infectious generosity, she supplied us with pleasures we might not otherwise have enjoyed. In Clara's endless stream of gifts, I see Jesus's generosity at work in my life. But I also see Jesus's generous spirit in the peace I feel sharing a quiet evening in prayer with Him and in the love He showers on me through family and friends. It's in the hope I feel each new day. And like Clara, every gift Jesus offers is handpicked perfectly for me. —HEIDI GAUL

FAITH STEP: *What items can you donate to or buy for a friend? Let your generosity reflect Jesus's generous gifts to you.*

Friday, May 15

In their hearts humans plan their course, but the L<small>ORD</small> establishes their steps. Proverbs 16:9 (NIV)

A<small>HHHH</small>. I <small>SIPPED MY COFFEE</small>, reflecting on my plans for the day ahead. I had none! I'd caught up on my work, the laundry was done, the house was clean, and there was a casserole in the fridge for dinner. The blissful uneventful day stretched ahead of me with infinite possibilities. Just then the phone rang.

"Mom," panted my daughter Melissa, "I need to switch cars with you. I'm running late with no time to get gas. Be right there!" And just like that, my day blew up. Melissa roared in the driveway, toddlers Sloane and Jameson scrambling out of their car to get into mine. I pressed the garage door opener, but the door only went up halfway and stuck. Now what?

"Mom, do you have gasoline?"

The lawnmower gas! I grabbed the can and hurried to squirt it into Melissa's tank, spilling some on my shoes in my haste. We reinstalled the kids in their car seats, just as Sloane whispered, "Potty." I picked her up and ran inside. Sloane back in her car seat, I was making my getaway when Melissa asked to borrow my credit card. I sprinted into the house, grabbed it, tossed it through Melissa's window, and prayed my loved ones would make it safely on time.

I smiled. My coffee was cold, and I smelled like gasoline. But I had to admit the impromptu pit stop energized me. I was eager to see what other exciting possibilities this day held. —P<small>AT</small> B<small>UTLER</small> D<small>YSON</small>

F<small>AITH</small> S<small>TEP</small>: *Ask Jesus to help you embrace interruptions, be helpful, and pray for those you encounter, whether they are a part of your plan or not.*

SATURDAY, MAY 16

Follow God's example, therefore, as dearly loved children and walk in the way of love, just as Christ loved us and gave himself up for us as a fragrant offering and sacrifice to God. Ephesians 5:1–2 (NIV)

My mom and dad call regularly to check in on me. When I picked up the phone the other morning, my dad asked, "Is this the beautiful Susanna Aughtmon?" This is their usual early morning phone greeting. I responded, "Yes. Is this the beautiful Richard and Ruth Foth?" They chuckled and answered, "Yes!" Even though it has been decades since I have lived with my parents, they still want me to know that they are thinking about me. I know that I am wanted and loved.

I want to follow my parents' example with my own kids. I've been contemplating the best way to let my three sons know I am thinking about them. They would not respond well to early morning calls, but I feel certain they would enjoy being told they are beautiful. (They are, of course.) They may not appreciate all the hugs and kisses I try to lavish on them, but I know they feel wanted and loved.

Jesus loves me the most of all. He loved me so much He gave His life for me (John 3:16). His thoughts about me outnumber the grains of sand (Psalm 139:17–18). When I am anchored in Jesus's goodness and love, I can follow His example and model His love to those around me. And that is beautiful. —Susanna Foth Aughtmon

Faith Step: *Reach out to someone by phone or text and tell them they are beautiful, you love them, and Jesus loves them.*

Sunday, May 17

Therefore encourage one another and build one another up, just as you are doing. 1 Thessalonians 5:11 (ESV)

Though my son Isaac hasn't taken a spiritual gifts assessment, I'm confident he would score off the charts for the gifts of encouragement and gratitude. I've never known anyone as enthusiastically supportive and thankful. It's almost as though he's constantly looking for something to praise. He does it with such earnestness that I can't help but be buoyed.

At the drive-through: "Mommy, you're a good orderer."
At the dinner table: "Mommy, thank you for my dinner!"
Before church: "Mommy, you look beautiful."
Doing housework: "Mommy, good job cleaning."
Driving to school: "Mommy, you're a good driver," followed by, "Thank you for taking me to school."
Playing a game: "Good job, Mommy. Thank you for playing with me."
My personal favorite, "Thank you for being a great mama," which he'll say unexpectedly for no particular reason.

Isaac's praise is constant and doesn't come with strings attached. My actual performance seems to be irrelevant. His compliments are spontaneous acts of loving attention and genuine gratitude. This would delight most anyone, but I receive it as an especially thoughtful gift from my heavenly Father, who knows I suffered a deficit of praise and gratitude for a very long time. I aspire to be more like Isaac with liberal compliments and heartfelt gratitude and will begin today: Thanks so much for reading! —Isabella Campolattaro

Faith Step: *Set a personal goal to give at least three people specific compliments and thanks every day this week. Remember to praise and thank Jesus too.*

Monday, May 18

Trust in him at all times, you people; pour out your hearts to him, for God is our refuge. Psalm 62:8 (NIV)

LAST WEEK I CONFIDED IN someone about a personal struggle I've been dealing with—and I instantly regretted it. Their response was, "You shouldn't feel that way." Then I heard a mini-lecture on why my feelings were wrong. I didn't find the conversation helpful. I thought about another friend who would probably have asked questions for a deeper understanding of my situation, offered to pray with me, shared an encouraging scripture, or maybe talked about similar experiences she'd faced. Being told my feelings were wrong only added to my burden.

Some people are better listeners than others. But I can always feel safe sharing my struggles and negative emotions with Jesus. Many passages in the Psalms urge readers to trust Him enough to express hurt feelings openly and honestly. Nothing I tell Jesus will ever shock Him because He already knows my deepest thoughts (Matthew 9:4). Jesus will help me find solutions to my problems while handling my emotions in a godly way.

I'll keep on sharing some personal feelings with close friends, but my favorite listener will always be Jesus. I can trust His response. He may remind me of a Bible verse or truth that speaks to my situation. He may point me toward a helpful resource or person. Either way, I will know the freedom of unburdening my emotions with the One who understands me better than I know myself.
—DIANNE NEAL MATTHEWS

FAITH STEP: *Ask Jesus to reveal any struggles or feelings you have held back. Pour out your heart to Him knowing He is your refuge.*

TUESDAY, MAY 19

I will give you treasures hidden in the darkness—secret riches. I will do this so you may know that I am the LORD, the God of Israel, the one who calls you by name. Isaiah 45:3 (NLT)

MY HOME OFFICE IS A MESS. Old meeting notes, books, journals, notepads, folders, bills, and more are piled high on my desk. There's so much stuff that I can hardly make heads or tails of it. I'm really not in the mood to tackle the clutter, but my dislike for disorder finally wins out. I slowly start to sort through the piles.

I pick up my iPad along with a stack of papers and find buried underneath them a lovely quilt square, a gift handmade by my friend Janet. I had totally forgotten about it. I could have been enjoying its beauty the past several months if I had only kept the clutter at bay.

The assortment of papers and books aren't the only things that need to be cleared away in my life. I am constantly turning to Jesus to clean up the dark places within me—impatience, anger, stubbornness, unforgiveness, selfishness, and self-reliance, just for starters. Even though I may not want to admit these things lie deep within me, Jesus knows they are there. He beckons me to come to Him so that He can remove the darkness to make room for the good things He has in store for me. Just like my beautiful quilt square that was buried by my unsightly piles, treasures from Jesus await me. —BARBRANDA LUMPKINS WALLS

FAITH STEP: *As you clean a dark space in your home, ponder the dark places within your heart. Ask Jesus for help cleaning them both.*

Wednesday, May 20

My old self has been crucified with Christ. It is no longer I who live, but Christ lives in me. So I live in this earthly body by trusting in the Son of God, who loved me and gave himself for me. Galatians 2:20 (NLT)

PLEASE DON'T BE HORRIFIED, BUT I watch *The Walking Dead,* a television series set in contemporary America about life after a zombie apocalypse. In the show, a virus caused masses of people to die and turn into zombies, who take over the world, except for pockets of survivors who depend on one another. They try to carve out a civilized existence—survive and hopefully thrive against all the odds in a totally different world. I don't like all the blood and gore that comes with being a zombie, but I like seeing the characters reveal who they are under extreme pressure. Watching their inner strengths and failures interests and entertains me. Of course, I know it's purely fictional.

This past year, I've been under more pressure than I can ever remember. Like the characters in *The Walking Dead,* my world looks totally different than it did before. My life has been turned upside down by divorce. Everything I imagined when I walked down the aisle thirty years ago has changed. I'm trying to carve out a civilized existence, despite my fear and trepidation.

Sometimes the pressure has brought out the worst in me. But when I look to Jesus, I find His strength is sufficient for my failure. Depending on Him, I know I will not only survive but thrive no matter what the odds. And that's a fact! —GWEN FORD FAULKENBERRY

FAITH STEP: *Make a word cloud of ways you depend on Jesus. Pray and trust Him to help you thrive.*

Thursday, May 21

Always giving thanks to God the Father for everything, in the name of our Lord Jesus Christ. Ephesians 5:20 (NIV)

For someone who works indoors, you wouldn't think it would bother me that we've had day after day of soaking, drippy rain. Several neighbors sympathize with my weather weariness. One doesn't—the farmer. He says the constant rain helps make up for the near record-low snowfall last winter. He'd been concerned about the autumn harvest until the rain came. He was ecstatic about the mud.

Lesson learned. Or so I thought.

Then our family heard hard news. The kind that warrants informing all the kids and grandkids, siblings, close friends. Looking for comfort, I read Ephesians 3:20, the verse about how when we trust Jesus, we can count on Him to provide much more than we could ever ask or imagine. But I landed instead on Ephesians 5:20, two chapters away.

"Always giving thanks." Always? Even now? Even in this? Even in this flood of disheartening news? Jesus has never failed me. He cannot fail. So I trusted that the principle applied to *my* always.

Within minutes, a grandchild who had gotten offtrack spiritually texted to say, "Praying for you." Would that message have come, that acknowledgment of the power of Jesus to answer, if the need had been minor?

We're heading toward the far side of the crisis now, but I'm already thanking Him for it. Not everything about it, but I'm grateful that Jesus can work through anything for our good and His glory.
—Cynthia Ruchti

Faith Step: *What is the hardest thing for you to be thankful for right now? Jot it in the margin of your Bible near Ephesians 5:20 or in a journal. Then mark the date when you thanked Jesus for it.*

Friday, May 22

Do you not know that your bodies are temples of the Holy Spirit, who is in you, whom you have received from God? You are not your own; you were bought at a price. Therefore honor God with your bodies.
1 Corinthians 6:19–20 (NIV)

While hand-washing some dishes, I jerked my head upward toward a cacophony of chirping. Out the kitchen window, I watched three tiny sparrows chase a large hawk across and out of my backyard. The little birds individually would have been no match for the mighty hawk. Yet I marveled at their success when they bonded together.

Watching from the kitchen table, my daughter Ana suggested the hawk was probably prowling a nest of eggs. Hawks are lazy and prefer easy prey.

Finishing the dishes, I wondered how many times I was like that hawk. How often did I succumb to doing what was easy instead of what was better? It was a struggle I often had with food and exercise. I was more likely to grab a quick processed snack rather than take the time to put together a healthy plate. I knew that by treating myself well and fueling my body with nutritious choices, I honored the life Jesus gave me. But it's not easy. Like the sparrows, maybe I needed a buddy to join me. Accompanied by Ana, I added thirty minutes of exercise to my day. I also added a few healthier recipes to our weekly meal plan. Changing some eating habits and adding extra movement to my day remind me to honor and be grateful for my body. —Gloria Joyce

Faith Step: *Try a new recipe this week or add more movement to each day. Honor Jesus by caring for your body.*

Saturday, May 23

While he was still speaking, a bright cloud covered them, and a voice from the cloud said, "This is my Son, whom I love; with him I am well pleased. Listen to him!" Matthew 17:5 (NIV)

THE HIGHWAY TO MY DAUGHTER'S home in northern British Columbia is populated with signs meant to alert people to local dangers. For instance, a curvy stretch of road leads through several tunnels that keep travelers safe in the event of rockslides and avalanches. Signs located prior to the tunnels warn drivers to remove their sunglasses and turn on their headlights before entering them. As the miles roll on, signs warn of icy surfaces on bridge decks. The most foreboding appears farther north in forested areas. They depict images of antlered deer leaping from the ditch and moose approaching the highway.

These signs are posted for good reason. Nighttime driving is especially dangerous because trees lining the road provide a hiding place for the animals until seconds before they dart into traffic. By then, it's nearly impossible to avoid a collision.

I consider highway signs a kindness shown to travelers. Someone more knowledgeable than I am about the local dangers decided they're a worthy investment to keep us safe, and I appreciate the effort. Heeding them is both wise and necessary as I journey toward my destination.

I consider Jesus's teachings in the same light. He's more knowledgeable than I am about this journey called life, and He wants to help me navigate it well. Like heeding the road signs, paying attention to Jesus's words is the wise and necessary thing to do. —GRACE FOX

FAITH STEP: *Identify one danger you've avoided by heeding Jesus's words. Write about it and keep the page in your Bible.*

SUNDAY, MAY 24

Do not forget to entertain strangers, for by so doing some have unwittingly entertained angels. Hebrews 13:2 (NKJV)

WHILE ON A ROAD TRIP, my friends and I discussed how risky it is to help a stranger in need nowadays. I shared my recent encounter with a suspicious-looking man who followed me out of a convenience store and to my car at the gas pump. He asked for the $2 in my hand. Caution alarms went off in my brain. But I handed him the money, got into my car, and looked to see where he'd gone. He was nowhere in sight. Where had he disappeared to in just a few seconds? Had I interacted with an angel unaware?

We discussed that scary scenario, angels, and safety, not knowing that a few miles ahead, we would find ourselves in need of a stranger's kindness. Traffic had slowed on a bridge crossing the Mississippi River. The driver behind noticed too late and plowed into our car. A white pickup truck whipped into the empty space in front of us. The driver named Jonathan rushed out, asked if we were OK, then checked on the other driver. While we were stranded on the bridge, he waited with us as vehicles whizzed by on both sides, keeping us calm and making sure we were safe. When the police arrived, I mentioned we'd been discussing angels, and Jonathan was ours. "No," he insisted. "I was just driving to the bank."

I'm still not sure I did the right thing by getting close enough to hand that stranger $2, but Jonathan reminded me how much a simple kindness matters to someone in need. —KAREN SARGENT

FAITH STEP: *Seek an opportunity to do something kind for a stranger this week.*

Memorial Day, Monday, May 25

Be devoted to one another in love. Honor one another above yourselves. Romans 12:10 (NIV)

My friends Sarah and Amelia visited for our annual get-together weekend. We shopped at a clothing boutique, and I noticed a man when we walked toward the fitting area. He sat on a chair outside the dressing room and wore a Vietnam War veteran's ball cap, the kind my father, a Korean conflict veteran, had worn when he was alive.

"Thank you for your service," I said, extending my hand. He shook my hand, nodded, and introduced himself. As we chatted, I learned where Don had served in Vietnam. His eyes lit up, eager to talk about his military time. As a former United States history teacher, I enjoy hearing stories from veterans. I used to share such stories in the classroom to help my students understand the personal sacrifice behind the experiences they read about. I try to honor the stories of servicemen and servicewomen often by asking about and listening to their stories now.

I got so caught up that I didn't notice Sarah and Amelia had finished shopping and were waiting by the door. "We can't take you anywhere without you striking up a conversation," said Sarah, as she and Amelia laughed. "I'll never apologize for talking to a hero," I said with a smile. My friends nodded in agreement. A few minutes of my time is the least I can do for those who risked their lives for my freedom. —Brenda L. Yoder

Faith Step: *Take a moment today to thank a veteran or active-duty military serviceman or servicewoman for their commitment and acts of service. Listen to his or her stories.*

Tuesday, May 26

"The gatekeeper opens the gate for him, and the sheep recognize his voice and come to him. He calls his own sheep by name and leads them out." John 10:3 (NLT)

Most nights when my husband, Kevin, and I are eating dinner, one of the cats will walk to the back door and cry to go outside. I can tell which kitty it is, even if I'm sitting at the dining room table around the corner. Because I know their voices, I'll ask Kevin to open the door for Princess or Fred. Each cat has a distinct cry. I suppose if I had twenty-seven cats (God forbid), I'd still recognize their individual voices because they are mine.

The cats may irk me when they wake me at 5 a.m. They may annoy me when they act as if they want outside but then sit in the doorway and sniff the air. They may even anger me when they fight with each other or climb the drapes. But they are still mine. And I love them dearly.

I cry for the sins of my past that bring regrets. I cry for children who are hurting or lost. I cry for people who refuse to believe that Jesus is God. I often cry tears of joy for the kind, generous things Jesus does for me and the sweet relationship we have.

When I cry, Jesus doesn't simply hear a random person weeping; he hears my specific voice, whether broken or joyous. He calls me by name. And just as I love Princess and Fred, Jesus loves me dearly because I am His. —Jeanette Levellie

Faith Step: *Find a picture of a shepherd with his flock of sheep. Thank Jesus that in all the millions of those who belong to Him, He knows your distinct voice.*

WEDNESDAY, MAY 27

The LORD's lovingkindnesses indeed never cease, For His compassions never fail. They are new every morning; Great is Your faithfulness.
Lamentations 3:22–23 (NASB1995)

WE FACED A CHALLENGING PERIOD in our homeschool journey a few weeks ago. Nearing the end of the school semester, the routine of books and computer programs had become dreary for my children and for me. To be honest, it wasn't even fun anymore—for any of us.

I decided to shake things up by planning a day trip to the Arkansas Museum of Fine Art. For years, the thought of taking my rambunctious children to a place filled with fine art seemed daunting, but I felt a prompting that it was time to try something new.

As we walked through the museum, the change of scenery was refreshing. It wasn't just an escape from our daily routine but an enriching experience that sparked curiosity and creativity in all of us. The kids were surprisingly engaged, asking questions about the artwork and discussing what they saw.

This day trip to the museum reminded me that education isn't only about structured learning. It's also about exploring new experiences that can ignite passion and wonder. I couldn't help but know that Jesus's kindness extended to inspiring me to provide moments of joy and discovery for my family when we most need them. Shaking up our routine refreshed our spirits and guided us to unexpected joys. Weary students and teachers both can benefit from a little fun at the end of the school year! —TRICIA GOYER

FAITH STEP: *Pinpoint one area of your life that feels monotonous or challenging. Ask Jesus to show you how to bring new excitement and perspective to it. Pray for the openness to embrace these opportunities as gifts from Him.*

Thursday, May 28

"Although you wash yourself with cleanser and use much soap, I can still see the stain of your guilt," says the Lord God. Jeremiah 2:22 (NCV)

WHAT HAPPENED HERE? THIS LOOKS like the scene of a homicide! Having seen too many murder mystery movies, I was startled by a three-foot-long reddish-brown swath on my mother-in-law's dining room floor. She explained it had mysteriously appeared one afternoon. She'd tried multiple cleaning products on the vinyl floor, all to no avail. The huge, unsightly stain of unknown origin plagued my mind, keeping me awake all night after seeing it, as I mentally rehearsed various possible ways to remove it.

Ruminating on such a stubborn, obvious stain brought to mind my own stains—mistakes, sins, and shortcomings that were removed at the cross (1 Peter 2:24), which is why it was so hard for me to accept that this particular strange spot could not be removed using bleach, cleansers, or solvents. Ultimately, my mother-in-law's badly stained flooring had to be replaced.

The stain was a visual reminder of how impossible it is for me to remove the stain of sin by my own power. Although I like having an arsenal of cleaning supplies at my disposal, there's nothing I can do to relieve myself of my own sin stain. Only Jesus can remove the stain of sin (Hebrews 9:22). Jesus's blood washes me white as snow (Isaiah 1:18). Such a miraculous mystery! What a relief to have a Savior who can do the impossible—replace my sin and guilt with a renewed, cleansed spirit. —CASSANDRA TIERSMA

FAITH STEP: *Find a recording of "Nothing but the Blood of Jesus" online and sing along about how only Jesus cleanses sin and makes us whole again.*

Friday, May 29

The Spirit of the LORD will come powerfully upon you, and you will prophesy with them; and you will be changed into a different person. 1 Samuel 10:6 (NIV)

CHEERING WITH BLUE POM-POMS, I shouted "Congratulations!" as my oldest daughter, Cassidy, crossed the stage to receive her diploma. Having homeschooled her from kindergarten through high school, in some ways I felt it was as much my accomplishment as it was hers. Taking her seat, Cassidy hugged her diploma and silently mouthed "Thank you" to me. I blew her a kiss, feeling the moment deeply.

My mind went back to when I was Cassidy's age. I ran away from a loveless and abusive home. I never could have imagined the life I now shared with my husband and children, nor did I ever dream Matt and I would have homeschooled Cassidy and her sister, Ana, for the last thirteen years. But as we prepared for this moment, I was able to happily look back over a path I never saw myself taking. Only Jesus did. Jesus led me to a future that I could not see (Jeremiah 29:11). He led me down righteous paths when I surrendered my life to Him (Psalm 23:3). Though not always easy for me, Jesus changed me into the woman He knew I could be because I am His (Romans 1:6). Resting my pom-poms on my lap, I mouthed a silent "Thank you" to Jesus. In my mind's eye, I caught the kiss Jesus blew me. —GLORIA JOYCE

FAITH STEP: *Write a thank-you note to Jesus today, thanking Him for your path, for the way He has encouraged you and cheered you on.*

SATURDAY, MAY 30

They are carried to the grave, and watch is kept over their tombs.
Job 21:32 (NIV)

BENDING TO MY KNEES, I began to wash the marker of my son's grave. Pouring water over the metal letters of his name, Steven McCormick, I made sure to scrub every letter. Next, I replaced the flowers with blossoms in bright shades of blue, his favorite color.

I worked quietly. Performing this service for Steven, who died in a car accident at twenty-one, is balm for my soul. I don't believe there is a correct way to grieve. I think Jesus understands my heartache and accepts my rituals. As I stood, I admired my son's decorated grave. It makes me feel better to tend this well-kept site as a tribute to how much he was loved. Leaving, I spotted a dilapidated grave that was obviously long forgotten. Grass had grown over the marker, and the vase was empty. I felt a nudge from Jesus.

I clipped the grass until the marker revealed the name of a veteran. I wanted to honor this man and find a way, however small, to try to repay him for his service. I scrubbed the marker and wiped away years of neglect. Lastly, I offered him Steven's former silk flowers and arranged them in a lovely display.

Standing back, I smiled at the transformation. I know in my heart that one day all these graves will be forgotten, but the One who served when He was on earth remembers. Jesus made the ultimate sacrifice, and he stays near to those who also gave their lives and to those who grieve. —JEANNIE HUGHES

FAITH STEP: *Notice some of the neglected graves in your neighborhood cemeteries. Choose one to honor with your loving care, knowing your quiet service honors Jesus as well.*

Sunday, May 31

Don't put it off; do it now! Don't rest until you do. Proverbs 6:4 (NLT)

I LOST A BANANA TODAY. It's around here somewhere. I'd recognize it anywhere because there's a bite out of it. I don't like bananas—the texture, the taste, the spots. But I know bananas are good for me, so I eat one every day. Breakfast would be the ideal time to choke that banana down, but I can't always face one so early. It doesn't seem to go with lunch, and a banana for supper makes no sense. So I generally put off eating that banana. And sometimes I lose it.

I'm ashamed to admit sometimes I also delay my precious devotional time with Jesus. It's nothing like my banana procrastination. I love spending time with Jesus! It's just that often other things get in the way. Occasionally I have an early appointment. I sometimes need to keep grandkids. I may have an important email that should be answered immediately. The cat might be scheduled to go to the vet for shots. So off I go, willy-nilly, promising Jesus I'll meet with Him in the afternoon. But then I need to get groceries and to fix supper. Suddenly, it's bedtime, and I'm too tired to offer Jesus anything but a quick prayer of thanks.

I've determined I must schedule my devotional time for first thing in the morning, before the world gets in the way. There's no more important thing in my life and no better way to start my day.

Being a procrastinator with Jesus is a lot worse than putting off a banana. He deserves better. —PAT BUTLER DYSON

FAITH STEP: *Set a devotional time to meet with Jesus. Don't deviate from it!*

Monday, June 1

I became a servant of this gospel by the gift of God's grace given me through the working of his power. Ephesians 3:7 (NIV)

I DUG A HOLE IN the softened dirt for my tomato plants, just as my father had shown me decades ago. I smiled as I remembered how he tolerated my small hands making his farming chores more difficult. He made growing vegetables look so easy. Tomatoes, green beans, and potatoes graced our table every night. Placing a tomato cage around each tender plant, I stood and could almost feel my father's hand on my shoulder.

Every day I watered and fussed over each vine. Were they looking a bit droopy today? Dad's would have been twice this size by now. The next day, the plants were wilted, flat on the ground. I felt like crying. I wanted to ask Dad where I had gone wrong.

I realized that happened a lot in my life. In fact, I could think of several times I fell flat like those tomato plants. Unfortunately, Dad wasn't here to tell me what to do. I remembered complaining to him when I couldn't do something. He always told me, "God gave everyone a gift. Isn't it exciting to discover what yours might be?"

I removed the tomato cages and pulled up the dead plants. I thought I felt that same hand on my shoulder. Gardening was certainly not my gift. But I was definitely going to keep trying, until I found mine. —JEANNIE HUGHES

FAITH STEP: *Write down three things you have a talent for. Are you overlooking your God-given gift?*

Tuesday, June 2

Do not merely listen to the word, and so deceive yourselves. Do what it says.
—James 1:22 (NIV)

When my husband and I went on a cruise this year with three other couples from church, I was excited to participate in my first ever silent disco. I knew the unusual spin on a classic dance party was popular with teenagers and youth groups, but I'd never had the opportunity to experience the craze myself. We each got a pair of large neon headphones to wear when we arrived and instructions on how they worked. At any given time, four different songs were available through the headphones by turning a dial on the side. The fun came in choosing which song you wanted to dance to, then discovering others who were dancing to the same song.

Even with my headphones on, lost in my own little world of music, it was easy to see who was listening to the same song as I was. We'd both be moving to similar beats or mouthing identical lyrics as we responded to the music in our ears. A few times, I took my headphones completely off and was surprised that I could still figure out which songs people were listening to, even in the absence of the music. Their words and actions revealed the songs in their ears.

To me, it was a perfect picture of what it looks like when I immerse myself in the words of Jesus and read my Bible regularly. My own speech and actions begin revealing what I'm hearing, and it becomes impossible to merely listen without responding in tune.
—Emily E. Ryan

Faith Step: *Hone your ability to hear from Jesus by listening to worship music through headphones or earbuds. Dance if you want, praising Him.*

Wednesday, June 3

Now, dear brothers and sisters, one final thing. Fix your thoughts on what is true, and honorable, and right, and pure, and lovely, and admirable. Think about things that are excellent and worthy of praise. Philippians 4:8 (NLT)

During dinner with colleagues while on a work trip, we started talking about our hotel accommodations. I shared that I loved the huge walk-in marble shower with dual showerheads. But others started to complain about how difficult the shower was to operate—one even griped about the pattern of the shower tile.

Then we began discussing the view from our rooms. One coworker said she could see the river, which I immediately envied. Then I told them my room overlooked the hotel's unsightly heating system and parking lot. My friend and colleague Shanda quickly piped up, "Barb, you have a nice view. You can see the swimming pool and city streets." She was right. I felt ashamed that I had so easily joined the complaint crew.

In his letter to the Philippians, Paul encourages the church to dwell on the good, honorable, and beautiful. I take that to mean to meditate or focus on the good things around me. What I choose to put into my mind is what feeds my thoughts, actions, and beliefs. So focusing on the good will help me to see it and do it. There's little room for complaints and dissatisfaction if I look for and think about what is praiseworthy, pure, and godly. Good thoughts can go a long way—including Jesus's loving-kindness toward me, which includes a view of a lovely hotel pool. —Barbranda Lumpkins Walls

Faith Step: *What are you complaining about in your life? Instead, write down three good things you can focus on today and thank Jesus for them.*

Thursday, June 4

I have hidden your word in my heart. Psalm 119:11 (NIV)

I LIVE IN NEW HAMPSHIRE, which feels like the vanity-plate state of the United States. Everywhere I look, people have personalized license plates to represent something. Often, I can decipher the meaning of the six- to eight-letter/number combination. For example, 4EVRL8 is for the person who is forever late. MY3KDZ is for the proud mom of three children.

Some take a little longer, like FLD+IC. It took me a solid 10 minutes to figure out that it means the driver is into hockey—on the field and ice. There are some letters and numbers I can't figure out. I don't necessarily keep them front and center in my thoughts, but they tuck themselves into my subconscious. Sometimes, they occur to me like a bolt of lightning out of the blue, or I may never figure them out.

The same thing happens when I read scripture. A lot of the verses make complete sense and resonate right away. Others, I have to ponder to discover their meaning. As I tuck them away in my heart and go about my day, I find myself returning to them over and over again, sometimes actively, sometimes passively. If Jesus wills it, the meaning is revealed to me like a surprise gift on an ordinary day, unexpected and greatly appreciated. I've also come to realize there will always be those verses that I'll never understand, and that's OK. Like so many of the mysteries of faith, I trust they will still touch my heart and draw me closer to Him. —CLAIRE MCGARRY

FAITH STEP: *Memorize a Bible verse that doesn't quite make sense. See if Jesus will reveal its meaning to you over time.*

Friday, June 5

Praise be to the God and Father of our Lord Jesus Christ, the Father of compassion and the God of all comfort, who comforts us in all our troubles, so that we can comfort those in any trouble with the comfort we ourselves receive from God. 2 Corinthians 1:3–4 (NIV)

I spotted the boy and his family entering the Savannah hotel. His left arm looked similar to mine, missing the forearm and hand. Pointing at my prosthesis, I asked the dad if I could talk with his son. He nodded. "Hello. My name is Becky. I have an arm like yours."

His eyes widened. "I'm Lucas."

"Nice to meet you, Lucas. How old are you?"

"Seven." He paused. "My friends think there are no other people like me."

I dramatically gasped and put my hand on my hip. "Well, they're wrong, aren't they? There are lots of us!" He giggled and then touched my prosthesis. His dad whispered, "Thank you!"

I was uniquely suited to speak words of encouragement to Lucas. I had lived through being a seven-year-old with one arm and clearly understood his challenges. I had also experienced the compassion of Jesus for a lifetime and could now pass that on to him.

Some might call the encounter a chance meeting, but I feel sure Jesus orchestrated it. Lucas and I were from two different states, visiting Georgia on the same day, staying in the same Savannah hotel, walking across the lobby at the precise moment—too exact for coincidence. I pray our unexpected conversation gave Lucas hope for his future via a glimpse into my world as an active, happy adult. —Becky Alexander

Faith Step: *List three personal situations that equip you to share compassion in unique circumstances.*

SATURDAY, JUNE 6

Because your love is better than life, my lips will glorify you. I will praise you as long as I live, and in your name I will lift up my hands. Psalm 63:3–4 (NIV)

MY FRIEND CHRISTA IS THE women's ministry director at our church. We met for coffee last week, and she invited me to a ladies' worship night at church. I told her I would be there. I love worship services. I like to sing loudly. My loud singing makes my husband, Scott, nervous. He feels like I may draw attention to myself. I feel like I want to sing loud so Jesus can hear how much I love Him.

When I arrived at the worship night, I chose a row close to the front. The musicians on the stage were preparing to sing. A whole family of ladies scooted into the row in front of me. We all smiled and introduced ourselves. Then the mom turned to me and said, "I hope it's OK with you, but we like to jump." I laughed and said, "Go right ahead." I had a good feeling that these fellow worshippers wouldn't care if I sang loudly.

Jesus likes it when I worship Him. He inhabits the praises of His people (Psalm 22:3). Each time I praise Jesus for all He has done, I remind myself of His faithfulness and love. And that's something to sing about, as loudly as possible. —SUSANNA FOTH AUGHTMON

FAITH STEP: *Turn on your favorite worship playlist. Take time to worship and sing loudly, praising Jesus and thanking Him for all He has done.*

Sunday, June 7

You, my brothers and sisters, were called to be free. But do not use your freedom to indulge the flesh; rather, serve one another humbly in love. Galatians 5:13 (NIV)

Summer vacations from my school counseling job are usually welcomed with their unstructured schedule. But this summer, I worked daily on a book writing deadline. I missed having carefree days for leisurely coffee or meals with friends. I said no to most invitations, often feeling guilty, even though I knew the project was God's plan for this season.

By limiting time with those I invested in, including family members and those I mentored, I worried they wouldn't understand as I hunkered down and worked on the manuscript, often leaving my desk only for meals or laundry.

One afternoon, a young mom I mentored texted me. She was stopping by with a surprise. When she arrived, she and another young mom brought freezer meals and snacks to get my husband and me through my long days of focused writing. I was speechless at their act of kindness and reciprocity. As the mentor, I was supposed to be feeding them. Instead, they were feeding me—literally!

Jesus showed me I didn't need to feel guilty for prioritizing the work He had given me. The thoughtful kindness of my younger friends was His way of validating the boundaries I set around the work He called me to do and His way of feeding my body and soul.
—Brenda L. Yoder

Faith Step: *Think of how you can serve, feed, or encourage someone working for Jesus. If not a home-delivered meal, maybe a gift certificate or card of encouragement would be a welcomed surprise of support.*

MONDAY, JUNE 8

Then I heard something like the voice of a great multitude and like the sound of many waters, and like the sound of mighty peals of thunder, saying, "Hallelujah! For the Lord our God, the Almighty, reigns."
Revelation 19:6 (NASB)

I LIKE TO START MY times of prayer with praise and worship. I often sing to Jesus, and a few months ago I was singing a song, "Hallelujah, Jesus Is King!" which my husband, Kevin, wrote for Vacation Bible School. I love the simple tune and snappy rhythm. I was enjoying myself as I sang, my hands and face lifted, when the telephone rang. I raced across the room, still singing, and surprised myself when I answered with, "Hallelujah!" Both the caller and I laughed. I later thought that would be the perfect way to answer the phone every time, with a greeting that exalts Jesus.

What if I answered each problem that confronted me in the same way? Praising the name of Jesus in the face of misfortunes and maladies. Standing on the promise of God's good plans (Jeremiah 29:11), even amid life's difficulties. I don't praise Jesus for suffering since He's not the author of trouble; I praise Him despite them. I trust Him to teach me perseverance and to help me grow more like Him because I walked through a tough season.

In fact, I'd like my life to be one big hallelujah to Jesus.
—JEANETTE LEVELLIE

FAITH STEP: *Look up the definition of* hallelujah. *Use it to praise Jesus right now, no matter what else is calling you.*

Tuesday, June 9

A friend loves at all times, and a brother is born for a time of adversity. Proverbs 17:17 (NIV)

When you have ten children, it's easy for other relationships to take a back seat. However, last year, in a moment of divine intuition, my husband and I felt a spontaneous urge to visit friends in Florida, just the two of us. Initially, the plan was to meet up with another couple and relish three days going to theme parks or relaxing. Little did we know God had a different purpose for our trip.

Twelve hours after booking our tickets, our Florida friends' teenage son suffered a critical accident in a swimming pool. Instead of enjoying roller coasters, we found ourselves in the ICU, supporting our friends during the most harrowing time of their lives. As the days passed, it became evident that they would soon face the unimaginable task of saying their final goodbyes to their son.

During this intense period of sorrow, I felt a real sense of Jesus being near. Thousands were lifting prayers for this family. Jesus had made a way for me and my husband to be at our friends' side. As sad as it was, I knew this tragedy was in His hands. It felt as if heaven itself extended into that hospital room, preparing to welcome their son into eternal peace.

This profound experience confirmed that our seemingly spontaneous decision to visit friends in Florida was guided by Jesus's foresight. He orchestrated our presence to provide comfort and support precisely when and where it was most needed. —Tricia Goyer

Faith Step: *Pray for the awareness and sensitivity to respond to Jesus's spontaneous nudges, wherever they might lead you.*

WEDNESDAY, JUNE 10

All these blessings will come on you and accompany you if you obey the LORD your God. Deuteronomy 28:2 (NIV)

JESUS HAS BEEN ASKING ME to do something for quite a while now, but I'm resisting. He knows it. I know it. But I fear it's time to make a move. "I'm holding the door open for you," He tells me. "Yes, I see that," I reply. Then to erase any doubt, in a matter of days, Jesus lines up a random podcast I listen to, an unexpected Zoom with a key individual, an online article in my inbox—all arrows pointing me in the same direction.

So why do I drag my feet toward that open door instead of sprinting through it? Because this thing is not easy, and, from my perspective, the chances of success are close to nonexistent. But I know what Jesus can do, and His measure of success probably isn't the same as mine. And as each day passes, I wonder what blessings I'm robbing from myself.

I'm acting like the Israelites in the Promised Land, the land flowing with milk and honey that the nomadic people could call home, with rich soil for planting, a climate for thriving livestock, and mountains for protection. Yet Israel only occupied a small portion of the Promised Land because of rebellion and faithlessness (Numbers 14:6–10). Sounds a little like me. I don't want to settle for only a portion of the blessings Jesus has planned for me. So I'm going to double down, attempt the hard thing, and walk in confidence that while I may not know where this path leads, Jesus does. —KAREN SARGENT

FAITH STEP: *List your reasons for not following where Jesus is leading. Then mark out each one and write "OBEY JESUS" in bold letters on the list.*

Thursday, June 11

I myself am convinced, my brothers and sisters, that you yourselves are full of goodness, filled with knowledge and competent to instruct one another. Romans 15:14 (NIV)

SOME FRIENDS INVITED ME TO play mahjong. It's a game similar to rummy, but it uses tiles instead of cards. I felt confused the first time because it's complicated and has different rules from other games I've played. But they patiently taught me. They explained the tiles and the strategies and answered my questions. My first game, an experienced player sat next to me and helped me with each move. The others showed all their tiles so I could see what they were doing. After three or four sessions, I began to understand the game. Now I can help other friends who want to start playing.

Just as my friends mentored me in mahjong, the Apostle Paul encourages us to mentor new believers in this complicated game of life. As mentors, we don't need to be perfect or be an expert; we just need a willing heart and a desire to pass on to someone what Jesus has taught us. And, like my friends teaching me mahjong through showing me their tiles, we can strive to be authentic, not hiding our mistakes or challenges—willing to answer questions as they come up.

As I've grown in my faith and mentored young believers, I've had the joy of watching them take others under their wings to lovingly instruct them and experience the abundant life of following Christ, together. —JEANNIE BLACKMER

FAITH STEP: *Pray for Jesus to inspire you with someone you could mentor. Give her a call. Perhaps a game night would be a good start.*

Friday, June 12

God is the one who makes us patient and cheerful. I pray that he will help you live at peace with each other, as you follow Christ. Romans 15:5 (CEV)

A LEFTOVER PIZZA BOX SITTING at eye level on top of the coffee maker convicted me. Not because of anything to do with pizza. But because of the words printed on the side of the box, which I'd never noticed before. Four words of reproach: "Be Buddies, Not Bullies." A silent reprimand. Convicted by a pizza box!

For several days, I'd been in a bad mood. Irritable. Easily annoyed. For no reason at all. My dear husband, John, bore the brunt of my impatient, brusque attitude. Besides feeling out of sorts, I also secretly felt guilty about having been unnecessarily short with John for no fault of his own. So, when I entered the kitchen, after yet again waking up on the wrong side of the bed, and saw "Be Buddies, Not Bullies," I knew Jesus was showing me something. He got my attention. And I got the message.

Those four words of kindness reminded me of His Word: "Be kind to one another, tenderhearted, forgiving one another, as God in Christ forgave you" (Ephesians 4:32, ESV). I'm still replaying the gentle reminder over in my mind: *Be buddies, not bullies.* Thank You, Jesus, for your kind encouragement in reminding me of the cheerful and harmonious way You want me to live. Now to find John and ask him to forgive me. —CASSANDRA TIERSMA

FAITH STEP: *Consider ordering pizza for dinner. When you say grace tonight, thank Jesus for the patience and cheerfulness to be able to live in peace and harmony with others.*

SATURDAY, JUNE 13

A merry heart does good, like medicine, but a broken spirit dries the bones. Proverbs 17:22 (NKJV)

MY FRIEND BETTY ATTENDS MY church. She has asked me on several occasions to go with her to the monthly "Circle of Sisters" meeting, but I've always turned her down. Working full time and the demands of my family keep me pretty busy. The circle is basically the ladies of the congregation spending quality time together and getting to know one another on a deeper level. I just didn't think I had the time to spare.

I almost turned Betty down yet again due to another busy week, but something stirred in my spirit, and I found myself saying yes. The moment I walked through the door, I was greeted with smiling faces and friendly hugs. We played a get-to-know-you game, ate pizza, and then had a wonderful devotion. I met so many encouraging women. The laughter and conversations comforted me. I hadn't realized how much I needed it. I cherished my time with my Christian sisters.

Something else I realized I needed more of was quality time with Jesus. Prayer, Bible study, and just sitting quietly listening to worship music can soothe my spirit, but there is nothing like spending time in His presence. Jesus is my encourager and my comforter. Thankfully, I can be with Him anytime. I can stay as long as I want with Him and talk about whatever I choose. I cherish my time with Him. I need it so much. —RENEE MITCHELL

FAITH STEP: *Find a few extra moments to be alone with Jesus today. Unload all your thoughts and cares, dreams and hopes. He's never too busy to spend quality time with you.*

Sunday, June 14

"The city streets will be filled with boys and girls playing there."
Zechariah 8:5 (NIV)

My husband, Ron, and I keep the same busy rhythms we'd maintained for years when our kids lived at home. With four kids active in sports, including two college athletes, we often rushed from one event to another in addition to our full-time jobs. Even now, we arrive home most evenings with several chores to do on our small farm. We often feel as though the work never ends.

But separate near-fatal accidents we each experienced in the last two years have caused us to rethink our priorities. We want to slow down and enjoy life together. We can't retire yet, so how can we work less and play more? I've often asked Jesus to provide ways for Ron and me to have more fun.

I was pondering the dilemma when, on a whim, I bought tickets for a local concert featuring 1950s music. Growing up, I loved oldies music and often danced to vinyl records in my bedroom. The event made me happy and gave us something fun to look forward to.

The night of the concert, I was as excited as a kid. During the show, the musicians encouraged the audience to dance, so I bebopped the whole night. Driving home, Ron and I both laughed and reflected on the enjoyable night. We felt as though Jesus was giving us permission to go out and play—a new rhythm I'm intentionally making room for in my busy life. —Brenda L. Yoder

Faith Step: *What playful activities can you add to your life? Take a class, try a new sport, or get tickets to a local event. Pray for Jesus to show you how to have fun, regardless of the amount of work in front of you.*

MONDAY, JUNE 15

> *Therefore, as God's chosen people, holy and dearly loved, clothe yourselves with compassion, kindness, humility, gentleness and patience.* Colossians 3:12 (NIV)

RESIDENTS KEEP MOSTLY TO THEMSELVES in our marina. I was clueless when we moved in, so I invited our neighbors for desserts and occasional meals. Surprise, surprise—they came, and friendships sprouted.

Gene and I felt a special kinship with one fellow through a shared interest: Poland. We visited his homeland often for ministry purposes, so we brought him Polish-produced tea and chocolate. Kindness built trust, and soon he told us about his escape from communism. As a result of atrocities witnessed, he said he didn't believe Jesus existed and wasn't interested in spiritual discussions. We respected his feelings and refused to let them build a wall between us.

One day, my path crossed his in the parking lot, and he tearfully told me about being diagnosed with pancreatic cancer. I asked permission to pray for him right then and there, and he said yes. Gene and I visited him in the hospital twice after his surgery a month later, and he eagerly accepted my offer to pray for him on both occasions.

Chemotherapy followed. Our friend's energy and appetite waned, so we served him by bringing occasional meals to his boat. One evening when we delivered dinner, he said his chemotherapy had stopped working. He drew Gene and me into a group hug and then, for the first time, invited us aboard his boat—an action akin to inviting us into his life.

Gene and I are rejoicing in the breakthrough and trusting that he'll invite Jesus into his life too. —GRACE FOX

FAITH STEP: *Ask Jesus to help you build a relationship with someone whose spiritual beliefs differ from yours. Be open to how this friendship unfolds.*

Tuesday, June 16

"All that the Father gives Me will come to Me, and the one who comes to Me I will by no means cast out." John 6:37 (NKJV)

RETURNING HOME FROM THE GYM this morning, I entered the kitchen. As I grabbed a cold drink from the fridge, I glanced at the breakfast nook, then did a double take. There, beside a sunny window, on the table we'd set up for our orchids, sprawled a cat. The sleek Siamese mix, white with chocolate point markings and eyes as blue as the Caribbean Sea, lifted his head and greeted me. Butters is his name. He must have snuck in through the cat door, but he's not my cat. Or is he? I smiled at the thought.

No one knows the beginning of Butters's story. He simply showed up one morning a few doors down the street. A true wanderer, he's chosen to adopt the entire neighborhood as his family. And we all care for him, supplying food, toys, catnip, even veterinary visits. He belongs to us and we to him.

Like Butters, I spent years wandering, never seeming to belong anywhere or to anyone. But Jesus took me in, welcoming me as one of His own. He provides me all I need and more. He delights in me and I in Him. The past no longer concerns me; Jesus fills my today and all my tomorrows. And He will never turn me away because I've found my home in Him. —HEIDI GAUL

FAITH STEP: *Do you know a wanderer—human or otherwise—who doesn't seem to belong? Find ways to show your acceptance as you offer Jesus's nurturing kindness.*

WEDNESDAY, JUNE 17

"If ever you were willing to listen, listen now!" Matthew 11:15 (TLB)

THE RAINSTORM HAD ARISEN SUDDENLY, making it impossible for shoppers to exit the store without getting drenched. I complimented the woman beside me on her basket loaded with fruit and vegetables. "My son is coming for a visit and has Prader-Willi syndrome," she said.

She explained to me that Prader-Willi is a rare genetic disorder, characterized by an insatiable appetite, leading to obesity. She told me Prader-Willi patients often have behavioral difficulties, and most adults live in a group home, as her son did.

I like chatting with strangers, but I was eager to get going as soon as the rain let up. Just then, my spirit quieted. *Listen.* The rain continued as the woman talked about her life. She'd been married when her son was diagnosed, but her husband couldn't cope and abandoned them. It hadn't been easy, but Jesus had been with her every step of the way—and He still was. She trusted Him to bring people into her son's life who would help her determine what was best for him.

I nodded, told her how much I admired her, and thanked her for telling me about Prader-Willi syndrome. The rain had stopped, but I still felt prompted to stay. Surely Jesus had placed me in the store so I could hear out a lonely fellow believer. We walked to our cars together, and the woman waved to me. "Thanks for listening," she said. "And eat kale!" —PAT BUTLER DYSON

FAITH STEP: *The next time Jesus places someone in your path who wants to talk, listen.*

Thursday, June 18

"See, I am doing a new thing! Now it springs up; do you not perceive it? I am making a way in the wilderness and streams in the wasteland."
Isaiah 43:19 (NIV)

A FEW MONTHS AFTER MY husband and I moved back to Tennessee, we discovered an 850-acre nature area that we had no idea existed. Just three miles from our house, Middle Fork Bottoms Recreation Area includes paved trails; spots for kayaking, canoeing, and fishing; and retriever training. The scenery features microcosms of the different habitats found in the state. Programs are designed to protect endangered species and to offer environmental education. The most amazing part is the history: The low-lying land was farmed for more than a century but frequently flooded, so eventually farmers gave up the battle. Now this area is used to mitigate flooding in nearby communities.

Walking along the trails, I marvel at how seemingly useless land has been transformed and given new beauty, purpose, and value. It reminds me how Jesus is transforming me and everyone else who belongs to Him. The more I get to know Him, the more I find new meaning and fulfillment in my life. The more I obey His leading, the more He allows me to serve Him in ways that honor Him and impact others beyond what I could have imagined.

In 2024 Tennessee designated Middle Fork Bottoms as a state park; more plans are under way to transform the area. Jesus has ongoing plans for my transformation as well. I'm grateful to be designated as His follower. —DIANNE NEAL MATTHEWS

FAITH STEP: *Think about your skills, talents, possessions, and personality traits. Are any of them being underused or wasted? Ask Jesus to show you how to use these in new ways to bless Him and others.*

JUNETEENTH, FRIDAY, JUNE 19

The blood shall be a sign for you, on the houses where you are. And when I see the blood, I will pass over you. Exodus 12:13 (ESV)

When Juneteenth became a federal holiday in 2021, I decided to incorporate its celebration into my annual summer plans. Thankfully, the city of Memphis—where I live—is home to several Juneteenth celebrations, filled with food, music, singing, and dancing. The mood of attendees is always festive as we remember the joy that must have been present among the last enslaved African population in America when they learned of their independence on June 19, 1865.

Celebrating Juneteenth reminds me of the Passover feast that began in Exodus 12. Centuries after the Exodus, Jews would flock to Jerusalem to remember how God instructed the Hebrews to apply the blood of a spotless lamb to their doorposts, marking them as safe from the destruction that was to come.

Juneteenth and Passover are wonderful reminders of God's providential liberation throughout history. Although important, both events point to deliverances that were limited to a specific time and audience. How grateful I am today for the sacrificial work of the Lamb of God that offers a different kind of deliverance—freedom from sin—to anyone, at any time, who applies the blood of Jesus to their heart, marking them as saved in this world and the one to come (John 3:16). These freedoms are worthy of a celebration! —Ericka Loynes

Faith Step: *Find something in your house that symbolizes your ancestry, examine it closely, and then take a moment to celebrate Jesus's gift of salvation to all nations.*

Saturday, June 20

You prepare a table before me in the presence of my enemies. You anoint my head with oil; my cup overflows. Psalm 23:5 (NIV)

As a director of human resources, I cross paths with people from all walks of life. Day in and day out, I sit with folks as I coach, counsel, and encourage them. It's given me a front-row seat to some of the most common fears and worries that we humans wrestle with. And you know what I've noticed? The root of so many struggles is the belief that Jesus won't provide. That He's not enough. Boy, can I relate.

Jesus also crossed paths with people from all walks of life. He fed five thousand men (plus additional women and children) with five loaves and two fish in Luke 9 and had twelve baskets of leftovers. Ten people with leprosy in Luke 17 were physically healed and had their very lives restored. The women in Luke 8 who supported Jesus and His ministry were blessed with deliverances, healings, *and* the forgiveness of sins. People who crossed Jesus's path left with an overflow. Not "just" enough—more than enough. He not only filled their cup; He made it run over. The same is true today. Jesus is enough. He will provide for us even more than we can imagine. Our cup will run over, and we'll be drinking from the saucer! —Kristen West

Faith Step: *Put a cup and saucer near your kitchen sink. Overflow the cup to the brim and watch the excess pour into the saucer. Leave it there until you drink in this truth: Jesus is more than enough.*

FATHER'S DAY, SUNDAY, JUNE 21

Be kind and compassionate to one another, forgiving each other, just as in Christ God forgave you. Ephesians 4:32 (NIV)

MY DAD WAS THE WORST! The once-close relationship we'd enjoyed disintegrated when I turned thirteen. I made good grades and behaved myself, but Dad found reasons to ground me. I couldn't go to the creek with my friends, and I couldn't have sleepovers. I repaid Dad's strictness with sulking and surliness. Considering our rift, I was shocked when he asked if I'd like to go fishing, a pleasure we'd mutually enjoyed in past years. I couldn't imagine anything worse than spending hours in the broiling sun, alone in a boat with this man.

Rising before dawn for the hour drive to Black Lake, I questioned my sanity for agreeing to what was sure to be torture. As the sun rose over the water, I studied Dad's face. He looked tired. And where had all those wrinkles come from? He worked long hours selling insurance to support our family of five and was a church and civic leader. A trickle of compassion seeped into my stone-cold heart. Out of the blue, Dad said, "Growing up is hard. I'm proud of you, Hon."

"Thanks, Daddy," I replied, as my rod bent double. Dad shouted, "You've got one!" He helped me land the big bass and told me I'd always been a better fisherman than he was. We stayed on the water till our skin was baked and our ice chest was full. Fences and hearts were mended that day, and I have no doubt the Great Fisherman had cast this reconciliation. —PAT BUTLER DYSON

FAITH STEP: *Ask Jesus to soften your heart toward a loved one from whom you are estranged.*

Monday, June 22

God said, "Let there be lights in the vault of the sky to separate the day from the night, and let them serve as signs to mark sacred times, and days and years." Genesis 1:14 (NIV)

Waking before dawn, I dragged myself to the beach. I must admit, I've been coming to the Jersey Shore every summer for fifty years and never witnessed a sunrise. My husband has shared the annual tradition with our two girls since they were young. Oftentimes, they have tried sweetly cajoling me into joining them, but I always valued my sleep more than the experience. However, with my daughters now in their teens and college looming on the horizon, my heart coaxed me along.

I sleepily set a blanket in the sand as my family poked for seashells nearby. Eyeing the horizon, dawn broke around us with a swath of light that colored the sky. The early peeps of sandpipers skittering alerted me to the scent of salt on the breeze. As waves rolled against the shore, I breathed deeply, filling my lungs. I sat in awe of God, who created all of this and still took the time to create me. And to think I'd been sleeping through it! How could I have valued sleep more than this experience?

Like an excited child at her father's knee, I awoke over the next several days to witness the sunrise again and again. I can nap later.
—Gloria Joyce

Faith Step: *When was the last time you witnessed a sunrise? Wake up early and sit with God to show you value experiences with Him more than sleep.*

Tuesday, June 23

How beautiful on the mountains are the feet of the messenger who brings good news, the good news of peace and salvation. Isaiah 52:7 (NLT)

My family is in Lucerne, Switzerland, today. It's one of the cities on a European trip we are enjoying this summer. It's been a dream for which I feel deep gratitude.

We've traveled by train through the Alps, which are massive and stunningly beautiful. I commented to my husband that the scenery prompted me to search for verses I recalled about mountains. My faith was boosted by reading that my help comes from the mountains (Psalm 121:1–2) and that faith in Jesus has power to move mountains (Matthew 21:21).

But a third verse, Isaiah 52:7, is sticking with me the most today because it feels like a link between the power of a faith that can move a mountain and the beauty of that faith on someone else's behalf. When I step out in faith toward someone who needs His beautiful news of salvation, Jesus moves a mountain in yet one more life. In my time on earth and on vacation, I'm here not only to enjoy His beauty wherever my feet go but also to share His good news. In that way, my faith is part of His mountain-moving work too. —Erin Keeley Marshall

Faith Step: *Your feet may be limited by age, injury, or illness, but you still can have unlimited faith that moves mountains. Treat your feet to a foot scrub, massage, or pedicure. Thank Jesus for allowing you to carry His beautiful news of peace and salvation.*

WEDNESDAY, JUNE 24

"I am the vine; you are the branches. Whoever abides in me and I in him, he it is that bears much fruit, for apart from me you can do nothing." John 15:5 (ESV)

WHILE WAITING ON THE PLATFORM in a busy train station, I noticed that nearly everyone had a phone in their hand. Some wore earbuds to listen to music. Others were texting. A few scrolled through social media feeds. And still others were having phone conversations. Literally hundreds of people around me were engrossed in their smartphones. I saw very few people standing quietly or reading a book.

I have to admit that I'm often guilty of being glued to my mobile phone. I'll pull it out during my work commute to check email, make to-do lists, or listen to an audiobook. But on this day seeing so many folks gripping their phones, I had to ask myself if I am attached like that to Jesus, the true vine. Am I tethered to my phone, or am I seeking, listening, and talking to Jesus? Well, not all the time. But instead of aimlessly passing the time on my phone, I could spend those minutes connecting with Jesus in prayer or silently praising Him by quietly humming a worship song.

I believe I can better use my so-called idle time to further strengthen my bond with Jesus and cut the cord on those worldly things that draw me away from Him. I know my soul and spirit will certainly blossom by being unplugged. —BARBRANDA LUMPKINS WALLS

FAITH STEP: *Intentionally put away your phone the next time you wait in line or for an appointment. Use the idle time instead to connect with Jesus.*

Thursday, June 25

"These were your traders in choice wares, in wrappings of blue and embroidered work." Ezekiel 27:24 (WEB)

I WAS HORRIFIED WHEN NEW owners of a derelict neighboring house repainted their fixer-upper. Who in their right mind paints a house black! Previously a putrid shade of aged pink, the now black house wasn't what I wanted to see from my big picture windows that face the forlorn place. A neighbor friend insisted the house was blue. Eventually, I conceded that the house is somewhat blue, a dark midnight blue.

The color grew on me, and I now appreciate that house. Even on the bleakest, dismal rainy days of winter, it's a vividly pristine welcome sight in my daily routine. And what an improvement over its former self! The transformation from its wretched, forlorn coat of peeling paint to this new cloak of midnight blue is a daily source of inspiration. I marvel at the transformative difference a fresh coat of paint made on this old, neglected place. It gave it new life.

Likewise, this old house, called myself, experienced a similar home improvement when Jesus, in His compassionate kindness, transformed me from my wretched old self into a restored new person by wrapping me in a fresh coat of His love and forgiveness. Now, every time I see that midnight house, I can't help but appreciate what Jesus did for a fixer-upper like me by giving me new life in Him.
—CASSANDRA TIERSMA

FAITH STEP: *Find something in your home you've been meaning to give a fresh coat of paint. While painting, reflect on how Jesus transforms you into a better version of yourself.*

Friday, June 26

> As it is written, "What no eye has seen, nor ear heard, nor the heart of man imagined, what God has prepared for those who love him." 1 Corinthians 2:9 (ESV)

I'VE LIVED IN FLORIDA FOR eight years now, and there are a few things that still make me sigh with wonder. I love crossing the palm-lined causeways to gorgeous beachfront destinations. I still marvel at the abundance of lizards and exotic vegetation and at hearing seagulls in the Costco parking lot, some five miles away from the Gulf of Mexico. When I'm pushing my loaded cart to my minivan, usually rushing to my next stop, and hear the familiar seabird cry, I tingle with delight that I live that close to the beach. It's surreal to be in an otherwise totally nondescript big-box suburban shopping center and hear sounds I once associated with vacationing, feet in the sand, and an ocean view. It feels positively magical and incredibly special.

One day, I know that I will journey to an eternal paradise full of indescribable delights that I expect will fill my heart and soul with wordless wonder. There, I'm promised a "glorious body" (Philippians 3:21), living forever without "mourning, nor crying, nor pain" (Revelation 21:4). I'll stroll through pearly gates on streets of gold (Revelation 21:21) to my heavenly mansion (John 14:2), surrounded by glistening, jewel-laden walls (Revelation 21:18–20).

As positively magical and incredibly special as living in Florida is for me, I know living in heaven with Jesus will be even better!
—ISABELLA CAMPOLATTARO

FAITH STEP: *Search the Internet for images that evoke paradise for you. Create a collage to paste into your prayer journal along with this verse.*

Saturday, June 27

"Again, the kingdom of heaven is like a merchant seeking beautiful pearls, who, when he had found one pearl of great price, went and sold all that he had and bought it." Matthew 13:45–46 (NKJV)

My beloved sister is in the process of paring down her belongings and recently gifted me her pearl bracelet and necklace set. I marveled at her generosity and remain deeply grateful. The pearls are baroque, meaning they are irregular in size and shape, lending them a fascinating appearance. Like me, they are perfectly imperfect.

Among gems, pearls are unique in that they're created inside a living creature. Other jewels are formed by pressure or heat underground, while some are made in a laboratory using advanced technology.

Jesus compared the kingdom of heaven to a merchant seeking beautiful pearls, teaching that heaven is more valuable than anything else and a person must be willing to give up everything to obtain it. In the same way, Jesus gave His life not so He would have a place in heaven because He already had that (John 17:5) but so we could enjoy eternity in flawless freedom with Him.

Today, as I slip on my heirloom jewelry, I bask in the love I share with my sister. But as I run my fingers along the spheres, I will remember the unique sacrifice it took to create a priceless pearl offered to me and to all believers in Jesus. And I am eternally grateful.
—Heidi Gaul

Faith Step: *Spend a few minutes researching the way pearls are created, and meditate on why Jesus chose that gem to describe heaven and the immeasurable price He paid.*

Sunday, June 28

This same God who takes care of me will supply all your needs from his glorious riches, which have been given to us in Christ Jesus. Philippians 4:19 (NLT)

Two weeks had passed since I'd submitted my manuscript for a ninety-day devotional book, and already the time had come to start writing the next. I sat before my computer, stared at the blank screen, and whispered a prayer. I waited for a heavenly download, but nothing came. The clock ticked. I moved from my chair to my knees and asked God again for help. This time, He responded with undeniable clarity.

Into my mind popped the Old Testament story of the widow who faced financial ruin. She stood on the verge of losing everything, including her two sons, to pay off her late husband's debts. The prophet Elisha told her to collect empty jars and pour oil from her flask into them. She trusted him and obeyed, and the oil multiplied to fill every jar. She sold the oil and paid the debts (2 Kings 4:1–7).

Like the widow, I suffered from a lack of resources. That morning, I envisioned ninety empty pages and asked Jesus to give me enough ideas to fill them. Every day following became an adventure. I'd pray for words to fill three or four pages, and fresh ideas flowed. By day's end, I'd met my desired quota. Before long, the manuscript was complete.

God supplied oil for the widow and ideas for my devotional book. His resources know no limit. Rest assured, He'll provide for your needs too. —Grace Fox

Faith Step: *Begin the habit of remembering the provisions God has given you. Write each on a small slip of paper and place them in an empty jar on your table or cupboard.*

MONDAY, JUNE 29

The LORD watches over the strangers; He relieves the fatherless and widow; But the way of the wicked He turns upside down. Psalm 146:9 (NKJV)

I HAD THE OPPORTUNITY TO go to Guatemala with The MomCo, an international ministry to moms. We visited a shelter for teen moms, all who had escaped abuse and violence. Many of them arrived carrying cardboard for beds, assuming they and their children would be sleeping on a dirt floor. Instead, they each received their own furnished room, counseling, job training, and the support and love of other moms. After a year, these moms were given a place to live in a safe community, a job, furnishings for an apartment, food, and regular visits from the staff.

We were privileged to be with them the night before they left the shelter for their new lives. After doing a craft, we heard their stories and prayed with them. One young mom, Abigail, shared how Guatemala needed more shelters like this one, but her prayer was there would be no more violence. I saw strength and determination in her eyes and imagined she would be a woman to run her own shelter in the future.

As believers, Jesus calls us to help the fatherless and widows. We live in a sad time where women and children are abused and sold into slavery in astounding numbers worldwide. Thankfully, shelters everywhere are providing safety and relief to women and children. I'm determined to join the battle alongside Jesus, to turn the ways of the wicked upside down and support organizations doing just that. Will you join me? —JEANNIE BLACKMER

FAITH STEP: *Ask Jesus how you can help the fatherless, widows, or the oppressed. Join Him in making the world a safer place until He comes again.*

Tuesday, June 30

Whoever refreshes others will be refreshed. Proverbs 11:25 (NIV)

ON MY WAY TO BED every night, I walk into my kids' rooms, say the same prayer, and bless them with holy water. One night, years ago, Mason was awake for his blessing. After I said, "Jesus, please bless and watch over Mason. Keep him healthy, happy, and safe. Bring him good, true, and faith-filled friends. Help me be the mom he needs me to be," he stood up and prayed the same blessing over me. It was incredibly powerful to experience the reciprocal impact of my child blessing me. I felt my heart swell with grace.

In the same way, when I bless others with kindness and love, that blessing returns to me twofold. It may not be as overt and profound as my experience with Mason, but amazingly I have felt Jesus touch my soul with grace each and every time. To be clear, it's not in the sense of hash marks on a tally He keeps of my good works, nor in a way where I have to earn my way into His heart. Instead, it's in the sense that love breeds more love, grace multiplies into more grace, and blessings expand as they ripple out on their journey.
—CLAIRE MCGARRY

FAITH STEP: *Look back and recall a well-intended kindness you did for someone that led to them reciprocating that same kindness to you. Did you feel your heart expand with the grace Jesus placed there? Consider journaling about your experience.*

WEDNESDAY, JULY 1

"He reached down from on high and took hold of me; he drew me out of deep waters. He rescued me from my powerful enemy, from my foes, who were too strong for me." 2 Samuel 22:17–18 (NIV)

WHEN I WAS WALKING DOWN the 29th Street beach access in Ocean City, New Jersey, for a day in the sun with my daughter, my arthritic knees made the trek difficult and slow. I stopped multiple times on the path to rest. Cassidy happily grabbed my beach bag and chair and soldiered ahead, promising to secure my chair in the sand. She'd offered to carry my things before we set out, but I refused. Now, she still helped without so much as a harsh word or an "I told you so."

My willingness to accept help from others has always been a constant battle. As my daughter walked away, I admonished myself for succumbing to pride yet again. Even though the Bible reminds me that pride leads to destruction (Proverbs 16:18), I hold tightly to my independence and want to do everything myself. If I'm honest, I sometimes turn down Jesus's help instead of turning to Him. Yet I know it's the offering *and* accepting of kindness that allows both the giver and receiver to grow closer to Jesus. Happily, Jesus never says, "I told you so."

Next time, I will graciously say yes to Jesus and Cassidy.
—GLORIA JOYCE

FAITH STEP: *What burdens have you been carrying alone? Lay down your pride, and allow someone to help. Ask Jesus to bless them for their support.*

Thursday, July 2

Fearing people is a dangerous trap, but trusting the LORD means safety. Proverbs 29:25 (NLT)

My daughter's last major event before moving up to the youth ministry at church was attending her final year of kids' camp. I'd served as a counselor for her grade level every summer since she was in second grade, so I knew this would be my last year at kids' camp as well. She and her friends were ready to graduate, but a part of me wondered if they would be OK around students who were so much older and more mature than they were.

On the last day of camp, I watched as an older boy from the youth group came to my daughter's table in the cafeteria and sat down among her large group of friends. He fist-bumped some of the boys and high-fived a few girls, but I couldn't help but wonder why he was there in the first place. Just when I was about to casually meander across the cafeteria to investigate, I saw the entire group bow their heads in prayer as the older boy began praying. My daughter told me later that the boy said he wanted to personally welcome the group and pray for them because he remembered how nervous he'd been to transition from fifth to sixth grade himself.

I knew Jesus had allowed me to see that moment to remind me that each time I have to let my children go, He holds them tighter and tighter. They are safe in His presence, even when I'm not around. —Emily E. Ryan

---

Faith Step: *Identify an area of your life where you need to let go of some control and trust Jesus with a loved one. Memorize Proverbs 29:25 as your prayer.*

Friday, July 3

Then they said to each other, "What we're doing is not right. This is a day of good news and we are keeping it to ourselves." 2 Kings 7:9 (NIV)

As the weather gets warmer, I've seen more ants. I've learned that ants, when they encounter a rich food source, collectively take it back to their nest to share with the colony. Furthermore, ants also secrete pheromones that mark a path to the food source so that other ants can find their way to this newfound supply. If they weren't invading my windowsill, I'd be impressed!

Oddly enough, this trait of ants reminds me of my childhood best friend, Roberta. Whatever she had or experienced, she shared with me. Whether it was a new pencil, a piece of candy, or her favorite snack, Roberta's generosity knew no bounds. She was even generous with sharing things she learned, including new words she read.

In 2 Kings 7, four lepers facing death from famine entered an empty camp of the enemy and found it filled with abundant food, drink, silver, gold, and clothing. Rather than keep it to themselves, they shared the good news with their countrymen, saving their people in the process.

I have been called by Jesus to do the same. I am privileged to have read the rich Gospel of Jesus Christ, and now I am called to generously share the good news of God's forgiveness in Jesus to a world in spiritual famine. This news is too valuable to keep to myself, and like the ant, my friend Roberta, and the four lepers, I want to share it.
—Ericka Loynes

Faith Step: *What special treasures do you have? Choose one and pray about the possibility of sharing it with a friend or family member.*

Independence Day, Saturday, July 4

Jesus replied: "'Love the Lord your God with all your heart and with all your soul and with all your mind.' This is the first and greatest commandment. And the second is like it: 'Love your neighbor as yourself.'" Matthew 22:37–39 (NIV)

A RED, WHITE, AND BLUE cloth covers the table, which I top with matching paper plates, napkins, and plastic cups decorated with the American flag, as is my T-shirt. A breeze lifts the flag bunting stretched across our front porch railing, and Old Glory waves from the pole in our yard. Miniature flags border the edge of the flower beds. Even the mailbox post is wrapped in red, white, and blue and topped with a bow. It's Independence Day, and our national flag is on full display.

Two hundred and fifty years ago, Betsy Ross was commissioned to sew the first American flag as a symbol of national pride and unity only weeks before the Declaration of Independence birthed a new nation in July 1776. She was chosen for the job, in part, because she attended Christ Church in Philadelphia along with General George Washington, whose shirt ruffles and cuffs she had embroidered.

The US flag hasn't changed much in two and a half centuries. We've just added a few stars to the original thirteen. But I wonder how well our flag symbolizes national pride and unity today. In a prayer for America, George Washington asked the Almighty to help citizens "entertain a brotherly love and affection for one another." Surrounded by red, white, and blue on this Fourth of July, that is my prayer today. —KAREN SARGENT

FAITH STEP: *As you celebrate today, reflect on Matthew 22:37–39. As Christians, may we be united in our love of God and our neighbor.*

SUNDAY, JULY 5

Impress them on your children. Talk about them when you sit at home and when you walk along the road, when you lie down and when you get up. Deuteronomy 6:7 (NIV)

ONE WEEKEND, MY HUSBAND, RON, and I babysat for our almost two-year-old grandson, Ben. He lives two hours away, so we gladly watch him whenever possible. I soaked up the time with him. It brought back memories of when our kids were young.

But not all those memories are good—there are many things I wish I could redo as a parent. As we took Ben to church this weekend, I remembered how stressed and irritable I often was on Sundays. Children stay in the sanctuary during the entire worship service, and keeping them quiet is challenging.

Ron and I took turns entertaining Ben with books and small items. At the end of the sermon, it was time for prayer. I placed him on the floor beside us while we stood and prayed. Without prompting, Ben folded his little hands and scrunched his eyes closed too. He held this posture for a while, creating an unforgettable memory as I peeked at him from the corner of my eye.

I couldn't take credit for Ben's prayer posture—that belonged to his parents. But Jesus reminded me that these faith-building practices started for Ben more than thirty years before, when our son, Mark, learned about prayer and prayed with us during his growing-up years.

Ben and Jesus graciously showed me that parental priorities, like prayer and worship, are just as significant as the things I wish I could do over. —BRENDA L. YODER

FAITH STEP: *Note things in your life you often regret. Submit them to Jesus, asking Him to reveal the significant, faithful acts you often overlook.*

Monday, July 6

When Jesus saw his mother there, and the disciple whom he loved standing nearby, he said to her, "Woman, here is your son," and to the disciple, "Here is your mother." John 19:26–27 (NIV)

"The doctor taxi has arrived to pick me up," Mom said.

I chuckled because she was right. For two months, my little red Beetle had transported my eighty-three-year-old mother on countless trips to the heart center, the heart failure clinic, the hospital, and various doctors' offices.

I switched on her portable oxygen tank and helped her to my car.

The Beetle wasn't the best vehicle for medical transport. Mom had to drop and plop into the seat because the car was low to the ground. Though I positioned the passenger seat as far back as possible, she had to use her hands to lift and pull each leg into the limited floor space. And once buckled in, the heavy door presented a challenge for her to close. Yet the doctor taxi got Mom where she needed to go.

We made the most of these days together, catching up on family news and listening to gospel music. We stopped at Blue Plate Café for a meal, peach cobbler included, when she felt strong enough.

Jesus showed concern for His mother too. Even on the cross, He spoke to Mary and arranged for John to take care of her. Such a kind and loving Son.

Mom is doing better now. No more oxygen tanks and far fewer medical appointments. I'm on my way to pick her up again in my little red taxi but just for fun today. —Becky Alexander

Faith Step: *Meet the need of a parent or other special person. No red car required.*

Tuesday, July 7

Not only so, but we also glory in our sufferings, because we know that suffering produces perseverance; perseverance, character; and character, hope. Romans 5:3–4 (NIV)

I WENT ON A GIRLS' fly-fishing excursion to become better at the sport my husband, Zane, enjoys so much. This lodge in Montana is situated on a famous fly-fishing river. A guide took me in a river boat and gave me a lesson, teaching me how to cast, where the fish were, what flies they were attracted to, and more. He also taught me about perseverance.

After a few hours of not catching anything, I was cold and ready to stop for the day, but he refused. He believed I would catch a fish, and he wouldn't stop rowing the boat until I landed one. Inspired, I kept trying. After nearly eight hours of fishing, I finally caught a twenty-eight-inch-long brown trout. I better understood my husband's passion for fly-fishing because after persevering, finally catching a giant fish was a thrill. Isn't that similar to what walking through this life with Jesus is about too?

When I face trials of different kinds, I put my hope in Jesus. He gives me strength and encouragement to endure, grow in character, and ultimately find hope. I want to continue to learn more about fly-fishing and enjoy it with Zane. I also want to continue to persevere even in difficult times, knowing Jesus is cheering me on. What a thrill it is to live with that kind of hope! —JEANNIE BLACKMER

FAITH STEP: *Write your own definition of what it means to persevere with Jesus. How can you put that into practice today?*

WEDNESDAY, JULY 8

You came near when I called you, and you said, "Do not fear."
Lamentations 3:57 (NIV)

I CALL IT "DEAD WOMAN'S CURVE." It's the spot where I had my bike crash two years ago. I face my fear and ride past it every day, giving it a wide berth. I don't bike after a rain anymore, so a mud slick won't bring me down. But something else might.

I've read that the phrase "fear not" is written in the Bible 365 times—a reminder to live each day fearlessly. I've never counted to be sure, but what a concept! A recent call from our granddaughter's pediatrician struck fear in my heart. Blake had been running a slight fever for several weeks, but she seemed OK otherwise. The doctor ordered blood tests, the results of which were alarming. "Blake's white cell count is the highest I've ever seen," the doctor said. "Get her to the Texas Children's Hospital emergency room now!"

When I heard the news, I panicked. I fell to my knees racked with fear and beseeched Jesus for help. For days, Blake didn't have a diagnosis. Finally, doctors determined she had a severe UTI, and they needed to do a culture to discover which antibiotic to use. With medication, Blake's white cell count returned to normal. Her temperature decreased, and she was cured.

And with Jesus's help, I fought my fear until I knew Blake would be OK. It's a fight I need to address daily, and thankfully I have 365 biblical cures for it. —PAT BUTLER DYSON

FAITH STEP: *Google "fear not" and read over the list of Bible verses. Write your favorites on a note card and commit a few to memory to recall when fear threatens to bring you down.*

Thursday, July 9

Each of you should give what you have decided in your heart to give, not reluctantly or under compulsion, for God loves a cheerful giver.
2 Corinthians 9:7 (NIV)

CHERRY PICKING WAS HARD WORK. Farmer Charles, as my husband and I lovingly called him, had phoned asking for our help harvesting his cherries. With six trees, it took most of the day. The buckets slowly filled with juicy, red fruit from our work. We were thrilled when the elderly widower unexpectedly insisted we take some home.

Once we arrived home, I started washing and pitting the cherries. I texted Farmer Charles a thank-you, but that just didn't seem like quite enough. I had no harvest to share with him. I didn't know what to do to thank him for his kindness. I knew he didn't expect anything. He gave out of a place of love.

I bit into a delicious ripe cherry. As the juice dripped on my chin, the perfect solution came to me. A cherry pie. I rolled out the dough for the crust with great excitement. Farmer Charles would be so surprised!

After the pie cooled, my husband drove me back to the farm. When I handed it to Farmer Charles, tears glistened on his cheeks. "No one's ever made me a cherry pie before," he said. I was surprised, but I should have known that Jesus would inspire me with the perfect gift to show my appreciation. I didn't have a harvest to share, but with inspiration from Jesus, I had the perfect way to return a delicious kindness. —JEANNIE HUGHES

FAITH STEP: *Find a creative way to repay someone who has been kind to you this week. Pray for Jesus to inspire you how you might surprise them.*

Friday, July 10

The righteous care for the needs of their animals, but the kindest acts of the wicked are cruel. Proverbs 12:10 (NIV)

MY KIDS HAVE ALL BECOME animal lovers. My son and his family own a farm and keep two horses, several cows and goats, fifty chickens, and two Great Pyrenees dogs. Parents and kids alike care for the menagerie by collecting eggs, milking goats and cows, feeding and watering all the critters, putting them in their pens at night, and letting them loose in the morning.

My oldest daughter and her husband adopted a lap-sized rescue dog. They've lavished love on the little guy from the moment they met him. She recently sent two pictures—one taken on the day they brought the dog home and the other taken exactly a year later. The animal's transformation was remarkable. His fur, once matted and shaggy, is well groomed. His eyes, once sad and scared, are happy and bright.

My youngest daughter recently fostered a litter of five kittens. They arrived traumatized and skittish, so she and her kids gave them space and time to settle in. Within a couple of days, one of the cats crawled into my four-year-old granddaughter's lap, began to purr, and fell asleep. This kitty found its forever home with them, and the other four were adopted elsewhere.

A little kindness goes a long way to help animals thrive. Our care for them demonstrates love in action. It also reflects Jesus's love for me and you. He provides for us, protects us, and—best of all—rescues us and adopts us into His family (Ephesians 1:5). Because of His kindness, we can have a forever home too. —GRACE FOX

FAITH STEP: *Visit a pet store or volunteer, if possible, at an animal shelter to lavish love on God's creatures.*

SATURDAY, JULY 11

[Jesus] touched their eyes and said, "According to your faith let it be done to you"; and their sight was restored. Matthew 9:29–30 (NIV)

WHEN I FIRST WITNESSED THE wonders of touchlessness—a touchless car wash—it seemed like such a great idea. Then touchlessness crept into other arenas in life. Touchless pizza delivery, faucets, or visits with a doctor; remote-control or voice-activated page-turning.

It seems as if the consuming drive is toward a completely touchless society. I wonder what Jesus would think of that. So much of His ministry involved touch—touching two blind men's eyes, touching a sick child (Matthew 9:25), touching those whom culture deemed untouchable—lepers, Samaritans, the unbelieving (Matthew 8:3).

Am I losing touch with the purpose of touch?

If I opt for and am satisfied with virtual-only visits with a grandchild instead of being present, face-to-face, eyeball-to-eyeball, and aging cheek pressed against smooth newborn cheek, I've lost so much more than the smells and textures of the experience. Something important happens inside when I touch the pages of God's Word, run my fingers over the words in red—the words of Jesus Himself. Far beyond virtually, my spirit touches the Spirit of Jesus.

How could He want anything less of me than to go from that place of peace in His presence, from in some ways "touching" heaven, to reach out and touch others in need of encouragement or a reminder of His love? And all the more so if it isn't in a touchless text message but a hand on someone's shoulder or a warm, concerned embrace.
—CYNTHIA RUCHTI

FAITH STEP: *Take a photo of the word* **touchless** *if it appears in your day or week. Use it as a reminder that Jesus touches us and makes us whole. (See Matthew 8:3.)*

Sunday, July 12

She opens her mouth with wisdom, and on her tongue is the law of kindness.
Proverbs 31:26 (NKJV)

My husband, David, and I entered the popular restaurant and approached the harried-looking young hostess. After giving her our name, I sensed a prompt, a need to say something. "Are you all right?" Those words left my mouth before I could even form the thought. An instant passed, then her placid expression crumbled. She replied, "How did you know?"

Know? I didn't know anything. I'd simply reached out to her the way Jesus did—and still does—for us. I glanced toward the entrance. We were the last in line. After leading us to our table, she opened up to me about her life, currently overfull with challenges and disappointments. A teardrop or two spilled from my eyes. I asked if we could pray for her. She nodded. I whispered for Jesus to encourage her and lighten her load. She returned to her station with a trace of a smile on her lips.

I looked at my husband, seated across the table from me, and stretched my arms toward him. David took my hands in his and nodded, his eyes filled with peace.

I knew the meal would be as nicely presented and tasty as always, but for now, I savored the deep nourishment my soul had received. Jesus had honored me with the privilege of using my ears, and my heart, to hear. —Heidi Gaul

Faith Step: *Look, really look, and listen to those you encounter today. How can you share Jesus's kindness, love, and encouragement with them?*

MONDAY, JULY 13

All Scripture is given by inspiration of God, and is profitable for doctrine, for reproof, for correction, for instruction in righteousness.
2 Timothy 3:16 (NKJV)

FEW THINGS EXCITE ME MORE than opening my mailbox to find an actual letter in it. I get excited when I see other people's mail sticking out of their boxes and wonder who may have sent them a letter. I've spent enough years now traveling around the sun to remember when landline phone calls and handwritten letters were the top two methods of communication. However, since the advent of the Internet and smartphones, folks are not as inclined to mail handwritten letters. So when I do receive one, I'm prone to break into a happy dance at the mailbox—right there in front of Jesus, my neighbors, and anyone who happens to be out walking their dogs at that moment.

It's not only the contents of a letter that thrill me; it's the fact that someone thought enough about me to take a moment out of their busy schedule and write meaningful and intentional words to me. Words of value. Words of purpose. Words of affirmation and encouragement. Just like God's Word. Every time I open it and leaf through its pages, it's like reading a personal letter from God. A magnificent letter detailing the life of His precious Son, Jesus. A letter that reveals His tender heart for us. A divine letter filled with purpose, hope, clarity, and instruction for our lives. A letter to help us look more like Jesus. —KRISTEN WEST

FAITH STEP: *Pray for Jesus to show you who you can affirm and encourage. Then sit down and write that person a purposeful letter to let them know how much you and Jesus value them.*

Tuesday, July 14

*I will instruct you and teach you in the way you should go;
I will counsel you with my loving eye on you.* Psalm 32:8 (NIV)

LAST MONTH, WE MISSED OUR planned excursion on a cruise because we didn't follow the instructions. Our excursion tickets stated that we were supposed to meet *before* debarkation, and we wrongly thought we were meeting the tour guide after we were off the ship. Unfortunately, we failed to read the directions. Like King Saul in 1 Samuel 13:1–14, who felt compelled to act without seeking the Lord's favor, I sometimes rush ahead without consulting the instructions provided to me. The prophet Samuel had told Saul to wait for him and he would come and show him what he was to do, but the king didn't. Similarly, our family had the necessary information for our excursion yet failed to follow it properly due to haste and presumption. Thankfully, the cruise staff accommodated us on a different excursion. This act of grace mirrored the greater kindness Jesus extends to us daily.

Jesus manages our missteps and redirects us. Like the staff who helped reroute our day, Jesus is always ready to assist and guide us back on track when we call out to Him. Whether we find ourselves lost in life's journey or distanced in our relationship with Him, a simple, heartfelt plea for help is enough, even when we've failed to follow directions. —TRICIA GOYER

FAITH STEP: *Reflect on a situation in which you might have acted hastily or without proper guidance. Consider how this has impacted your journey. Pray for the patience to wait on Jesus's timing and for the discernment to follow His instructions more faithfully in the future.*

WEDNESDAY, JULY 15

The mind of a person plans his way, but the LORD directs his steps.
Proverbs 16:9 (NASB)

I HAVE CONTROL ISSUES. EVERYONE who knows me knows this. In fact, it's a running joke in my family that Mom brings gauze, a nod to my planning for every contingency. It became a pocketbook staple after vacation one year. My six-year-old daughter, Ana, had loose baby teeth. And I felt one would fall out at the most unlikely moment.

My family and I were standing underneath the shark tunnel at Adventure Aquarium when it finally happened. Ana's tooth came out, and I whipped gauze from my purse. My family roared with laughter. Ana is in high school now, but each time we pack for a trip, someone still lightheartedly asks, "Hey, Mom, did you pack gauze?"

Several years later, I replaced the gauze in my purse with rosary beads. My life was not going as I'd planned. Praying through the beads was a tangible reminder of Jesus's presence in my life. Changing my focus to Him calmed my mind and allowed me to stop wrestling Jesus for control.

No matter the season of life I find myself in nowadays, whether I can plan for it or not, I know Jesus is by my side. He is a constant that I do not need to remember to pack. As Jesus set the path before me, I know He will bring me through it. Instead of holding on to control, I hold tightly to His hand. *Jesus is my gauze.*
—GLORIA JOYCE

FAITH STEP: *Make a list of any worries you carry today. When you finish, write "For Jesus" at the top of the page, and ask Him to take control.*

Thursday, July 16

"If I go and prepare a place for you, I will come back and take you to be with me that you also may be where I am." John 14:3 (NIV)

My husband's parents are moving from California to Idaho. We feel like we have won the jackpot. When we moved to Idaho five years ago, we moved away from Scott's family. We had lived near one another for more than twenty years, and the separation was painful.

Fast-forward to last spring. After visiting us several times, Scott's sister, Cheri, and her husband, Kevin, began to feel the pull of the Boise foothills. They were ready for a change and decided to join us here. We were thrilled. The only problem was that when they moved to Idaho, Scott's parents felt left out.

That problem will be solved in less than a week. Our family's pull is powerful. Scott's parents have bought a new home halfway between ours and Kevin and Cheri's. We couldn't be happier! There is something beautiful and sustaining about being close to family. We are meant to be together.

When I asked Jesus into my heart, I became a part of His family. Jesus has gone ahead to be with His Father and to prepare a place for His whole family, me included, in heaven. It is humbling and exciting to know that Jesus can't wait to see me! Being with Him will sustain me for all eternity. We are meant to be together.
—Susanna Foth Aughtmon

Faith Step: *When did you become a part of Jesus's family? Share the story of your salvation with a friend who you would like to see become a part of His family too.*

Friday, July 17

Your ears shall hear a word behind you, saying, "This is the way, walk in it," when you turn to the right or when you turn to the left. Isaiah 30:21 (ESV)

I LOOKED OUT THE OFFICE window and saw it was a beautiful sunny day. So I decided to briefly step outside to get a breath of fresh air before attending a meeting. I grabbed my key fob and headed out. But as I waited for the elevator, something within me told me to go back and get my phone. "No, I don't need it," I said to myself. But the prompting was strong, so I returned to my office to retrieve the phone.

As soon as I stepped outside and started my walk around the block, I spotted a man sitting on the sidewalk. I was led to approach him and ask if I could buy him something. Knowing that I could use my smartphone to make a purchase, I asked the man if he would like anything from the nearby Starbucks.

"A cup of hot coffee with cream and sugar," he said. As I entered the store, I realized I didn't have any cash. But then I suddenly remembered that I had a Starbucks gift card loaded on my phone! I purchased the coffee using the gift card and handed it to the man. "Thank you, ma'am," he said. "God bless you."

I'm so glad that I listened to Jesus's voice quietly telling me what to do before I left my office. Doing so enabled me to offer a cup of kindness to a stranger and be a blessing, just as Jesus wanted.
—BARBRANDA LUMPKINS WALLS

FAITH STEP: *What is Jesus's still small voice prompting you to do today? Listen to Him and see how you can bless someone.*

SATURDAY, JULY 18

"He has sent me to proclaim freedom for the prisoners and recovery of sight for the blind, to set the oppressed free, to proclaim the year of the Lord's favor."... "Today this scripture is fulfilled in your hearing."
Luke 4:18–19, 21 (NIV)

ON A FAMILY ROAD TRIP through Kentucky horse country, I was intrigued to see distinctive rock walls stretching for miles. They looked old and purposeful, constructed of gray rocks layered a few feet high and topped with a spiky cap of stones. I felt as if we were driving through the Scottish lowlands I'd visited decades earlier.

Curious, I searched online for their history. Turns out the masons of those Bluegrass walls did follow the work of Irish and Scottish craftsmen. Similar ancient limestone rock fences are found in New England, around Nashville, and in Texas Hill Country.

The Bluegrass walls carry mixed history because indentured servants and enslaved persons did some of the later work, earning the structures the nickname "slave walls."

My heart mellowed. I had wondered who built them and whether the walls were evidence of a tragic part of our country's history. As I read these details to my family, we quieted at the truth that freedom is fragile on earth.

Jesus quoted Isaiah about oppression that extended many generations before His earthly life. By doing so, He illustrated how we've always needed His freedom and healing. He knows all of history. When we struggle to make sense of and heal from the past, we can place our hope in Jesus. He is true freedom. —ERIN KEELEY MARSHALL

FAITH STEP: *No one is immune from generational wounding. In what ways does your family or community need Jesus's freedom and healing? Ask Him to work powerfully in those areas.*

SUNDAY, JULY 19

God has placed the parts in the body, every one of them, just as he wanted them to be. If they were all one part, where would the body be? As it is, there are many parts, but one body. 1 Corinthians 12:18–20 (NIV)

I LIKE TO COOK AND be creative while being efficient and thrifty at the same time. One way I accomplish all these goals is with a store-bought rotisserie chicken. My local food wholesaler sells a giant, juicy bird for less than $5, which is a great value. I make the very most of it—literally.

When I buy one, I immediately remove the breasts, with which I make pot pie and chicken salad. I'll serve the two leg quarters as a quick meal for my sons when we're on the run. Any stray meat on the bone along with the drippings I use to make chicken soup or an Italian pasta sauce. I pack each separately in freezer bags along with the chicken carcass, which will be employed when I make a delicious soup. Every last smidgen of chicken is used for something.

In the same way, every part of the body of Christ has great value too. Jesus designed us with different traits that are all intended to serve the common good. No attribute or member of the body has greater value; they all serve a vital function that depends on the others. Working together, we make the most of our collective and individual bodies to serve God and each other—every last smidgen of us. —ISABELLA CAMPOLATTARO

FAITH STEP: *Buy a rotisserie chicken, and use every part for recipes of your choice. Contemplate 1 Corinthians 12:18–20 as you work with the chicken.*

Monday, July 20

[Jesus] said to Thomas, "Put your finger here; see my hands. Reach out your hand and put it into my side. Stop doubting and believe." John 20:27 (NIV)

AFTER MOST OF HER MANY surgeries, my mother—always a nurse at heart—would often say, "Wanna see my scar?" I think she saw the scars, raw and tender as they were, as evidence of what she'd endured.

Reading in the Gospel of John today, I noticed a gem of wonder that increased my gratitude for Jesus's patience with me. I saw myself in the story of Thomas, who was often called the doubter.

While reading the passage, I had a "Wait a minute!" moment. Thomas hadn't told Jesus that he'd crossed his arms in defiance and stomped his spiritual foot, refusing to believe that Jesus had conquered death, as his friends had reported to him. Yet Jesus divinely knew Thomas had said he would never believe until he saw the nail prints, the scars, the physical evidence in His side. According to the biblical account, after appearing among His followers, Jesus stood nose to nose with Thomas and invited the doubting one to see, touch the scars, stop doubting.

Jesus knew Thomas's struggle and addressed it directly, not with condemnation but with a very personal, vulnerable invitation— "Wanna see My scars?" An invitation to believe, Jesus extended His nail-scarred hands for Thomas. And He does the same for me.
—CYNTHIA RUCHTI

FAITH STEP: *Find a photo of a time in your life when Jesus gave you clear evidence that He spared you—a car accident, a house fire, a potentially dangerous decision, a serious hospitalization. Let it serve as a "see My scars" reminder of the reality of His saving power.*

Tuesday, July 21

Cling to your faith in Christ, and keep your conscience clear.
1 Timothy 1:19 (NLT)

PHYSICAL RESTRICTIONS MAKE IT IMPOSSIBLE for me to clean like I used to, scrubbing obsessively and striving for perfection, even in places hidden from view. Now I'm trying to develop a more relaxed attitude. I thought I'd made progress until a few things occurred together. First, I received very short notice of overnight guests coming. Second, I'd neglected the house because of a pressing work assignment. Third, my husband had brought extra furniture, bedding, and boxes of papers and mementos into our already crowded house after a relative passed away. My relaxed attitude disappeared as I rushed around cleaning the areas the guests would use. I ended with a marathon session of stuffing everything I could under beds and into closets, baskets, and drawers.

Thankfully, I never have to hide things I'd prefer Jesus didn't see. He invites me to bring anything I feel ashamed of to Him openly and freely (1 Peter 5:7). I don't have to clean myself up to keep company with Him. He promises to cleanse me completely when I confess my sins (1 John 1:9).

Living out my faith includes being tuned in to the Holy Spirit's leading to do what is right. Each time I ignore that inner nudging, I risk my heart getting hardened and my mind cluttered. I may not keep my house as perfectly clean as I did when I was younger, but with Jesus's help, I can maintain a clean conscience. That's the best way to have a relaxed attitude. —DIANNE NEAL MATTHEWS

FAITH STEP: *Do you have a cluttered drawer, shelf, or other area in your home? As you purge this space, search your conscience for anything you need to confess to Jesus.*

WEDNESDAY, JULY 22

The holy LORD God of Israel had told all of you, "I will keep you safe if you turn back to me and calm down. I will make you strong if you quietly trust me." Isaiah 30:15 (CEV)

PRETEND YOU'RE A PRETZEL. One foot at a time. Bend, twist, sit, or stand. This is how I have to get out of my new (to me) car. It's a sharp-looking sports car that sits low to the ground. I need to slow down and focus when I get in and out of my vehicle. Otherwise, I may fall on my face.

I'm usually in a hurry. I rush to the market on my lunch break and rocket through my grocery list, barely speaking to acquaintances I meet. I zip home after work so I can rest on the couch. I hurry to doctor appointments so I can be on time. Scurrying, scrambling, and bustling is my routine, even when it comes to my relationship with Jesus, I'm sad to admit.

But when I read the Bible slowly and think about what I've read—even if it's only one verse or one passage—I learn and grow more than when I speed-read through a huge section of scripture. When I talk with Jesus, I hear His voice more clearly if I quiet my mind and take time to listen. When I hear a sermon, take the Lord's Supper, and sing praises, focusing on Jesus gives me a deeper experience with Him.

That focus on Jesus—not anything the world can offer, even a new car—is what I really need. —JEANETTE LEVELLIE

FAITH STEP: *Close your eyes and take three deep, slow breaths. Focus on Jesus as you sit quietly.*

Thursday, July 23

Do not let any unwholesome talk come out of your mouths, but only what is helpful for building others up according to their needs, that it may benefit those who listen. Ephesians 4:29 (NIV)

A GOVERNMENT-RUN PROGRAM PROVIDES INEXPENSIVE bus transportation between northern British Columbian communities and urban Vancouver. These coaches serve seniors and people requiring medical appointments that are unavailable in rural locations. My age qualifies me, so I've ridden these buses several times to visit our youngest daughter.

On one occasion, a woman boarded and settled herself comfortably only to discover minutes later that she'd left her purse at home. She flew into panic mode, phoned her husband to explain the situation, and asked the bus driver if he could postpone departure until her husband could bring her purse. The driver glanced at his watch and agreed to wait ten minutes. The woman apologized profusely and returned to her seat muttering self-abasing statements about her forgetfulness.

Passengers within earshot immediately jumped to her defense. "We all forget things," said a lady seated across the aisle. "This could have happened to any one of us." Another urged her to take a deep breath and assured her that everything would be fine. The woman gushed gratitude for their kindness and visibly relaxed.

With passengers eager to reach their destination, one unkind comment could have ignited tension aboard the bus. Thankfully, stress was diffused because people chose to speak encouragement to the distraught woman. Wholesome words benefited both her and everyone else who heard them. The woman got her purse, and the trip progressed with a sense of friendship and unity among strangers. —GRACE FOX

FAITH STEP: *Ask Jesus to help you speak wholesome words the next time you feel irritated at someone else's mistake.*

Friday, July 24

He canceled the debt, which listed all the rules we failed to follow. He took away that record with its rules and nailed it to the cross. Colossians 2:14 (NCV)

TODAY IS TAKEOUT DAY AT our house. By takeout day, I don't mean ordering takeout for dinner or my husband taking me out on a date. Takeout day came about because I wanted a positive way to refer to the day before the waste disposal truck comes to collect our trash. It seems so negative and ungrateful to regard an entire day every week as trash day. Convinced of the power of the spoken word, I no longer wanted to be in the habit of labeling an entire day of every week of my life "trash." Hence, takeout day.

Dealing with the physical debris of day-to-day life is a necessary reality. Contemplating this dilemma, I wondered, *What does the Bible say about taking out the trash?* I found several biblical scenarios wherein God's people are required to dispose of offal (waste by-products of sacrificed animals) by carrying it away outside of their camp, similar to the way we carry our trash to the curb for weekly garbage collection.

But unlike the trash, my inner offal, unholy thoughts and attitudes, cannot be scheduled for a weekly pickup. No, it can only be carried away by Jesus—left not at the curb but at the cross. Now when takeout day rolls around, as I purge my physical offal, I'm reminded also to take my mental, emotional, and spiritual nasty bits and pieces outside the camp by leaving them at the cross so Jesus can take them away. —CASSANDRA TIERSMA

FAITH STEP: *As you take out your trash this week, give your sin offerings to Jesus and thank Him for the opportunity to be free of sin.*

Saturday, July 25

Let us not grow weary while doing good, for in due season we shall reap if we do not lose heart. Galatians 6:9 (NKJV)

PLEASE DON'T LET ANYTHING SLOW *me down today*, I implored Jesus as I dashed into the grocery store to grab charcoal for our family cookout. Out of the corner of my eye, I glimpsed a woman who seemed to be wedged between her open car door and the return rack for grocery carts. *Jesus, I don't have time. Send someone to help her.* And like the Levite in the parable of the Good Samaritan (Luke 10:32), I crossed to the other side.

Nearing the entrance, I glanced back at the woman. Despite my plea to Jesus, no one had come to help her. Reluctantly, I jogged over to her, still hoping Jesus would send someone.

"Can you get back in the car?" I asked. She did, and I disengaged her door from the cart rack. I had her drive to the other side of the lot where there was more space. I met her and helped her into a motorized shopping cart. I walked beside her until we reached the store's entrance. She told me, through tears, that she was newly widowed and not used to doing things by herself, without her husband. I asked if she needed help getting her groceries, but she assured me she was good to go.

I felt good that I'd taken the time to be kind. Then it dawned on me. I'd asked Jesus to send someone, and He did. Me! —PAT BUTLER DYSON

FAITH STEP: *Follow Jesus's urging to help a fellow traveler in trouble.*

Sunday, July 26

Let us consider how we may spur one another on toward love and good deeds, not giving up meeting together, as some are in the habit of doing, but encouraging one another—and all the more as you see the Day approaching.
Hebrews 10:24–25 (NIV)

Our family, along with many others, have found alternative ways of attending church since the pandemic. Most weeks we utilize our large and small screens to experience a worship service. We still teach, hear the Word of God, worship, pray for, and exhort one another—all without seeing each other in the flesh, like the believers in the book of Hebrews did. It is good. But Jesus showed me through this verse that it was not best. I cannot hug that grieving sister, who just lost her husband, through the phone. I cannot look that young, struggling believer in the eye and tell her to hold on to faith when she is one of twenty-five tiny faces in little squares on my tablet. He reminded me, as I sat on my living room couch, that I can't lay my hands on the sick and hurting the way I could if I were physically present.

These are certainly trying times. Yet I don't want to forget the importance of believers being in one another's presence. The scripture writer exhorts us not to give up meeting together, "as some are in the habit of doing." So now my family tries harder to make our way to the house of the Lord more often. Technology is fine, but nothing beats a real hug from a brother or sister in Christ.
—Pamela Toussaint Howard

Faith Step: *Discuss your worship habits with Jesus. Consider attending church safely, in person, to see what you've been missing.*

Monday, July 27

He said to me, "My grace is sufficient for you, for my power is made perfect in weakness." Therefore I will boast all the more gladly about my weaknesses, so that Christ's power may rest on me. 2 Corinthians 12:9 (NIV)

HE COULDN'T HAVE BEEN BIGGER than my thumb. Tiny, green, and cute as could be, the tree frog squatted at the base of one of our rhododendrons, his eyes watchful and perhaps reflecting a wisdom greater than his size. Unfortunately, he wasn't wise enough to realize he sat directly in the path of the lawnmower.

As he and I entered a stare-down, at which he was clearly winning, my husband snuck up from behind and carried him to safer ground.

I couldn't help but think that teeny creature seemed a lot like me as I bounce along through life, landing myself in one fix or another. There I stand in defiance, facing off a giant capable of squashing my existence without ever noticing me. David-meets-Goliath without the slingshot.

But I have a Savior who saves me, gently removing me from harm's way: Jesus. Whatever approach He chooses, whether it be changing my surroundings or my perspective, or even the circumstances of the "giant" itself, I can depend on Him. I might seem petite, fragile, and foolish, but there's limitless power behind my weakness. And a wisdom beyond my size, for I know from where my strength comes. And from Whom. —HEIDI GAUL

FAITH STEP: *List ways you've unknowingly put yourself in harm's way and the different means Jesus used to rescue you. Keep the list handy for those days you need reminding.*

Tuesday, July 28

I praise you because I am fearfully and wonderfully made; your works are wonderful, I know that full well. Psalm 139:14 (NIV)

MY EIGHTY-NINE-YEAR-OLD MOM AND NINETY-ONE-YEAR-OLD dad have led a very active lifestyle. But now, they are mostly sedentary. So I had an idea to buy them a couch bike. It's a low-impact exercise machine that provides a cardio workout from a chair. It works like a bike for the legs with handles that move in a circular motion so you can move your arms too.

I wasn't sure if they would appreciate this gift or if it would make them sad. Would it remind them they won't ever ride a regular bike again? Then I realized I'm the one who is sad. It's difficult to watch my parents age, and I have my own fears of growing old. Jesus never promises aging would be easy, but He does promise to be with us (Matthew 28:20). And with aging comes wisdom and understanding (Job 12:12).

To my delight, my parents loved the couch bike and use it often to experience needed movement in their day. They were not offended or sad because they've accepted this season of their life. I guess I was the one who needed to accept them aging.

I do believe I am wonderfully made, and part of that is growing older. I pray I will age as gracefully as my parents have, and when my time comes for a couch bike, I will ride with gusto.
—JEANNIE BLACKMER

FAITH STEP: *What's one aspect of growing older that you're fearful about? Ask Jesus to quiet your fear and open your eyes to see yourself as wonderfully made at all ages.*

Wednesday, July 29

> *Peter came to Jesus and asked, "Lord, how many times shall I forgive my brother or sister who sins against me? Up to seven times?" Jesus answered, "I tell you, not seven times, but seventy-seven times."*
> Matthew 18:21–22 (NIV)

FROM MY DESK, I COULD discern every word of the heated conversation taking place in my manager's office. When her door opened, a disgruntled customer stormed past me. Then, Alberta stepped out, nose in the air, and said, "Don't worry about him. He's just an hourly employee at Armco."

I understood her inference. The man labored at the local steel mill for a blue-collar wage and didn't have a CEO's salary like her important husband.

Alberta created an arrogant work environment that conflicted with my Christian convictions. I struggled to tolerate her, let alone love her as Jesus commanded. I wrote Bible verses about patience, kindness, and love on sticky notes and pasted them all around my computer screen. Each evening, I asked Jesus to forgive me for the irritation I felt toward Alberta, even though I suspected I had surpassed the "seventy-seven" number Jesus mentioned.

For a year, I leaned on scriptures and prayers, but try as I might, I couldn't stand working with Alberta. I felt as if I'd failed when I prayed, *Jesus, I can't love her, so I'm trusting You to do it.* Weeks later, I found a new job with less stress, happy surroundings, and a congenial manager. Finally, with Jesus's help, I forgave myself for not being able to love Alberta as Jesus did. —BECKY ALEXANDER

FAITH STEP: *Are you beating yourself up for not loving a challenging person? Write down her name and give her to Jesus. Then ask Jesus to strengthen and forgive you.*

Thursday, July 30

"Sanctify them by Your truth. Your word is truth." John 17:17 (NKJV)

I HAVE MY MOM'S BIBLE. The leather is worn, and the pages are filled with her handwriting. I love reading the passages she underlined or highlighted, the prayers she wrote in the margins, and the names of her children and grandchildren scribbled beside specific verses. Her notes document trials in her life, prayers that were answered, her faith faltered and bolstered.

My friend and spiritual mentor, Pat, reads a different translation of the Bible each year. Like my mom, she highlights scripture and marks up the text with notes and prayers. Her goal is to pass on a Bible to each of her grandchildren someday. What a beautiful and personal way to ensure her faith legacy will continue.

Inspired by my mom and my friend, I purchased a journaling Bible a few years ago. The wide, lined margins provide space for me to engage with scripture; add my thoughts, reactions, and questions; and write prayers for my children and grandchildren. Adding this simple practice to my routine has deepened my morning time with Jesus more than I ever expected. I accidentally shifted from reading my Bible to studying God's Word.

As I continue to record my spiritual journey, I pray my words will point my family to Jesus when I no longer can. —KAREN SARGENT

FAITH STEP: *Do you write in your Bible or journal? Be intentional about the faith legacy you're leaving for future generations.*

Friday, July 31

Therefore if anyone is in Christ, this person is a new creation; the old things passed away; behold, new things have come. 2 Corinthians 5:17 (NASB)

I ADOPTED OUR SON'S CAT when Ron moved to an apartment of his own. Dr. Phibes, named after a cruel British movie character, is a lovable, sweet, and cuddly male tabby. Who, as it turns out, is only lovable and sweet for one person at a time.

When Ron was his owner, Dr. Phibes let him hold, cuddle, and carry him from room to room. But no one else could get near D.P. without him growling, hissing, even swatting at them with his claws extended. Now that I am D.P.'s owner, he climbs in my lap, purrs when I baby talk to him, and sleeps cuddled next to me. But to everyone else, he's a monster.

A few days ago, I decided to do something about this ugly situation. I changed his name to Fred. I think Fred has a sweet ring to it. But the main reason I chose Fred was to honor one of my kindness heroes, Fred Rogers. I hope it helps my kitty reflect kindness toward others.

The moment I decided to follow Jesus, He didn't just give me a new name in hopes that I'd stop sinning. He gave me a new nature. Jesus filled me with His Holy Spirit so I could reflect His character traits to others. Unlike Fred, who only received a new name, I became a new person when Jesus took over the ownership of my heart.

My past sins no longer exist. Jesus has erased every one. And given me a new heart. —JEANETTE LEVELLIE

FAITH STEP: *Reflect on how you changed after becoming a new creation in Christ. Pray for Jesus to reveal specific ways to become more like Him.*

SATURDAY, AUGUST 1

> *[Jesus] interpreted for them the things written about himself in all the scriptures, starting with Moses and going through all the Prophets.* Luke 24:27 (CEB)

IF A MOVIE IS BASED on a novel, I always do my best to read the book before watching the film. I want to see the story unfold in my mind and envision the characters according to the author's original creation. As I watched (and enjoyed) the first movie of a fantasy trilogy years ago, I thought about how much the viewers who hadn't read the books missed out on: incredibly beautiful writing, tons of background material, deep explorations of the characters' thoughts and motivations. I recently heard someone say that he was glad he saw the movies first because he already had a picture of the characters in his mind when he started reading. I wondered if he'd noticed how drastically different the movie versions of some characters were from what the author intended.

If I watch a movie about Jesus, I'm even more glad that I've already read the Book. Biblical productions can be powerful and worth watching, but I never want my view of Jesus to be influenced by someone else's opinions or portrayal. The Bible shares details about Jesus's life, including eyewitness accounts of His words and actions. It even includes prophecies about Him long before He was born and about what He plans to do in the future.

What a privilege to be able to go straight to the Bible and get a detailed image of Jesus the way the Author intended.
—DIANNE NEAL MATTHEWS

FAITH STEP: *Choose one of the Gospels—Matthew, Mark, Luke, or John—and commit to reading it through. Ponder anything that contradicts the way you've seen Jesus portrayed.*

SUNDAY, AUGUST 2

*Give praise to the L*ORD*, proclaim his name; make known among the nations what he has done. Sing to him, sing praise to him; tell of all his wonderful acts.* Psalm 105:1–2 (NIV)

BEFORE WE LEFT FOR A two-week family road trip from Texas to California, my husband gave us a day-by-day itinerary. The best part about his detailed outline was that he'd chosen special songs for every day of our vacation and added them to a shared playlist so our four children and I would all have a customized soundtrack of our trip. True to his plans, he opened the playlist each time we arrived at a new destination and allowed the song to set the mood of the moment. The children sometimes rolled their eyes or wandered away, but I enjoyed the way he'd intentionally paired music with memories. Even now, several years later, my memories of that trip become more vivid when I revisit the soundtrack he created.

I use customized playlists to remind me of other journeys as well—journeys I've taken with Jesus as He's walked with me through good times and bad. Sometimes I revisit the songs I learned as a child in Sunday school to recapture the joy of my salvation. Other times I play music from college and remember how Jesus guided me through my first years of independence. My playlist of gospel quartet songs reminds me how Jesus helped my family heal after my mother's death, and another playlist helps me trust Him when I'm feeling worried or scared. When I intentionally pair music with memories, my faith becomes stronger. Jesus is the beautiful soundtrack of my life. —EMILY E. RYAN

FAITH STEP: *Create a playlist on your phone with songs that represent what you're learning about Jesus right now.*

Monday, August 3

If we confess our sins to him, he is faithful and just to forgive us our sins and to cleanse us from all wickedness. 1 John 1:9 (NLT)

AT THE AGE OF FIFTY-SIX, I got my first speeding ticket driving Isaac to before-care at his school early one morning. I know. It's totally awful. How could I? My only excuse is Isaac and I have "dance parties" in my minivan, playing our favorite songs loudly while singing. I was happily distracted, mid-chorus.

As I pulled into the parking lot to drop Isaac off, red and blue lights flashed in my rearview mirror. I pulled over, and the policeman sternly alerted me to my infraction. Once we concluded our unpleasant business, we pulled away. Isaac was angry at the policeman. "I don't like him," he said. "He's mean!"

I explained that I'd broken the law and that the police officer was just doing his very important job, trying to keep people safe, especially kids. It wasn't the policeman's fault I received a ticket; it was mine.

I'll go to court, explain the circumstances and apologize. I'll take a safe driving course online beforehand to demonstrate my remorse. I'll admit my mistake, humble my heart, and hope for mercy.

My repentance over the ticket is the same way I repent over sins. I feel bad about my mistake, admit I'm wrong, commit to change, and make restitution. These four steps make for a genuine apology to Jesus and to anyone I've hurt. When I admit my mistake and humble my heart, Jesus always grants mercy. I hope the traffic court judge will be as gracious. —ISABELLA CAMPOLATTARO

FAITH STEP: *Memorize 1 John 1:9. Know that Jesus always forgives.*

Tuesday, August 4

I long to see you so that I may impart to you some spiritual gift to make you strong. Romans 1:11 (NIV)

Friends of mine recently had to declare bankruptcy. Their financial liabilities far outweighed their assets, and it was the only answer to relieve their deep debt. I have to admit, I've experienced bankruptcy myself, but it had nothing to do with money.

At times in my life, I've experienced spiritual bankruptcy and had nothing left in my Christian bank account. Let me explain. The liabilities of life were such a burden on my soul that I couldn't find an asset in sight. I went through the motions of what I believed a good Christian looked like. I mimicked the other parishioners' smiling faces when I felt empty inside. I made myself attend family luncheons and went to movies with friends with zero enthusiasm. I had so much grief from the burdens of life in the liability column—the death of my son, being the sole caregiver for my mother, and helping my husband during his cancer journey. I had trouble seeing any assets Jesus had deposited.

But the more I looked at these liabilities, I understood that Jesus had reconciled them—not with my spiritual strength but with His. On those days I felt I had nothing else left in my Christian bank account, Jesus made a deposit. His strength covered my overdrawn balance. Counting on Jesus is my biggest asset. —Jeannie Hughes

Faith Step: *Are you experiencing spiritual bankruptcy? Write down three liabilities. Then ask Jesus to make a deposit into your soul.*

WEDNESDAY, AUGUST 5

I have much to write to you, but I do not want to use paper and ink. Instead, I hope to visit you and talk with you face to face, so that our joy may be complete. 2 John 1:12 (NIV)

"Did you mean to FaceTime me?" I asked my daughter Brooke. I thought it must be a mistake because we usually text.

"Mom, I need you to look at something," Brooke replied. The image of a package of ground meat filled my screen. "Is this still good?"

I am the spoiled food inspector for my daughters. I always advise them to smell it. After Brooke's meat passed the sniff test and we continued to FaceTime, she placed it in her frying pan and began to brown it. I asked her about her school, where she teaches tenth-grade English. If we were texting, she'd just answer, "It's fine," but as the meat sizzled in the pan, she told me how she'd helped a student who'd come to her in a crisis. As she added spaghetti sauce to her meat, she mentioned a coworker with whom she was at odds and asked if I'd pray about it. As she ate, she told me she was worried about her dog, Hercules, who was lethargic. Looking into Brooke's sweet face, I considered how much more satisfying it was to see my girl than to type to her on a phone screen.

The Apostle John, like Jesus, understood the value of in-person communication, as he commented in a short letter to a friend. To make one's joy complete, John believed, it's best to talk face-to-face. FaceTiming Brooke, I couldn't agree more! —Pat Butler Dyson

Faith Step: *Find your favorite artistic rendering of Jesus. Look into His face and talk to Him.*

Thursday, August 6

Nevertheless I have this against you, that you have left your first love. Revelation 2:4 (NKJV)

"WE'RE KISSING ALL OVER FACEBOOK!" my daughter texted after the photographer posted sneak peeks of her engagement photos. "I'm so embarrassed."

The pictures were a little kissy for a couple that avoids PDA. But what I noticed even more was how skillfully the photographer captured emotion in the non-smoochy shots. As I scrolled through the poses, I noticed their smiles, their eyes, the natural placement of a hand on a cheek. I could see their devotion to each other—that all-consuming adoration of first love.

I remember that feeling, though, after forty years, love looks a little different for my husband and me. My heart doesn't flutter when he walks into the room, unless he's delivering a special cup of coffee from the French press with just the right amount of cream. Instead of talking into the late-night hours as we used to, he likes me to watch a Cardinals baseball game with him that goes into extra innings. An old married couple, we must be careful our expressions of love don't become simply routine or taken for granted.

Jesus doesn't want to become routine or taken for granted either. He wants to be my first love, always. Sometimes I can go through the motions—have quiet time, pray, serve at church—but my heart feels disconnected. So I remind myself why I choose to practice these spiritual disciplines. Because in all my messiness, Jesus first loved me and gave all of Himself to offer me a new life with Him. What a beautiful picture of the wonderful and overflowing joy of first love. —KAREN SARGENT

FAITH STEP: *Recall when you experienced your first moments in love with Jesus. Tell someone your story.*

Friday, August 7

He who is faithful in what is least is faithful also in much; and he who is unjust in what is least is unjust also in much. Luke 16:10 (NKJV)

OUR DISHWASHER HAS BEEN FLASHING an error code partway through its wash cycle. It's new enough that it's still under warranty, but we figured my handyman husband could fix it without calling a repairman. It's laughable to recount all we've tried these last weeks.

We'd even gone as far as tearing apart the cupboard that housed the dishwasher so we could access and observe all the mechanical workings underneath and behind.

The frustration has been beyond the minor inconvenience of handwashing dishes. The real problem is that the error message is intermittent. Sometimes the appliance works fine. Sometimes it doesn't. And we can't trace a pattern that will help lead us to an answer.

It's so hard to problem-solve an intermittent issue.

Ah. I'm listening, Lord. It's the same with me. When I'm randomly impatient but patience is my normal mode of operating, or when I'm oddly sharp-tongued one day, I'm not displaying consistent Christlikeness. It's as if an invisible error code starts flashing. If I quickly return to the procedure manual—the Bible—it will never fail to have me running smoothly again. Most homemade remedies will put me in a position much like the day we'd torn apart the dishwasher and had plastic hoses draped all over the kitchen, some draining into the sink, some into various five-gallon buckets. Solid effort but no real solution. —CYNTHIA RUCHTI

FAITH STEP: *Have you sensed an internal error code flashing regarding your habits, choices, relationships, or attitude? Forego the homemade attempts to solve it and run straight to what Jesus said in His Word.*

Saturday, August 8

> *Because the LORD kept vigil that night to bring them out of Egypt, on this night all the Israelites are to keep vigil to honor the LORD for the generations to come.* Exodus 12:42 (NIV)

HAVE YOU EVER KEPT VIGIL? Keeping vigil carries a weighty connotation. We don't keep vigil during a celebration or a joyous event. Vigils are loaded with import, sober countenances, protective ponderings, and contemplative prayer. They happen during times of serious concern, when we remain close with a guarding stance.

The Israelites were leaving behind captivity for freedom. They had much to fear because the Egyptians would not let them go easily. I love that the Bible includes how God kept vigil over them as they crossed out of danger into the unknown.

Jesus Himself asked His disciples to keep watch—or vigil—with Him in the Garden of Gethsemane (Mark 14:32–34). Each of us will experience times when we survive or overcome because Jesus keeps vigil over us.

I recall a season when I repeatedly woke in the middle of the night to intense spiritual distress. It was terrifying and included a gut-wrenching fear of others' ongoing actions. It was an utterly unsafe feeling.

Facedown on the floor in the dark, I called out to Jesus, desperate for Him to act on my behalf. I felt Him keep vigil with me. I knew He firmly held me. I'll never forget the reality of Him steadying me, guarding me, being supremely present and powerful.

When circumstances are most difficult, I can trust that Jesus always keeps vigil over me. —ERIN KEELEY MARSHALL

FAITH STEP: *Sketch a simple scene of Jesus keeping vigil over you. Put the drawing somewhere you can see it when you feel fearful.*

Sunday, August 9

We are God's handiwork, created in Christ Jesus to do good works, which God prepared in advance for us to do. Ephesians 2:10 (NIV)

The day after we moved my oldest child, Zack, into college for the first time, my friends Jess and Pam showed up at my door with a care package for me. It was filled with items to bring me comfort and ease the ache of Zack being gone. There were note cards to write and send to him so I could stay connected. There was Smartfood popcorn so I would feel loved and cared for through my favorite snack. There was a coffee mug with his college's logo and the word "Mom" on it to remind me each morning while sipping coffee that my pride in Zack far outweighs my loss.

Jesus may not drive up to my front door with a care package in His hands when I face a loss or a difficult transition, but He does fill the void with grace if I raise my eyes above the sadness to see it. He packages His love and care for me in everything that comes my way: the bright sun shining when my heart is cast in shadows, a kindness a stranger shows me when I'm out and about running errands, and even through my friends Jess and Pam, who become His hands and feet, delivering hope and love in a basket when I need it most.
—Claire McGarry

Faith Step: *Is there someone you know who is going through a difficult loss or transition? Consider making or ordering them a care package. Find a way to become Jesus's hands and feet to deliver love and care.*

Monday, August 10

Open my eyes, that I may see. Psalm 119:18 (NKJV)

I AM A COLLEGE PROFESSOR. At the beginning of the semester in one of my early-morning composition classes, a student kept falling asleep. I tried everything I could to keep her attention. But every day I watched her nod off, head slowly falling forward or back till she would startle herself awake. I work so hard on my lessons, and I am passionate about my subject. I could not imagine why she was bored during my lectures. I tried not to take it personally.

But her behavior irritated me. One day I asked her to stay after class. When I questioned her, big tears welled up in her eyes. "I'm sorry," she said. "I'm a single parent, and I work all night before coming to class. When I go home, I sleep a few hours till I pick my son up from school. We eat dinner and do homework, and then I take him to my mother's for the night while I go to work." I hugged her and worked with her the rest of the semester to help her get through the class.

Seeing that woman—really seeing her and understanding her situation—blessed us both. I could have taken her behavior to heart and let my irritation get the better of me. By reaching out to her, my eyes were opened. What first appeared to be a lazy, uninterested student was really a hardworking mama trying her best.
—GWEN FORD FAULKENBERRY

FAITH STEP: *Consider a frustrating or confusing situation you're facing. Practice two-way prayer by asking Jesus what is going on beneath the surface and then writing down what you hear Him speak to your heart. Pray that He opens your eyes to find a blessed solution.*

Tuesday, August 11

Do not be anxious about anything, but in every situation, by prayer and petition, with thanksgiving, present your requests to God. And the peace of God, which transcends all understanding, will guard your hearts and your minds in Christ Jesus. Philippians 4:6–7 (NIV)

WE OCCASIONALLY HAVE STUDENTS WHO experience separation anxiety at the elementary school where I work. Elise was one such student. The first grader screamed and clung to her mom when being dropped off one morning.

As the school counselor, I intervened. I coaxed Elise to my office as she continued to cry. Talking only agitated her. I set out several fidgets and calming tools, but she sat on the couch, refusing to be consoled or to go to class. I knew being stern would only escalate the situation.

"Lord, help me," I quickly prayed as I pushed down my anxiety, not knowing what may help her. I turned on calming music while I worked at my desk. Then, I printed some coloring pages and asked Elise if she wanted to join me on the floor to color. She didn't respond but watched as I colored.

A few minutes later, she joined me in silence. I watched her demeanor change as we colored together. Finally, I asked if she was ready for class. She smiled, said yes, and cheerfully went to her classroom.

How often I can be dysregulated like Elise! What a difference a gentle presence makes. The next time I get upset or anxious, I'll imagine Jesus inviting me to sit quietly and calm down in His presence. —Brenda L. Yoder

---

Faith Step: *Think of activities you can do when experiencing big emotions like anxiety—maybe sitting quietly, coloring, baking, or taking a walk. Whatever you choose, do it with Jesus.*

WEDNESDAY, AUGUST 12

Love is always supportive, loyal, hopeful, and trusting.
1 Corinthians 13:7 (CEV)

I WAS AT A LOSS on how to help my husband. Several weeks ago, Kevin received a medical diagnosis that required him to vastly change his eating habits. *Of course, I can cook healthier*, I thought. *And it won't hurt me to make some changes too.*

It was the emotional support he needed that I failed to grasp.

How do I show Kevin empathy without slipping into mothering mode? He's not fond of unasked-for advice.

So my prayers went something like this: "Please help Kevin, Jesus." "Please help me to help Kevin, Jesus." "Please give me divine wisdom and grace, Jesus." It was the best I could do.

And Jesus's sweet whisper in my heart told me simply to be with Kevin. I didn't need to do or say much. It wasn't advice my husband needed but love.

Kevin needed a much different type of love than I'm accustomed to giving. I'm a communicator with words. It's how I make my living. It's my love language. But in this new paradigm, Jesus gave me ideas for novel ways to show love. Longer hugs and more physical touch. Eye contact when Kevin talks, rather than cleaning the kitchen or making the bed. And listening more than I talk. That's the hard part.

But when Kevin stopped by my office after a difficult appointment this morning "just to see me," I knew I had hit the target.

Thanks to the asked-for advice from my best friend, Jesus.
—JEANETTE LEVELLIE

FAITH STEP: *Ask Jesus to help you love someone in a new way. Try that new way today.*

Thursday, August 13

The LORD himself goes before you and will be with you; he will never leave you nor forsake you. Do not be afraid; do not be discouraged.
Deuteronomy 31:8 (NIV)

MY DAUGHTER'S FAMILY OUTGREW THEIR Subaru upon the birth of their third child, so they asked my husband and me if we wanted to buy it. We said yes because our car was no longer reliable, and we'd discussed replacing it.

We bought the Subaru with an e-transfer, but taking possession meant driving ten hours to fetch it. My husband had recently undergone surgery and couldn't do the trip, so I hitched a one-way ride with a family member. The next morning, as I climbed behind the wheel of our newly purchased car, the thought of doing the return trip on my own seemed daunting. I'd never driven such a distance by myself, let alone in a new-to-me vehicle. Fear could have ruined my day, but I said no by envisioning Jesus in the passenger seat and conversing with Him.

I thanked Jesus for giving us this vehicle, with heated seats, nonetheless, and for the safety He provided during the years my daughter drove it. I thanked Him for the grandeur of the forests and tranquility of the farmlands through which I drove. I thanked Him for the beauty of the setting sun, for His eternal faithfulness and His unending love. When conversation paused, I played praise and worship music and sang along as loud as I wished.

Jesus's companionship made the miles roll quickly, and the day turned from daunting to delightful—a precious gift from my Savior's heart to mine. —GRACE FOX

FAITH STEP: *What activity gives you fear? Picture Jesus beside you wherever you are right now. Talk to Him and find peace.*

Friday, August 14

Why, my soul, are you downcast? Why so disturbed within me? Put your hope in God, for I will yet praise him, my Savior and my God. Psalm 42:11 (NIV)

I WENT IN FOR A routine medical procedure and ended up with internal bleeding and a bruised spleen due to a surgical mishap. I was shocked and angry. I had to cancel going to a close friend's sixtieth birthday party and a trip to Montana for the wedding of another friend's daughter. What happened to me was unexpected. But it happened. And I had no choice but to deal with it.

While I lay on my couch for three weeks to keep my spleen from bleeding again, I had plenty of time to think. Throughout my life, unexpected things have happened such as Zane's health issues, a son's addiction, and the loss of our home to a fire. With time I moved from disheartened to praising Jesus again. I've also watched friends endure unforeseen life events such as the suicide of a teenage child, a stage four cancer diagnosis, job losses, and more. I've also seen their faith carry them from discouragement to praising God, their Savior.

It was my time, again, to place my hope in God. I spent time reading my Bible, listening to worship songs, catching up with friends, and allowing my body to rest. Eventually, my spleen did heal, and my attitude shifted from discouragement to adoration. I gained wisdom in my time of healing. Now I can confidently lead others back from feeling downcast to praising God when the unforeseen touches their lives. —JEANNIE BLACKMER

FAITH STEP: *How do you deal with the unexpected? Write down three things you will do differently the next time life surprises you. How will you move from feeling downcast to praising God?*

SATURDAY, AUGUST 15

Remind them to be subject to rulers and authorities, to be obedient, to be ready for every good work, to speak evil of no one, to avoid quarreling, to be gentle, and to show every courtesy to everyone. Titus 3:1–2 (NRSVUE)

I HOLD JOYFUL MEMORIES OF staying at Grandma Selby's house as a child. She played games with me for hours—Parcheesi, Chinese checkers, rummy, and Old Maid. She made my favorite breakfast, waffles with homemade syrup, and my favorite lunch, creamed dried beef over toast. We walked to the dime store on Main Street and shopped for a sweet treat. At bedtime, we recited the Lord's Prayer together before falling asleep in her four-poster bed.

Once I grew up, I realized another reason I loved Grandma Selby so much—I never heard her utter a negative word about anybody. It seemed her sentences flowed through a filter of kindness before becoming audible. I wanted to be like that.

I recently pondered what Grandma would do if approached by a person sharing gossip. I pictured her saying something positive and skillfully changing the subject. I contemplated how she could refrain from making sharp remarks when someone upset her. I imagined her taking a slow, deep breath and pressing her lips together, preventing even one syllable from escaping.

My grandma patterned her life after the teachings of Jesus. I watched and learned from her throughout my childhood. Her example still influences me today, especially in situations where it would be best for me to bite my tongue. —BECKY ALEXANDER

FAITH STEP: *Evaluate your conversations from this past week based on Titus 3:1–2. Ask Jesus to help you filter out the negative and speak only positive words about others.*

SUNDAY, AUGUST 16

A word fitly spoken is like apples of gold in settings of silver.
Proverbs 25:11 (NKJV)

As my husband, Larry, and I were getting into our van to leave church that sunny afternoon, a glare in the passenger seat caught my eye. A shiny silver frame held a stunning picture of golden apples. Attached was a note: "Your words were needed this week."

Who could have left this? Normally we lock our doors, but we must have forgotten while hurrying that morning. My mind was reeling as to what this mysterious gift could be about. Later, Valarie, our pastor's wife, called and asked if I had received her gift. "Thank you, but I don't understand why you left it for me," I replied.

Valarie explained that I had called her last week right after she'd hung up from a difficult conversation with a church member. "I was feeling down, but your encouraging words spoke joy to my heart."

After we hung up, I racked my brain. I had no idea what I'd said. I had called her that day simply to chat and check in. Everyday words spoken. Nothing golden apple-worthy.

I was amazed that Valarie had experienced a completely different version of our conversation than I had. Jesus used my words to encourage another believer, and I wasn't even aware of it!
—Renee Mitchell

Faith Step: *Take a moment to send a text or call a friend. Simply checking in could be the apples of gold she needs.*

Monday, August 17

"Why is my language not clear to you? Because you are unable to hear what I say." John 8:43 (NIV)

My son Zack wanted me to take photos of his Social Security card and birth certificate and text them to him so he could apply for a new job at college. I've always believed one should never send documents with personal information electronically except through encrypted email, as it could make one susceptible to identity theft. Not wanting that for Zack, I asked him to drive home and pick them up, but he continued to argue his point and ask for me to send them via text.

In John 8, the religious leaders claimed that Abraham was their father. Jesus pointed out that if they were the children of Abraham, they wouldn't be trying to kill Him. Back and forth the argument went, like the text messages with my son. The religious leaders didn't want to listen to Jesus. If only they could have laid down their stubbornness.

It made me question whether I was guilty of the same thing in my argument with Zack. Was I refusing to listen when there was a chance I could be wrong? I consulted my husband to get his viewpoint. Sure enough, he saw it differently. I could text the images to Zack. He could print them out, then delete them immediately with little risk. I did and, in the process, learned that letting go of my stubborn stance and being open to advice can bring resolution and peace. —Claire McGarry

Faith Step: *The next time you're inclined to dig your heels in regarding your viewpoint, consult someone you trust to see if there might be another way to look at the situation.*

Tuesday, August 18

The LORD is near to all who call on him, to all who call on him in truth. He fulfills the desires of those who fear him; he hears their cry and saves them. Psalm 145:18–19 (NIV)

I RECENTLY FOUND OUT I have chronic inflammatory response syndrome (CIRS) due to mold exposure. Finding out has been both hard and good. It was hard because I didn't want to live with a chronic illness. It was good because I now have a path forward to healing.

Due to my CIRS symptoms over the last five years, I have often found myself wide awake at 2:30 a.m. Worrisome thoughts flooded my mind. They left me desperate for sleep. I asked Jesus to help me. He answered in an unusual way.

I discovered if I put on headphones and played Tim Keller and Rick Warren sermons, I could fall back to sleep. Not because their talks were boring but because the truth they spoke calmed my mind and spirit. They have helped shape my spiritual growth and theology. The power of scripture they share drowns out the loud worries in my mind. I am lulled to sleep by the goodness of God's Word.

When I awoke at 4 a.m. this morning, I reached for my headphones. With the healing words of scripture in my ear, I was able to rest.

Jesus knows me—body, mind, and spirit. It is no surprise that when I called out for help and healing, Jesus pointed me to His truth. He heard my cry and brought peace to my mind and healing to my spirit. —SUSANNA FOTH AUGHTMON

FAITH STEP: *Take a moment to reflect on any anxiety or worry that you have. Ask Jesus to help you. Know that He listens to your cries and is ready to save you.*

WEDNESDAY, AUGUST 19

Therefore, as God's chosen people, holy and dearly loved, clothe yourselves with compassion, kindness, humility, gentleness, and patience. Colossians 3:12 (NIV)

I RECENTLY STUMBLED UPON AN online video from a fast-food restaurant that featured the touching story of a man who went to pick up breakfast for his family on the day his daughter was leaving for college for the first time. He got so choked up that he couldn't speak when he got to the drive-through. The employee waiting to take his order could hear his sobs, so she went outside to see if he was all right. The man told her about his daughter's imminent departure and the employee leaned into the car window to reassure him. Such an unexpected act of caring brought tears to my eyes.

I started to think about how I've been a recipient of such kindnesses. Like the time a stranger anonymously picked up the bill for me and my parents at a restaurant. Or when I got an encouraging card from a friend while I was going through a difficult time. Jesus also has helped me to bless others. I've paid for items that a young couple needed at the grocery store when they ran short on cash. It was fun to surprise friends when I delivered my homemade banana pudding to their door. Small acts like these have been a blessing to me as a giver and as a receiver.

My next random act may not take me to a drive-through, but I believe Jesus is always in the driver's seat steering me to do something good. —BARBRANDA LUMPKINS WALLS

FAITH STEP: *Bless someone with a random act of kindness today. Send a handwritten note of encouragement, pay for someone's coffee, or drop off a meal.*

Thursday, August 20

> *Love is patient, love is kind. It does not envy, it does not boast, it is not proud. . . . Love does not delight in evil but rejoices with the truth.*
> 1 Corinthians 13:4, 6 (NIV)

I GET A BAD RAP sometimes for being too nice. Unlike some personalities that are blunt and straight-talking, I prefer to sweeten my words and soften my tone. I'm not oblivious to the truth of this world's harsh realities and shady people. I simply choose to focus on potential and to lead first with kindness when I engage with people and their situations. But I didn't always know how to speak truth in a kind way.

As a six-year old, I was pretty matter-of-fact when interacting with people. Critiquing my little sister's drawings one day, I shouted, "Ew, that's scribble scrabble!" My mother immediately shut down that commentary and coached me to respond with love. She emphasized the importance of using my words to encourage my sister. It was a highly successful coaching session because the next sentence I shouted was, "Ooh. That's nice scribble scrabble!" It was because of this early-age coaching that I began to practice addressing the truth with kind words.

Being open and honest with others is not always an easy task, especially when I need to provide constructive criticism or corrective action. However, Jesus's commandment when administering truth echoes my mother's coaching: love (Matthew 22:37–39). My mother and I both had the very best Coach, and His love, in word and deed, demonstrates kindness. —ERICKA LOYNES

FAITH STEP: *Have you spoken harshly to someone? Try conveying your message again. This time ask Jesus to help you deliver the words with His love and kindness.*

Friday, August 21

Just as you do not know how the life breath enters the human frame in the mother's womb, so you do not know the work of God, who is working in everything. Ecclesiastes 11:5 (NABRE)

OUR PLANNED WEEKEND TRIP TO the Pennsylvania Renaissance Faire to celebrate my daughter Ana was only hours away. It was a gift for her combined birthday and eighth-grade graduation. We sewed costumes all summer for the weekend-long event.

Barely a mile from home, our only vehicle began to sputter and shake. I was hardly able to safely ease the car to the roadside before it stopped cold. Calling my stepdad, he selflessly offered his only car to us for the weekend. We gratefully accepted and had a delightful time. Returning home that Monday evening, I learned that the issue with our SUV was an opportunity for my stepdad to repay a long-ago kindness. As a young man, a friend did a similar thing for him. He asked only that my stepdad pay it forward.

My version of the Bible doesn't use the term "pay it forward," but it is something Jesus asks believers to do. Love our neighbor unselfishly (Mark 12:31) and do for others what we would want them to do for us (Matthew 7:12). Giving of ourselves, sharing our possessions, and treating others with kindness are what Jesus commands. These actions can start a chain reaction that makes the world a kinder place. Now that's a gift I am happy to pay forward. —GLORIA JOYCE

FAITH STEP: *How can you pay it forward? While out and about today, look for someone who needs your help. Give the gift of your time or talent to ease their burden and brighten their day without accepting anything in return.*

Saturday, August 22

You will keep in perfect peace those whose minds are steadfast, because they trust in you. Isaiah 26:3 (NIV)

Every other day, my husband, David, and I head to the gym. We stand in the fully enclosed racquetball court, rackets and ball in hand, and we play. Our game has no rules but to keep the ball moving. We aren't concerned with things like taking turns or keeping score. As seniors, we don't chase after stray shots. We wait with the wisdom and patience of years for the ball to bounce its way over to one of us. The only goals we set are to get exercise and have fun doing it. It doesn't take long to find ourselves in the mental "zone," the coveted state of near elation, where our concentration is so focused that time seems to stand still. Also called the "flow experience," this state is conducive to mental health.

Jesus, our Great Physician, is the ultimate flow zone. It's easy for me to lose track of time as I study Jesus's teachings, my focus on Him alone. Plus, reading the Bible gives me hope and encouragement (Romans 15:4), strong assets for mental health. This collection of books strengthens my faith in Jesus and outlines my path to eternal life (John 20:31).

What other ways can I get in the flow zone with Jesus? Deep, heartfelt praying, singing praises, meditating, walking labyrinths, and Bible journaling, to name a few. The important thing to remember is that I need to keep my focus on Him and Him alone. I can't think of a better way to spend my time! —Heidi Gaul

Faith Step: *Let yourself get lost in the books of the Bible. Allow yourself to enter the zone as you meditate on Jesus.*

Sunday, August 23

"You can see the speck in your friend's eye, but you don't notice the log in your own eye." Matthew 7:3 (CEV)

I LOOKED UP AT THE screen displaying the pastor's first point. Unfortunately, my brain focused on what was *not* there: an *i* had been left out of the word *spirit*. My mind was stuck there until the screen changed. This familiar scene often plays out when I'm reading, browsing websites, or driving past billboards and signs. I don't want to notice every misspelled word, grammatical mistake, extra comma, or inappropriate apostrophe. But I do.

This natural bent helped when I worked as a proofreader for a textbook company. My supervisor always praised my work, so I felt confident about my ability to spot errors. When I discovered that my bio in a book said I have two children instead of three, I wondered who had made that mistake. Then I checked the info I'd submitted and found that I was the culprit!

That wake-up call reminded me of Jesus's warning against harboring a hypocritical attitude toward others. While it's helpful to discern the condition of someone else's heart, it's not my place to spot every little mistake and condemn them. My first responsibility is to examine myself and make sure I'm not oblivious to my own bad habits and behavior. If I want to help others, I first need to make sure that I can see clearly enough to proofread myself and make needed corrections. Only Jesus can help me do that.
—Dianne Neal Matthews

Faith Step: *The next time you feel frustrated by another person's fault, use it as a reminder to invite Jesus to examine your own attitudes and behaviors.*

Monday, August 24

For since the creation of the world God's invisible qualities—his eternal power and divine nature—have been clearly seen, being understood from what has been made, so that people are without excuse. Romans 1:20 (NIV)

When my son Gideon and his friends returned from the grocery store, he strutted into the kitchen and proudly hoisted a large, prickly, unidentifiable fruit onto our countertop. "It's a jackfruit!" he said with a huge grin. "And I have no idea what to do with it."

Together, we searched the Internet for tips on how to open the bulky, thirty-pound exotic fruit and had to work strategically to slice through the thick, pointy skin. Inside, we discovered dozens of yellow, spongy pods that made our hands stickier than tree sap as we tried to extract the seeds from the fleshy meat. The project took hours, but it felt like a fascinating science experiment with each step a new discovery of the Lord's creativity in nature. We tasted it both raw and cooked and concluded we'd need more practice to fully bring out the potential in such a versatile fruit.

That jackfruit made me wonder how many other species of fruits and vegetables exist that I've never been exposed to and if people around the world ever experience the same sense of awe that I encountered with the fruit. I learned that a single jackfruit can weigh up to 120 pounds! To some, that's a fun fact for a trivia night. For me, it's evidence of my Creator. —Emily E. Ryan

Faith Step: *Purchase a new-to-you fruit or vegetable and explore it through the lens of the beauty and majesty of creation. Research how it grows and its nutritional benefits. What does it show you about divine creativity?*

Tuesday, August 25

"Do good, and lend, hoping for nothing in return; and your reward will be great." Luke 6:35 (NKJV)

A St. Louis Christian radio station encourages listeners to share joy through random acts of kindness. Pay for a stranger's lunch. Do yard work for a neighbor. Drop off cookies for a friend. The station provides printed joy notes to be given to recipients so they'll know they have been JOY'd by a listener who loves Jesus.

Often a person who has been JOY'd calls the station and tells about the act of kindness. A single mom whose grocery bill was paid by the person behind her. A college student whose gas tank was filled by a stranger. My favorite callers are the fast-food drive-through employees who report that one person JOY'd the car behind, then the kindness was passed on from car to car ten or twenty times. The caller always says the act of kindness brightened their day.

I've been JOY'd a time or two myself in the drive-through, and I've JOY'd others. I love both! A simple act of kindness can be so powerful, even life-changing. I recently read about a study where people who suffered from anxiety and depression were separated into three groups. One group participated in social activities, one group attended behavioral therapy, and one group was assigned to do random acts of kindness. Guess which group experienced a greater sense of well-being? You got it. The kindness group. Researchers also found acts of kindness are contagious, which explains the JOY'd chain at the drive-through.

Kindness + joy = peace. Of course! —Karen Sargent

Faith Step: *Ask Jesus to inspire you and do a random act of kindness. Spread some JOY!*

WEDNESDAY, AUGUST 26

The boundary lines have fallen for me in pleasant places; surely I have a delightful inheritance. Psalm 16:6 (NIV)

MY INTEREST IN A VIDEO of a home renovation in Hawaii was piqued by the location and the major overhaul of a much-neglected house. As the couple neared final decisions about whether they could add square footage, they discovered to their surprise that the property boundary was not, as expected, marked by a low half-wall. Instead, the legal boundary for the property was several feet beyond that spot. The renovators had more than enough room for expansion, making the home more valuable for resale.

It's lovely when, as the Bible says, boundaries are set in pleasant places. In daily life, though, I, too, often push boundaries—working too long or hard, pressing deadlines to their limits, ignoring the need for rest, or making a self-imposed boundary way too close to something Jesus would define as unpleasant or unhealthy for me.

Technically, I'm sitting on my side of the fence. But it doesn't take much to peek over to catch a glimpse of what isn't good or worthwhile for body, mind, or spirit.

Some toe the edge of a boundary, thinking they're being clever and daring, and the result can be spiritually dangerous. My prayer is that Jesus keeps me aware of the lines He's drawn and content to stay well behind them for my sake and His glory. If I don't pay attention to His boundaries, I pray He'll renovate my mind and heart. —CYNTHIA RUCHTI

FAITH STEP: *In the imaginary boundaries you've set up in relationships, habits, or interests, consider this: How close do you sit to temptations? Is it time to put some distance between you and that edge?*

Thursday, August 27

"A new command I give you: Love one another. As I have loved you, so you must love one another." John 13:34 (NIV)

My supervisor, mentor, and dear friend, Darrell, had a remarkable reputation among our staff for his wisdom and thoughtfulness. Seldom rushed, he brought a warm, paternal presence into any room he entered. Beyond that, he had an incredible ability to deliver hard truths in the kindest of ways. The key? Darrell was intentional about building relationships.

When Darrell and I met five years earlier, I had jumped into my director of human resources role eager to please. I had an enormous amount of hurried, overachiever baggage that hindered my ability to process complex problems and issues in a healthy manner. Darrell could see it but was wise enough to know that tackling these issues without first building our relationship wouldn't be beneficial. Over our time of working together, he modeled Jesus to me as he kindly, patiently, and wisely mentored me, wrapping nuggets of coaching and constructive feedback with the gift of friendship and trust. I can look back and attribute much of my growth as a supervisor directly to Darrell and what he taught me.

Isn't that what Jesus does for us? He loves us, saves us, and then patiently helps us gradually grow to look like Him a little more each day. Thank heavens He doesn't show us everything we need to do differently all at once! Like my mentor Darrell, I'm so grateful Jesus is intentional about building relationships. —Kristen West

Faith Step: *Ask Jesus to show you someone you can mentor. Be intentional about building a relationship as you reflect Jesus's character.*

Friday, August 28

He refreshes my soul. He guides me along the right paths for his name's sake. Psalm 23:3 (NIV)

Recently motivated by a desire to improve my health, I considered joining a gym. After asking a friend for recommendations, I visited one nearby. My initial steps were hesitant. During early visits, I toured the facility and enjoyed a brief respite in a massage chair. It wasn't until my fourth visit that I truly began to exercise.

Trying something new often presents a challenge for me. I am filled with anxieties and uncertainties that can hinder me from taking the first step. Yet embracing a posture of openness and curiosity, I integrated this new routine into my life, accompanied by two of my teenage children.

After a few workout sessions, I realized that each visit strengthened my body and deepened our family bonds. This evolving journey at the gym is a testament to the small yet important steps needed to take toward growth. No matter how modest, each step forward is a step in the right direction. Throughout this process, I have exercised my spiritual muscles by finding comfort and direction in prayer. I ask Jesus to guide my steps and give me the perseverance to keep with it. And Jesus gives me strength to avoid the temptation of the massage chair until after I've worked out. —Tricia Goyer

Faith Step: *Consider something that would benefit you, but you have been hesitant to try. Pray that Jesus directs your steps, and take one small step toward that goal.*

Saturday, August 29

If we live in the light, as God is in the light, we can share fellowship with each other. Then the blood of Jesus, God's Son, cleanses us from every sin. 1 John 1:7 (NCV)

I'M NOT A LAUNDRESS BY trade. But for a decade, I've been laundering cleaning rags for a church in another town. I do it to help their church custodian, my husband. Although slightly creeped out by the idea of all the germs at first, I now appreciate the opportunity to bless another church family, many of whom I've come to know over the years of living in this rural area. I'm disinfecting, washing, and drying rags that clean the church of women I'd met long ago at Celebrate Recovery meetings, the man whose automotive garage repairs our vehicles, the friend who teaches at the Christian school, my mother's neighbor and best friend, and the pastor who officiated my father's funeral.

Naturally, Jesus uses this humble, routine task to remind me that in my human imperfection, as an unrighteous sinner, my own good deeds are like filthy rags (Isaiah 64:6). But when I confess my sins to Jesus, in His loving-kindness, He forgives and cleanses me. I'm not able to wash away anyone's sins, including my own, but I can wash away the germs and grime from the cleaning rags of fellow believers, so they can continue to praise, worship, and serve the Lord in clean quarters. —CASSANDRA TIERSMA

FAITH STEP: *Who does the laundry or washes the cleaning rags and kitchen towels for your church? Thank Jesus for their service, and ask Him to bless that person.*

Sunday, August 30

Love bears up under anything and everything that comes, is ever ready to believe the best of every person, its hopes are fadeless under all circumstances, and it endures everything [without weakening]. 1 Corinthians 13:7 (AMPC)

I SENT A TEXT TO my prayer group, and no one responded. This was odd. We've been praying together for years, but we had just discussed how frequently we want to meet because our prayer times together have dwindled. We decided to text prayer requests and updates to accommodate everyone's busy schedule, while meeting in person to pray a few times a year.

I sent a few more texts, and still no one replied. My feelings were hurt, and I felt ignored. I knew Jesus wanted me to believe the best of these women because that is love according to 1 Corinthians 13. But their silence discouraged me. A few weeks passed with no news from anyone. I assumed everyone was too busy. I felt unimportant.

While visiting with one woman from our group at her home, I noticed birthday cards on her kitchen island. I had missed her birthday. I apologized and asked if anyone from our group had texted her and she said they had. We compared phones. She had text messages from everyone. I expressed my discouragement, but she encouraged me to see if something else was going on. We searched my phone settings and figured out I had somehow turned off receiving messages from this group. I was ashamed of my wrong assumptions. I corrected my mistake, mentally and technologically, and immediately reconnected to this precious group of women.
—Jeannie Blackmer

Faith Step: *If you feel unimportant to someone or a group of people, assume the best of others as Jesus encourages us to do. Take the first step to reconnect.*

Monday, August 31

My God will meet all your needs according to the riches of his glory in Christ Jesus. Philippians 4:19 (NIV)

A SET OF THREE-YEAR-OLD TRIPLETS from somewhere in Asia keeps appearing on my social media feed. The quick little videos always show them doing mundane tasks like getting ready for the day. I'm not sure what the motivation is for their 117,000 other followers, but I'm mesmerized by how these little girls treat one another.

Seemingly unprompted, they help one another constantly: brushing one another's hair, straightening one another's clothes, passing food or sippy cups to the others. So in tune with one another, they intuitively know what the others need without being asked. It may be an identical triplet thing, but I can't help feeling that I have something to learn from them.

How often am I moving at the speed of light, so distracted by my own agenda that I overlook what others need? Grand gestures are great. But I'm talking about building community through little gestures, as those triplets do. I need to be more conscious of letting others go before me in the line at the grocery store, offering to unload the elderly gentleman's car at the transfer station, giving up my seat on the crowded train to the harried woman, and so on.

Jesus is lending me a hand with all the minute details of each and every one of my days. I don't have to be an identical triplet to do the same for others. —CLAIRE MCGARRY

FAITH STEP: *Make a list of small ways you can help others. Lend them a hand and feel a sense of community grow.*

Tuesday, September 1

I have tried hard to find you—don't let me wander from your commands. Psalm 119:10 (NLT)

THIS MORNING, I TURNED MY new favorite song on full blast. It filled the room with its rich chords and powerful lyrics. This song is a little on the old side. I've been listening to "Come Thou Fount of Every Blessing." It was written in the mid-1700s. Penned more than 250 years ago, the lyrics ring true today. Especially to me. This verse brings me to tears:

O to grace how great a debtor daily I'm constrained to be!
Let that grace now, like a fetter, bind my wandering heart to thee.
Prone to wander, Lord, I feel it, prone to leave the God I love;
Here's my heart; O take and seal it; seal it for thy courts above.

I keep thinking about the words and how true they are: I am prone to wander. I find myself giving into selfishness. Or leaning into fear more than my faith. Often, I want to chase after the life I think I deserve instead of waiting on Jesus's timing.

Jesus knows my wandering heart. He knows that I can go astray. He also knows that my true joy and satisfaction are found being wrapped in His grace and held in His mercy. Jesus is inviting me, one more time, to let Him bind my heart to His. —SUSANNA FOTH AUGHTMON

FAITH STEP: *Play "Come Thou Fount of Every Blessing." Listen closely to the lyrics. Examine your heart, and pray for Jesus to bind it to Him.*

WEDNESDAY, SEPTEMBER 2

"Watch and pray that you may not enter into temptation. The spirit indeed is willing, but the flesh is weak." Matthew 26:41 (ESV)

YEARS AGO, I USED TO take my lunch break at a local mall across the street from my office. One of my favorite clothing chains was always putting fresh merchandise out front, emblazoned with "new" and "sale" signs that were a siren call for my fashionista self. I'd often treat myself to the latest thing. Eventually, the lure made too much of a dent in my wallet, so I changed my strolling route to avoid the temptation to shop beyond my budget. I still employ variations of this strategy to stay out of trouble.

To battle against a middle-age spread, I guard against known culinary cravings. I have a terrible weakness for good cheese, so I watch the amount and type I have in the house, usually limiting it to slices for my boys' sandwiches, which don't tempt me.

The Bible acknowledges that we humans are prone to temptation. Jesus cautions to guard against the slippery slopes of sin in our lives by avoiding temptation or building hedges of protection against them. That's commonsense wisdom I can apply daily to stay out of trouble, big and small. —ISABELLA CAMPOLATTARO

FAITH STEP: *Do you succumb to certain weaknesses? Brainstorm and note some practical, doable methods to guard against falling prey, and ask Jesus to help you.*

THURSDAY, SEPTEMBER 3

Jesus spoke to the people once more and said, "I am the light of the world. If you follow me, you won't have to walk in darkness, because you will have the light that leads to life." John 8:12 (NLT)

"Do you want to walk?" my husband, Kevin, asked when I arrived home from work. That mild morning after two cups of tea and listening to the birds, I'd mentioned I wanted to walk when I got home. But eight hours later, my morning perkiness had flown away.

"I don't *want* to, but I think I should. I'm in a lot of pain." Nerve damage pain from two bouts with shingles attacks me most days on my drive home. Walking helps relieve the searing sting in my back. And the conversations Kevin and I have during our walks are good exercise for our relationship.

I started walking with Jesus when I was eight. I expected Him to tag along with my plans, and Jesus never forced me to do things His way. Just as Kevin asks what I want when I come through the back door at night, Jesus gives me a choice to walk with Him. Or not.

If I take Jesus's hand, ask for His help, and let Him lead me into His kind and good will, we have sweet conversations that deepen our relationship. I enjoy His wisdom, love, and strength. If I walk in my own way, I end up in darkness and pain.

So I'll continue to walk with Kevin and Jesus, even on days when I don't feel like it. —JEANETTE LEVELLIE

FAITH STEP: *Take a walk with Jesus. Listen to the birds and for Jesus's voice. What wisdom do you hear?*

Friday, September 4

Now I want you to know, brothers and sisters, that what has happened to me has actually served to advance the gospel. Philippians 1:12 (NIV)

My eyesight isn't what it used to be, so I check out large-print books from the library. It's ironic how great this is working out. I used to get overwhelmed trying to choose from the thousands and thousands of books in the building. Now, I head straight to the front display of the large-print new releases. Typically, there are fewer than ten to choose from. I can quickly scan the backs, select three or four that sound good, and check them out in under fifteen minutes. The other positive is I'm becoming more open-minded. With so few books to choose from, I'm now reading novels I would have otherwise left on the shelf.

When the Apostle Paul was thrown into jail for preaching the gospel, he didn't lament his limits. Instead, he recognized that being "in chains for Christ" had numerous advantages. It gave him access to the prison guards so he could preach to them. More importantly, his incarceration gave his followers so much courage that they put their fear aside and proclaimed the good news without restraint (Philippians 1:13–14).

As life continues to impose more restrictions on me as I age, I will remember that no obstacle is too great for Jesus. He is always working for my good despite and through them. Yet it's only when I stop focusing on my limits that I'm able to see the unlimited opportunities He's providing in their place. —Claire McGarry

Faith Step: *Think about your limitations. Ask Jesus to reveal the gifts He's offering through them. Focus on seeing the benefits.*

SATURDAY, SEPTEMBER 5

"My thoughts are nothing like your thoughts," says the LORD. "And my ways are far beyond anything you could imagine." Isaiah 55:8 (NLT)

I'D MADE THE DOUGH, ROLLED it out on parchment sheets, and chilled it for an hour. Now my granddaughters were chomping at the bit to start cutting and baking. But there was a problem: My daughter couldn't find her heart-shaped cutters, which was not surprising since the family had just moved. All we had available were round biscuit cutters. I turned the first few circles into hearts using a knife. Then I showed ways to crimp or mark the circles with a fork or spoon. Suddenly, my granddaughters took creativity to a whole new level, carving out girls' faces, a loaded taco, an alien, a dog, a setting sun complete with rays of light attached, and other little masterpieces.

What had looked like a minor problem turned our cookie-decorating session into more fun and laughter than I could have imagined. It made me wonder: How often does what I consider a hiccup in my plans actually represent Jesus nudging me toward something better than what I was going for? After all, His plans for me might differ in many ways from what I envision for my life. Since I trust that Jesus knows what is best, I want to embrace any detours that He allows instead of trying to conform to some preplanned design of my own.

Why would I want a cookie-cutter life anyway when I have such a creative Designer guiding my path? —DIANNE NEAL MATTHEWS

FAITH STEP: *Think about something in your life that doesn't seem to be turning out as you'd hoped. Tell Jesus that you trust the unique way He will work out the situation.*

SUNDAY, SEPTEMBER 6

"The thief comes only to steal and kill and destroy; I have come that they may have life, and have it to the full." John 10:10 (NIV)

"THIS IS THE THIRD OUTFIT I've had on today," I said to my husband, Kevin. "I hate changing clothes all morning, especially on Sundays." As the preacher's wife, I wanted to be centered on Jesus, not rushing to church.

I have a habit of pacing while praying every morning, and each time I passed the full-length bedroom mirror, I noticed pieces of my outfit that didn't look exactly right. That scarf didn't go as well with this sweater as I imagined it would. *Hunt for a better one.* I thought these pants fit, but I must have gained weight. *Sigh.* Change pants. And on it went.

As I changed earrings for the second time, the voice of Jesus stopped me. "This is a distraction, Jeanette. Focusing on your outward appearance is stealing from your time with Me." *Aha.* I asked Jesus to forgive me.

Distractions while I pray come in other forms besides changing clothes. I need a fresh cup of tea. I remember several pressing tasks and must write them down before they leave my brain. Or I notice the next-door neighbor's dog running in circles and stare at him for five minutes.

But after Jesus's loving correction, I'm aware of how my distractions are hurting my prayer life. Even a preacher's wife sometimes needs a Sunday lesson. —JEANETTE LEVELLIE

FAITH STEP: *Think of three distractions to prayer, and ask Jesus to help you focus on Him.*

LABOR DAY, MONDAY, SEPTEMBER 7

Whatever you do, whether in word or deed, do it all in the name of the Lord Jesus, giving thanks to God the Father through him. Colossians 3:17 (NIV)

FOR MANY, LABOR DAY MARKS the unofficial end of summer. Of course, there is a deeper purpose to this national holiday. Way back in 1887, Oregon, the state I call home, instituted this public holiday to celebrate the contributions of laborers to the development of our country. By 1894, it had become an official federal holiday.

Why should we as a nation honor our workers? Because those making up the labor force deserve recognition. Without the hard work they put forth, our nation would look quite different. Labor Day is a time to thank our workers. As Christians, we are called to an even higher standard. Everything we do or say should be in the name of Jesus. Attaching His name as we thank God for the opportunities we are given sets our work in a whole new light. Whether putting finishing touches on a job assignment or struggling with a cockeyed birthday cake, I am to strive my best as an offering to Jesus.

When I labor in His name, the Father sees Jesus's skill, not my feeble efforts. That is reason enough to give thanks! —HEIDI GAUL

FAITH STEP: *Every time you start a new task, no matter how small, offer your labors to God in Jesus's name. Give thanks that He sees your efforts through the sacred light of His Son, Jesus.*

TUESDAY, SEPTEMBER 8

Be wise in the way you act toward outsiders; make the most of every opportunity. Let your conversation be always full of grace, seasoned with salt, so that you may know how to answer everyone. Colossians 4:5–6 (NIV)

BROOKLYN CAME INTO MY CLASSROOM for seventh period and paused before going to her desk. "Mrs. Ryan, your fit is eating!" she said with a smile.

"Left no crumbs!" I replied and was taken aback by the chorus of whoops and high fives that followed from the others. Apparently, I had just used teenage slang correctly, and my students were impressed. The problem was I didn't quite understand what I'd said. I'd heard similar comments in the hallways and lunchroom, but I had not yet looked up the phrases to learn their meaning. (Later research confirmed she liked my outfit, and my reply suggested I gave it my best.)

I hear a lot of teenage slang I don't understand, and sometimes it makes me feel like an outsider. Awkward. Uncomfortable. My feelings have given me a greater awareness of how unbelievers and new believers may feel around followers of Jesus. I've used Christianese phrases like "born again," "quiet time," "the Lord's table," and "washed in the blood" without explaining what they mean. Instead, I need to remember Jesus's command to be empathetic toward outsiders in conversations about spiritual matters. Simple, straightforward language is often best. I can start with clear and direct statements like, "Jesus loves you" or "Jesus cares for you," and build from there. Even around teens. —EMILY E. RYAN

FAITH STEP: *Examine your speech this week and eliminate any Christianese words or phrases an unbeliever may not understand. Strive to share the love of Jesus in simple terms.*

WEDNESDAY, SEPTEMBER 9

"There is nothing hidden which will not be revealed, nor has anything been kept secret but that it should come to light." Mark 4:22 (NKJV)

BECAUSE OF MY FOOD ALLERGY, one of my husband's favorite restaurants is now off-limits. It was a favorite for both of us, actually, and it was hard to take it off the list of places where we could enjoy a date night dinner and both be happy chewing on barbecue ribs.

I stumbled upon an online recipe the other day that sounded intriguing. It promised fall-off-the-bone ribs enjoyment from a pork roast. The recipe was a little complex, with several extra steps, but sounded worth a try.

A big hit with my husband. He didn't just thank me but oohed and aahed over the tenderness and flavor. "Better than the restaurant," he said.

The next time I wanted to make the recipe, it was nowhere to be found.

Eventually I sank onto the sofa and said to my husband, "Looks like tuna melts tonight, Hon. I can't find it." Then I prayed, "Jesus, You're the only one who knows where it really is. Would You be so kind as to show me where I—"

The answer didn't come as a whisper. Just an impression. "You sent it to yourself in an email."

Human and frail, I'd forgotten. But even though it was such a minor request in light of all the other needs around me, Jesus dropped the message into my mind and answered that short prayer. Asking Jesus's help is the best recipe for finding lost things.
—CYNTHIA RUCHTI

FAITH STEP: *Designate a page in your prayer journal to record all the lost things Jesus has helped you find.*

Thursday, September 10

When he finished, one of his disciples said to him, "Lord, teach us to pray." Luke 11:1 (NIV)

"I'M SURE THERE'S SOMETHING WRONG with how I pray." My friend confessed her prayers are often snippets and whispers rather than full-on, beginning-to-end conversations with Jesus. Was she right?

I consider how my daughters communicate with me. Scrolling through texts, I see a picture of my granddaughter sucking her thumb and another of a new recipe my daughter tried. I read their quick messages: "Good day at work." "Maranda's in town!" "Olivia has a fever." "Love you."

These brief connections allow me to experience life with my girls in real time as they express their joys, concerns, and feelings. I think Jesus values prayer snippets as much as I value my daughters' texts. Even when the disciples asked Jesus to teach them to pray, He kept it short. "Our Father in heaven, hallowed be Your name..." (Luke 11:2–4, NKJV).

But as much as I appreciate my daughters' texts, typed messages cannot replace a phone call, even if the call is during a commute to work to help their drive go by quicker (I take what I can get). When I hear my daughters' voices, our communication feels richer. Our exchange is deeper as we ask and answer questions, react, share ideas, and say rather than type, "I love you." If left up to texts, my relationship with my daughters would lack so much.

I think Jesus wants to hang on the line with me, too, while I talk about my day, work out my worries, and invite Him to respond. Even so, I know snippets and whispers reach heaven too. Jesus is always listening. —KAREN SARGENT

FAITH STEP: *Are your prayers like texts or like phone calls? Practice praying both ways today.*

FRIDAY, SEPTEMBER 11

Who among you fears the LORD and obeys the word of his servant? Let the one who walks in the dark, who has no light, trust in the name of the LORD and rely on their God. Isaiah 50:10 (NIV)

I HAVE ALWAYS ENJOYED THE comfort of candles. Their flickering light, especially in the absence of other lights, gives me a sense of serenity. I attribute that to my great-grandmother Victoria. I fondly remember the votive candles in the foyer of her home. Each one represented a member of our family who served in law enforcement or the military. With each candle she lit, she prayed for that person individually. When she blew them out at night, she prayed again. Whenever worry for them overcame her midday, she would stop, walk to the candles, and pray. If she received a letter or call that they were safe, she would offer prayers of thanksgiving. Her foyer was her own personal sanctuary. When with her, I would do likewise. Her compassionate example taught me to turn to Jesus not only in the face of worry and fear but also in thanksgiving.

It is easy to become anxious over a loved one's safety. But balancing that emotion with praise and thanksgiving grants the peace that only Jesus can give. Keeping candles lit at home or in my church, I will hopefully pass along Jesus's light of peace to the world. One candle at a time with prayer, just like Grandma Victoria taught me.
—GLORIA JOYCE

FAITH STEP: *Light a candle in memory of those involved with 9/11. As you do, offer up a prayer for safety and thanksgiving for those serving in law enforcement and the military and for their families.*

SATURDAY, SEPTEMBER 12

The fruit of the Spirit is love, joy, peace, longsuffering, kindness, goodness, faithfulness, gentleness, self-control. Against such there is no law. Galatians 5:22–23 (NKJV)

MY HUSBAND AND I COLLABORATE well on home improvement projects. Recently, we gave our old fireplace a fresh update. The pretty stones reached from the floor to the ceiling but went unnoticed because of the black grouting around them. As we covered that dark color with a creamy one, the transformation was stunning.

I set a peach-colored candle on the left end of the mantel and a yellow pot of green plants on the right. Then I tied it all together and hung a whimsical canvas of forest trees with leaves of gold, orange, purple, blue, and pink in the middle.

The fireplace looked lovely alone. The candle and pot added warmth to the setting. Yet the bright picture in the center held the place of prominence, the focus of the eyes, the image to coordinate the whole wall.

When I examine the list of the fruit of the Spirit, I notice the word in the middle. *Love, joy, peace,* and *longsuffering* are on one side; *goodness, faithfulness, gentleness,* and *self-control* are on the other. *Kindness* is in the center, tying those characteristics all together with an element of emphasis and attention. As I seek to be more like Jesus, I pursue each of the nine attributes. And like the canvas hanging over my mantel, kindness can capture that position of importance and help me beautifully display the rest of the fruit of the Spirit in my life. —BECKY ALEXANDER

FAITH STEP: *List the fruit of the Spirit on a note card and circle kindness. Place it on your mantel or somewhere you can see it often.*

Sunday, September 13

"You are my friends if you do what I command." John 15:14 (NLT)

There's a Sunday worship song that I love called "Friend of God" by Israel Houghton. I sing it with gusto because the words remind me that my relationship with God is not only one between a sovereign deity and a lowly human but also one between friends. How great to know I am God's friend! As I grew in my relationship with Him, He began to challenge me, as His friend, to be His arms and legs in my community. Whoa...um, OK.

One day He asked me to comfort a woman who heard voices and sat mumbling loudly in our courtyard each day. He said to lay my hand on her shoulder and simply say, "It's OK. Jesus loves you." I did, and she stopped mumbling. Then my Friend asked me to offer prayer to an older man who scraped his cornea while tending his rosebushes. I did, and the next day he called and told me his optician said the scratch had disappeared! One winter afternoon, my Friend God asked me to give my scarf to the homeless woman who sat shivering in her giant garbage bag at a busy bus depot. I did. She took it, said thanks, and got up and moved. I feel His pleasure when I partner with Him to do these things.

This friendship I sing about on Sundays is not just skipping through the tulips hand in hand with Him through life. There is another level of responsibility to this awesome friendship with God—doing what our Friend wants done on earth. —Pamela Toussaint Howard

Faith Step: *Look up the song "Friend of God" on YouTube. Practice following the promptings of your Friend.*

Monday, September 14

If I rise on the wings of the dawn, if I settle on the far side of the sea, even there your hand will guide me, your right hand will hold me fast.
Psalm 139:9–10 (NIV)

ONE EVENING A WHILE BACK, I pulled up a map app on my iPad to find the Arctic archipelago of Svalbard, halfway between Norway and the North Pole. I follow an Instagrammer who lives there and am intrigued by the concept of the two seasons of polar night and polar day. Traveling there by the app's satellite imagery is the closest I'll come to visiting the place, so I took a virtual trip to satisfy my travel bug.

After I explored Svalbard, I spent the rest of the evening island-hopping and clicking on tourist sites, resorts and other lodging, airports, and so on, all over the globe. I covered a lot of miles and had fun zooming in on streets and shops and businesses in locales I'd never heard of.

The tiniest dots of islands in the middle of vast blueness left me in awe, and I wondered if the people living on them felt isolated in the bigness of Earth. How do they produce all they need for survival? What opportunities do residents enjoy? I think it would unnerve me to live so remotely.

And to think that Jesus sees it all. That's the greatest wonder. He knows every inch of deep blue sea and faraway land. And His watchful eye never misses a single moment of any person's life. Our satellite images can't compare to His omnipresence.

I am never isolated from Him. —ERIN KEELEY MARSHALL

FAITH STEP: *Open a map app and zoom in on your home. Thank Jesus that it's impossible to be isolated from Him.*

TUESDAY, SEPTEMBER 15

"Take the yoke I give you. Put it on your shoulders and learn from me. I am gentle and humble, and you will find rest." Matthew 11:29 (CEV)

THOMASINA IS IN MY PLACE on the love seat, snoozing in a sunbeam shining through the window. I wish I could be lounging in the sunshine. *It must be nice to be a cat.* I could handle that job. Contemplating Thomasina's mellow life, I'm imagining the job description for applying to be my cat. Based on current performance, it would be something like this: Always look cute and adorable. Take naps. Stretch luxuriously. Follow the sun; bask in its warmth. Follow me around. Relax. Watch me. Look at me. Stare at me. Have fun. Greet me every morning. Talk to me. Check in frequently to connect with me. Hang out with me. Stay close to me all day.

As Thomasina's owner and caretaker, I place no conditions, demands, or requirements on her. She isn't laboring under the heavy burden of my expectations. Thomasina's carefree, gentle, restful life reminds me that Jesus wants the same for *me*. He wants me to be completely devoted to Him (1 Corinthians 7:35). Scripture encourages me to release my worries (Matthew 6:34), take pleasure and delight in Jesus (Philippians 4:4), spend time in His presence (Luke 10:39, 42), and bask in His warmth by abiding in Him (John 15:7). These are the expectations of my Lord, Jesus, the One who cares for me.

Thomasina is showing me how to be a devoted follower of Jesus. Now if only she'd let me have my place on the love seat.
—CASSANDRA TIERSMA

FAITH STEP: *Seek out a beam of sunshine. Bask in its warmth, reflecting on all the ways Jesus wants you to live a life devoted to Him.*

WEDNESDAY, SEPTEMBER 16

When [Jesus] saw the crowds, he had compassion on them, because they were harassed and helpless, like sheep without a shepherd. Matthew 9:36 (NIV)

YEARS AGO, A FRIEND PASSED away unexpectedly. Although at one time we were very close, marriage, family life, and our careers caused us to experience a separation—not only in distance but also relationally. To my shame, I was not even aware she had fallen ill. My sister represented our family at her funeral, but what bothers me is the fact I was not there—for my friend or, upon her passing, for her family. Instead of reaching out afterward and sharing the pain of loss, I shied away, protecting myself.

I wish I could say it was the only time I exhibited that type of behavior, but it wasn't. When this same friend had suffered a miscarriage, I was similarly absent. I could not comprehend how to console someone who suddenly fell from the heights of joy to the depths of grief. Eventually, I mustered up enough strength to call her and offer condolences for her loss and apologies for my absence, but it took me a year to get to that point.

When others are hurting, I've found that my good intentions aren't good enough. I feel the pain of others deeply, but true compassion is characterized by presence. In the same way that Jesus gives us His Spirit as a comforter (2 Corinthians 1:3–4) and comes alongside us, I, too, want to demonstrate the loving compassion of Christ by being present alongside others when they are at their lowest point. With His Spirit, I will. —ERICKA LOYNES

FAITH STEP: *Set aside your intentions and ask Jesus to help you practice being fully present with a loved one today.*

Thursday, September 17

A man who has friends must himself be friendly, but there is a friend who sticks closer than a brother. Proverbs 18:24 (NKJV)

ONE DAY, MY FRIENDS CAROL and Laura came over for our weekly bike ride. Carol held her bike gloves in her hands, which caught the attention of Ody, my chocolate Lab. He quickly leaped and grabbed one. "Drop it," I hollered. Ody looked at me and gulped it down. We abandoned our bike ride, and I rushed Ody to the vet on call, where he induced vomiting. He even rinsed off the glove and gave it to me in a baggie. Knowing Carol, I figured she would want it back because those things are pricey.

Throughout scripture, Jesus values and encourages friendship. Jesus had twelve close friends, His disciples. Together they faced awe-filled moments such as feeding thousands (Matthew 14:13–21) and intense incidents like casting out demons (Mark 1:25–26). He promises He'll always be with us (Matthew 28:20). He even calls us His friends (John 15:15). I'm blessed to have friends who are like sisters, experiencing the joys, challenges, and sometimes intense moments in between. Friends who know me and love me and even love my naughty dog. It's my desire to know Jesus even better than I know my friends.

Later that day, Carol called to check on Ody. I asked if she wanted her glove back because I had kept it and washed it. She said yes, as I knew she would. —JEANNIE BLACKMER

FAITH STEP: *After you spend time with your friend Jesus, call another close friend today and let her know how much you treasure her.*

Friday, September 18

Do not forget this one thing, dear friends: With the Lord a day is like a thousand years, and a thousand years are like a day. 2 Peter 3:8 (NIV)

I LIKE TO KEEP AN ongoing list of grocery items on the Amazon Echo that sits on my kitchen table. It's so convenient when I am almost out of something just to say, "Alexa, add sugar" and presto, the device will put sugar or whatever I say on the list.

One day I told Alexa to add thyme to my shopping list. When I looked to double-check if it had done as I had instructed, Alexa had added "time," instead of the herb. I chuckled. Then I thought, *Wouldn't it be nice to be in control of time?* What would I do with more of it? I could add hours when I needed or wanted to—perhaps more time to sleep, complete tasks, enjoy family and friends, or even be still. I could make time go faster when the workday seemed to drag or the departure for a long-awaited vacation appeared far away. Wouldn't that be great?

I know that Jesus is the ultimate timekeeper, the One who is not limited by time or space. A wait that may seem like forever for me is nothing in the Lord's eyes. He sees the big picture so much better than I ever could. I just need to trust Him to work it all out for my good.

Jesus always knows what I need and when I need it, unlike Alexa. It's best to leave my time in His hands. —BARBRANDA LUMPKINS WALLS

FAITH STEP: *Ask Jesus to help you make the best use of the time He's given you.*

SATURDAY, SEPTEMBER 19

Who can discern their own errors? Forgive my hidden faults.
Psalm 19:12 (NIV)

THE PAST MONTH PILED ON my shoulders like a heavy weight as I sat before our checkbook ledger. Burst pipe. Broken sump pump. Unexpected travel. It would take months to dig out of the financial hole created. Tears filled my eyes as I balanced the columns. The final number was way less than I thought it should have been. *I don't understand.* Just then, my phone rang. It was my husband's daily lunch call. I shared my despair, unsure how we were going to pay our bills over the next few months. My thoughts spiraled as they tend to do. "Don't worry," Matt said. "It's probably just a math error. We'll figure it out together when I get home."

Hanging up, I was still unsure. It was true that arithmetic was not my strong suit, but I had worked the numbers twice. Yet Matt's calmness over the situation ceased my inner spiraling. He is usually the voice of tranquility in our relationship. Well, Matt and Jesus.

I put the checkbook aside and picked up my Bible because, like Matt, Jesus also tells me not to worry (Matthew 6:25–34). And while I don't always listen to my husband, I do listen to Jesus. When troubles shake my core, I trust Jesus to calm my emotions and provide a balanced foundation.

Oh, and my husband was right. It was my math. —GLORIA JOYCE

FAITH STEP: *Keep a ledger this month and add up the times Jesus has helped you calm your fears. Thank Him specifically for each and every one.*

Sunday, September 20

Each of you should use whatever gift you have received to serve others, as faithful stewards of God's grace in its various forms. 1 Peter 4:10 (NIV)

My husband, Ron, and I became empty nesters during the pandemic. It was odd to be without any youth in our home but more so in our lives. For years, we had been educators, coaches, and church volunteers while raising our family, but now I felt old without the youthful energy and perspective one gets being around teens.

When church activities resumed after the shutdown, the youth group was one program that didn't restart due to small numbers of teens attending church. I was sad at the lack of a ministry for young people and felt a nudge.

Considering our empty-nest schedule, Ron and I offered to restart the youth program. We had simple plans, meeting twice a month with activities and Bible studies. I was surprised when anxiety arose as we planned each activity. You'd think I was hosting a major event! *Would the kids like it? Would they even come?*

The first meetings went well, but I couldn't shake my insecurities. I asked Jesus why youth night created such stress. He showed me the gatherings weren't about my inadequacies but about making a welcoming place for teens to connect with caring adults, one another, and Him. Youth group wasn't about me; it was about Jesus—that simple.

The new perspective removed the pressure I'd put on myself. It also allowed me to enjoy the youth, have fun, and feel young again!
—Brenda L. Yoder

Faith Step: *Do you experience anxiety over outcomes? Have a heart-to-heart with Jesus, let go, and give Him control.*

Monday, September 21

Do not be anxious about anything, but in everything by prayer and supplication with thanksgiving let your requests be made known to God. Philippians 4:6 (ESV)

I HAVE A FEW CHILDREN who struggle with learning. Navigating the balance of encouraging them, correcting them, and overwhelming them is delicate. After my children had a year of limited social interactions due to the pandemic, one of my primary goals was to find a homeschooling community where my children could thrive socially and academically. For two years, this community was a blessing. My kids formed strong friendships and were challenged by tutors who recognized their potential and equipped them with tools for success.

However, as the academic demands increased, I noticed a shift. Two of my children expressed a desire to leave, feeling outpaced and overwhelmed. The third tried valiantly to keep up, but I saw the strain grow each week, the challenges stacking up like boulders on his young shoulders.

I wish I could say I acted immediately upon noticing these signs, but it took several phone calls about my children struggling, many conversations with them, and much prayer before I recognized that a change was necessary. Making the decision to leave our community was difficult, but it was what my children needed to alleviate stress and regain confidence.

This parenting experience underscored the Lord's kindness in providing us the discernment to make tough decisions that align with our children's best interests. After all, I'm always learning too.
—TRICIA GOYER

FAITH STEP: *Consider a situation in your own life where you might need to make a change for the betterment of yourself or others. Pray for wisdom and courage. Trust that Jesus will guide you through these transitions and bring peace to your decisions.*

Tuesday, September 22

"I will repay you for the years the locusts have eaten—the great locust and the young locust, the other locusts and the locust swarm—my great army that I sent among you." Joel 2:25 (NIV)

THE AUTUMN DAY WAS CLEAR and sunny, so I took our dog to a county park for a walk. We trotted along a lake, into some woods, and emerged in a meadow. I marveled at the scenery. The sky was a bright blue. The trees burst with vibrant fall color, while the prairie grass was golden. Everything looked like it was in Technicolor.

Several benches were positioned along the route at scenic spots. I enjoyed the picturesque spaces by sitting, reflecting, and praying. Jesus really met me here.

I usually dread the autumn season. It means a long, dark Midwest winter is ahead. My father and my in-laws all died during the fall. It's also when my husband, Ron, and I had separate, near-fatal accidents. Nature's grandeur invited me to consider how God brought us through these hard seasons. As I marveled at autumn's beauty, my dread dissipated. It was time for a different perspective. While I was sitting in the sun, Jesus seemed to wrap me in His arms. I realized the fall season and sadness don't have to coexist.

I asked Jesus to redeem the fall season, my losses, and my perspective. My ordinary afternoon walk became a significant milestone that moved me beyond the past and into a new season of hope with Him. —BRENDA L. YODER

FAITH STEP: *Is there a season, holiday, or certain time of the year that is difficult for you? Acknowledge it and ask Jesus to redeem that milestone or anniversary and prepare your heart for a new season of hope.*

Wednesday, September 23

I am convinced that nothing can ever separate us from God's love. Neither death nor life, neither angels nor demons, neither our fears for today nor our worries about tomorrow—not even the powers of hell can separate us from God's love. No power in the sky above or in the earth below—indeed, nothing in all creation will ever be able to separate us from the love of God that is revealed in Christ Jesus our Lord. Romans 8:38–39 (NLT)

A COUPLE OF YEARS AGO, a sudden realization startled me—I have trouble accepting Jesus's love. I know in my mind that He proved His love for me by dying on the cross. But have I fully embraced His extravagant, unconditional love? Do I live out that truth? Sometimes I find myself going through the motions of the Christian life but not feeling loved.

I'm not alone in this struggle. Lack of affirmation in childhood, past hurts, dysfunctional relationships, or personal sin can make someone feel unworthy to receive love. This often leads to a lifelong pattern of worry, poor self-esteem, jealousy, depression, or anger. I don't stand a chance of overcoming such ingrained attitudes on my own. I need Jesus to transform my thinking, to remind me that no matter what happened in the past or what the future brings, the reality of His love never changes.

Like a physical condition that requires daily medication, my struggle requires daily treatment: prayer, scripture reading, and meditation on His promises. I'm trusting Jesus for the cure. —DIANNE NEAL MATTHEWS

FAITH STEP: *Jot down past or present circumstances that tempt you to question Jesus's love. Insert each one into this sentence:* I am convinced that _____ can never separate me from Christ's love. *Cross everything off your list.*

Thursday, September 24

Yet you, Lord, are our Father. We are the clay, you are the potter; we are all the work of your hand. Isaiah 64:8 (NIV)

A PETITE GIRL I DIDN'T know paused at my classroom where I was standing at the door greeting students between classes. She tilted her head, looked up at me, and said, "So, you're one of the short teachers at this school." I choked back laughter and nodded. I certainly couldn't argue with that. She smiled brightly and concluded, "Cool. I like you!" then disappeared around the corner into a sea of mostly taller middle schoolers. Later, I told the story to my son Solomon, who is now taller than me and his older sister. He admitted he'd given us both nicknames when he added us as contacts in his phone. I'm now listed as "Strive for Five" since I'm just shy of five feet tall, and Adelle is listed as "Lowercase Sister."

People often ask me how I feel about being short. Does it bother me that I'm "vertically challenged"? Does it offend me when others point it out or poke fun? Is Zacchaeus my favorite Bible character because he was too short to see Jesus in a crowd? While I can't say it's *never* bothered me (I have daydreamed of reaching the top shelf, after all), I can say that any frustration I feel always fades when I remember that I am clay in the Potter's hand, purposely formed and fashioned in every detail. How could I ever bemoan my stature when God is the artist? He only creates masterpieces (Ephesians 2:10, NLT). —EMILY E. RYAN

FAITH STEP: *Read about Jesus and Zacchaeus in Luke 19:1–10. Thank God for every inch of your stature.*

Friday, September 25

His Son paid the price to free us, which means that our sins are forgiven.
Colossians 1:14 (GW)

Hanging my new jacket in the car for the trip my husband, Jeff, and I were taking, I noticed something dangling from the underside of the sleeve. The price tag! Oh, no. I'd already worn this jacket twice—once to a funeral in which I'd passed out programs and once to a sports banquet. In both instances, I would have lifted my arm. How embarrassing! My grandmother always liked Minnie Pearl on the Grand Ole Opry, the woman whose hat had a price tag hanging from it. Now I was Minnie Pearl.

I don't like to shop for clothes, and if I must shop, I usually look for items on sale. A friend told me about a woman she knew who never looked at the price tag. If she liked something, she simply bought it and didn't consider the cost. I can't even wrap my mind around that.

Something else I can't wrap my mind around is the fact that Jesus gave His life for me. He died for the sins of everyone in the whole world. In fact, 1 John 2:2 (GW) states that Jesus is the payment for our sins. Knowing that Jesus paid the ultimate price for me, I must continually strive to live a life worthy of His cost.
—Pat Butler Dyson

Faith Step: *Next time you study a price tag on an item to determine if it's worth the cost, consider the price Jesus paid for you.*

Saturday, September 26

Therefore, if anyone is in Christ, the new creation has come: The old has gone, the new is here! 2 Corinthians 5:17 (NIV)

The wooden dock to which our sailboat-home was tied was deteriorating. One stretch, about 100 feet long, became dangerous. At low tide, it tilted side-to-side on a 40-degree angle. I managed to walk across this section safely in dry weather, but doing it in the rain and snow unnerved me. The dock became especially hazardous when winter temperatures covered it with frost. If Gene was with me, I held his arm for support. The last thing a boat dweller needs is a fall resulting in a broken ankle!

Everyone living here sighed with relief when the marina managers decided to replace the dock. Workers took out the old wooden structure and hauled it to the marina yard to be crushed. Then they built a new dock system using materials that wouldn't become slick.

Watching the dock undergo change gave me a new appreciation for 2 Corinthians 5:17. When I trusted Jesus for salvation, He didn't respond by merely placing temporary patches on the broken places in my life. Instead, He began to fulfill His promise to permanently transform me by addressing the roots of those broken places. He took out patterns of wrong thinking and replaced them with truth. He removed old, selfish desires and behaviors and built in godly desires and behaviors.

The new dock on which I walk offers more than a sense of security. It serves as a daily reminder of Jesus's desire and power to transform me. The old has gone, the new is here, and I am grateful. —Grace Fox

Faith Step: *Take a walk, as you're able, and ponder the ways Jesus has changed your life.*

SUNDAY, SEPTEMBER 27

He Himself is the propitiation for our sins, and not for ours only but also for the whole world. 1 John 2:2 (NKJV)

As I wiped the delicate goblet dry with a dish towel, it slipped from my fingers and shattered on the floor. For a moment, I froze to stare at the mess. How could one glass break into so many pieces? The floor was littered with them. I grabbed the broom and dustpan and swept the area.

But the next day, I found a shard atop the counter on the opposite side of the kitchen, and the day after that, I spotted a large chunk in the breakfast nook. How could this be?

Sin is like that. It creates a mess in one part of my world. I clean it up, only to notice it has shattered into other areas, appearing in unexpected places over time. Even then, the jagged pieces can cut just as deeply as the day that sin was first committed.

Because Jesus sacrificed His life on the cross, my misdeeds have been cleaned up. Jesus not only atoned for sins but also sent the Holy Spirit to continue the work of helping us recognize our brokenness on a daily basis. We are made clean of every repented transgression.

Never capable of being repaired, my smashed goblet was bound for the trash. But because of Jesus, I can be whole again, no matter how broken I become. —Heidi Gaul

Faith Step: *As you wipe counters in your living space today, recognize how Jesus has wiped your slate clean with His sacrifice. Thank Him for restoring your brokenness and making you as beautiful as new.*

Monday, September 28

The tongue has the power of life and death, and those who love it will eat its fruit. Proverbs 18:21 (NIV)

Sometimes I struggle with knowing what to say on Jesus's behalf—or what I shouldn't say. A friend I pray for often, who is a great person but a fickle believer, started walking a destructive path. I feared if I said too much, I could damage our relationship and lose any spiritual influence. But how much was too little, and how much was too much?

While I debated with myself, she received a soul-crushing text from a fellow believer that brought tears to my eyes. Right message, wrong delivery. I found myself wanting to judge on both sides, pointing at one and saying, "You shouldn't do that," and to the other, "You shouldn't say that." I sound so self-righteous, don't I?

While the text was sent with the best intention, I fear the eternal damage that could result from the hurtful words. And shouldn't a message that important take place face-to-face? But who am I to criticize? I've hardly addressed my friend's destructive choices at all.

But now I had to say *something*. She was seeking comfort. With her sin clearly exposed, I remembered how gentle Jesus was with sinners during His earthly ministry (and with me) and prayed for the right words. I texted: *Don't ever let another person stand between you and the love of Jesus. There's no room for anyone in that space.*

Did I say enough? Maybe. Maybe not. But Jesus is enough (Philippians 4:19). What happens in my friend's heart isn't up to me, but Jesus is always the right message. —Karen Sargent

Faith Step: *Feeling judgmental about someone else's sin? Demonstrate Jesus's gentle love today.*

Tuesday, September 29

Then said Jesus to them again, Peace be unto you: as my Father hath sent me, even so send I you. John 20:21 (KJV)

I'VE BEEN PLAYING ON REPEAT (both through my device and in my brain) a song that reminds me how Jesus speaks peace over us. What a comforting sound. So unlike the noises that so often aggravate, disrupt, or disturb.

Some days, even the sound of a mosquito or the slightly out-of-balance squeaky fan can irritate. A whining child, precious as the child is. The ding of the microwave.

I can't imagine, though, what it's like to suffer from misophonia—a disorder that causes sufferers to have strong reactions to specific sounds, like other people's chewing (or their own), leaves moving in the breeze, or the tick of a distant clock. Some sounds are admittedly more pleasant than others. Many of my favorites are associated with family memories, waves washing against the shore, birds waking with the dawn, my husband saying, "I love you," or my children and grandchildren's loving words and laughter.

A ringing phone is jarring. But it becomes a sweet sound when the caller is revealed to be an old friend or someone I cherish.

What sound do I treasure most? The whispers of Jesus reminding me "I am with you" (Matthew 28:20, KJV). His voice in the middle of the storm: "Peace, be still" (Mark 4:39, KJV). His intentional message to those who follow Him: "Peace be unto you."

And I will never tire of the sound when His presence draws so near I can almost hear His heartbeat. —CYNTHIA RUCHTI

FAITH STEP: *What sounds or words from Jesus do you cherish most? Find a way to share them with someone you care about today.*

WEDNESDAY, SEPTEMBER 30

So then, dear friends, since you are looking forward to this, make every effort to be found spotless, blameless and at peace with him. 2 Peter 3:14 (NIV)

AS MUCH AS I WISH I did yoga every day, I'm just not that disciplined. When I do finally hit the mat, I approach it as I do everything else—all in and determined to do my best. Consequently, I sometimes strain my muscles trying to do the poses as perfectly as the instructor on the video. Then, I remember: Yoga is not about might; it's about gentleness and breathing. So I refocus. When I finally reach the point when I truly exhale, I relax into it and everything changes. That's when my tension releases. That's when I stop striving. That's when my muscles actually stretch farther of their own accord because they're no longer clenched.

My pattern continues in prayer. When I first sit before Jesus, I search for the right words to sound eloquent as I pepper Him with my problems and petitions. It's as if the more I strain to find Him, the faster He'll show up. It isn't until I've poured it all out before Him and then pause to catch my breath that I truly exhale all the chaos, making room for His grace. As my spirit becomes pliable, I refocus on the awareness that Jesus has been beside me all the time; I've just been wound too tight to notice. The more time I spend in His presence, the more I relax into His grace, soaking up His blessings, going deeper into His peace. —CLAIRE MCGARRY

FAITH STEP: *Take a moment to focus on your breathing. Inhale slowly; exhale deeply, making space to receive Jesus's grace.*

Thursday, October 1

"Peace I leave with you; my peace I give you. I do not give to you as the world gives. Do not let your hearts be troubled and do not be afraid."
John 14:27 (NIV)

"It's not a mass, so that's a good thing," the doctor said. He studied the ultrasound screen as the technician ran the wand back and forth across my chest. "It looks like a collection of something. We need to do a biopsy."

The technician, a friend of mine, scheduled the appointment for the earliest available date. Sensing my fear, she said, "Try not to worry too much between now and Friday. The doctor is being cautious, and nothing is certain."

I went home and read the statistics. One in eight women faces breast cancer at some point in her life. The median age of diagnosis is sixty-two—my exact age. Early detection, surgical options, and innovative treatments allow many patients to survive and even thrive afterward. Sobering, for sure.

I tried to follow my friend's advice and not worry too much. I prayed, worked my usual hours, visited my granddaughters, and completed a project on my to-do list. What helped me most, though, was reciting the gentle words of Jesus: "Do not let your hearts be troubled and do not be afraid."

The procedure begins at 8:30 in the morning. My technician friend will be there to offer assurance, and Jesus will be present to give me peace. Whatever the results, I know my kind and loving Savior will keep me in His care for all my days ahead. —Becky Alexander

Faith Step: *Write John 14:27 on a note card, and memorize it so you can recite the words of Jesus when you're fearful.*

Friday, October 2

Look, there on the mountains, the feet of one who brings good news, who proclaims peace! Nahum 1:15 (NIV)

YEARS AGO, THE IDEA OF public speaking terrified me. I would shy away, lowering my head and avoiding eye contact whenever the opportunity arose. However, as I began to accept more speaking engagements, I discovered something powerful: People connect deeply with stories. My role wasn't just to speak but to share how Jesus has shown up in my life, doing extraordinary things through ordinary moments. My perspective shifted dramatically when I stopped worrying about people's opinions of me and focused on how I could direct them toward Jesus.

This transformation in my approach to public speaking was not just about overcoming fear; it was about recognizing the Lord's ability to use my voice as a tool to bring the good news to others. It reminded me of what Jesus told the Apostle Paul: "My grace is sufficient for you, for my power is made perfect in weakness" (2 Corinthians 12:9, NIV). Embracing this public speaking calling was a profound reminder that Jesus's strength illuminates my weaknesses. He equipped me to share my story and transformed my apprehension into a conduit for His work. Overcoming my fear of public speaking is another way Jesus has extraordinarily shown up in my life. —TRICIA GOYER

FAITH STEP: *Write down one fear, weakness, or task you've been avoiding that can be transformed into an opportunity to demonstrate Jesus's power. Pray for courage and guidance to turn this challenge into a strength.*

SATURDAY, OCTOBER 3

By grace you have been saved through faith. And this is not your own doing; it is the gift of God. Ephesians 2:8 (ESV)

I WATCH TONS OF DO-IT-YOURSELF videos. How to cut my own hair, how to upcycle thrifted clothing, how to mend and darn, how to alter clothes that don't fit, how to exercise while sitting on a chair, and so on. I love learning how to do things to make my life better.

I used to think I could DIY my spiritual life with various spiritual self-help methods. I thought I could make my life better by reading the right books, praying particular prayers, repeating positive affirmations, attending seminars. My DIY method of attaining spiritual peace was an endless to-do list that didn't make my life better.

When Jesus became my personal Lord and Savior, my never-ending spiritual DIY quest ceased. With Jesus, I finally experienced and understood what the Bible calls "the peace of God, which surpasses all understanding" (Philippians 4:7, ESV). All my desire to DIY my spiritual life was gone. Jesus made me whole and complete. He made my life better.

Now my DIY interests are of a more mundane nature. I still want to know how to turn my skinny jeans into flare-legged pants, but I'm no longer obsessed with trying to DIY my own salvation. Jesus is in charge of that. What could be better than that?
—CASSANDRA TIERSMA

FAITH STEP: *Jot down a short to-do list of three things you're planning to do. Add one more item to your list:* Save Myself. *Cross that out and write Ephesians 2:8 in the first person:* By grace I have been saved. And this is not by my own doing; it is the gift of God.

Sunday, October 4

Sing praises to the Lord with the lyre, with the lyre and the sound of melody! Psalm 98:5 (ESV)

To say my husband, Roger, and I made a joyful noise to the Lord would be a giant lie. I often pictured Jesus with His fingers in His ears just so He could drown out our sour notes. I knew the biblical directive to sing praises to the Lord, but could our off-key singing even be considered music?

I had visited other churches where their chancel choir made my heart swell with emotion. The thought of our small church having a choir was laughable. Even if it did, membership would not be extended to me.

Standing in the pew on most Sundays, I just mouthed the words. Lip-synching each stanza so those around me wouldn't have to endure my singing. Moving my mouth to yet another hymn, I thought about singing praises to the Lord. I realized, Jesus didn't say, "Make perfect music to the Lord." He never said, "Be quiet unless you sound like an angel." I had been looking at singing to the Lord all wrong. I opened my mouth and softly whispered the words. Then, I decided to increase the volume just a little—not much, but a little. Don't get me wrong—Roger and I still sound like screaming cats. But we were singing praises to the Lord. And for the first time, my heart filled with emotion. —Jeannie Hughes

Faith Step: *Practice singing hymns or other praise songs in your home until you are comfortable with the tune. Realize Jesus doesn't care how musically gifted you might be, only that you are making music in His name.*

MONDAY, OCTOBER 5

"You have heard that it was said, 'Eye for eye, and tooth for tooth.' But I tell you, do not resist an evil person. If anyone slaps you on the right cheek, turn to them the other cheek also." Matthew 5:38–39 (NIV)

I'M ALL FOR "EYE FOR eye, and tooth for tooth" when it comes to fictional stories. One of my pet peeves is when the villain commits a heinous act against a hero and arrogantly expects the hero to simply tolerate the offense. When the hero fights back, the villain has the audacity to seek revenge. The conflict makes for a great story, but (not-so) secretly, I always want the hero to get revenge.

Perhaps strong feelings bubble up for me because I was sometimes picked on in grade school. I was labeled a Goody Two-shoes in grade school and grew tired of the moniker by eighth grade, when I agreed to meet in the girls' bathroom to fight. The altercation was more of a light scuffle with no clear winner or loser. When I returned to my desk, my teacher expressed her disappointment in me. I didn't feel great about seeking revenge.

I may root for everyone to get what they deserve in fictional worlds, but I'm glad Jesus doesn't give me what I deserve. If He did, I'm sure I would be a one-eyed, toothless woman! Jesus forgives me even when I'm in the wrong, and He commands me to forgive others despite what they've done. Jesus is the hero of His factual story of loving-kindness. —ERICKA LOYNES

FAITH STEP: *Write the name of someone you need to forgive on a sheet of paper. Add your name and ask Jesus to help you both extend and experience His forgiveness.*

Tuesday, October 6

Let the redeemed of the LORD tell their story—those he redeemed from the hand of the foe, those he gathered from the lands, from east and west, from north and south. Psalm 107:2–3 (NIV)

A FEW WEEKS AGO, I flew to Colorado to hang out with my sisters and my mom for a girls' weekend. Our get-togethers include evening chats by the fire, coffee runs, and, of course, shopping. But over the last few years, we have started frequenting thrift stores instead of retail shops.

My sister Erica is a thrifting expert. She has started an online business reselling her resale treasures. She finds the most amazing designer clothing for unbelievable prices. I'm not as knowledgeable as she is, so I peppered her with questions on this last trip. "Is this a good brand?" "Do you think this is a good deal?" "How can you tell if something is a great find or trash?"

Erica has learned all about the art of redemption. She sees things differently than I do. To me, a top can look like an old cable-knit sweater. To Erica, that same sweater could be a designer steal. She knows what things are worth and redeems them—selling them for far more than she paid. Erica recognizes their value.

Jesus also knows all about redemption. He sees things differently than I do. He sees past all my issues, struggles, and insecurities. Jesus is the Great Designer who made me. I may not feel worthy, but He thought I was worth dying for. Jesus recognizes my value. And He has redeemed my life. —SUSANNA FOTH AUGHTMON

FAITH STEP: *What is your redemption story? Take time to meditate on Psalm 107:2–3, and thank Jesus for redeeming your life.*

WEDNESDAY, OCTOBER 7

To all who believed him and accepted him, he gave the right to become children of God. John 1:12 (NLT)

"DIANNE, YOU'RE RELATED TO GEORGE WASHINGTON!" I thought this email from one of the major genealogy websites was cool. That night I joked with my husband that we just needed to discover that he was related to Abraham Lincoln and then we would really be somebodies. A few months later, an email informed me that I'm a descendant of Lincoln. One month later, Elvis Presley, followed by Benjamin Franklin. This culminated in an email listing twenty-six famous people supposedly in my family tree, including dancers, authors, inventors, suffragettes, and royalty in Great Britain.

I enjoy researching genealogy, but I've always taken the findings with a large grain of salt. I routinely see mistakes copied and passed around online, even about living relatives. Just a year after my father died, that same website displayed a death certificate with a stranger's name listed as Dad's spouse. So I don't take much stock in information about relationships dating back to the 1500s or earlier. If we trace our family trees back far enough, wouldn't we all share a common ancestor anyway?

I'll keep tabs on my favorite genealogy website, but the relationship I value the most will always be the one that Jesus made possible through His sacrificial death. When I accepted Him as my Savior, I became an adopted child of God. According to His records, I am now part of "a chosen race, a royal priesthood" (1 Peter 2:9, CSB). That's as much of a somebody as I could ever hope to be. —DIANNE NEAL MATTHEWS

FAITH STEP: *Slowly read 1 Peter 2:9–10 aloud. Tell Jesus how grateful you are for your identity in Him.*

Thursday, October 8

"I know that even now God will give you whatever you ask."
John 11:22 (NIV)

Darkness had fallen, and rain pummeled our sailboat as I cooked dinner. My husband, Gene, was listening to the news when he suddenly realized that one of his hearing aids was missing. He searched the boat's interior but came up empty-handed. Then he scoured the cockpit where he'd worked briefly in the late afternoon, but he found nothing. Retracing his day's steps through the marina parking lot was his last recourse, but the chances of finding the device there seemed nil, especially in the stormy dark.

Gene strapped on a headlamp, grabbed an umbrella, and then paused at the door while we asked Jesus to lead him to the hearing aid. I stayed behind and continued praying as I finished cooking our meal. An undeniable peace filled my heart, and I felt confident that even now, even amid a seemingly impossible situation, Jesus would somehow answer our cries for help. And He did! As Gene walked toward the parking lot, Jesus reminded him about an app on his phone designed to track the device. When Gene turned it on, it led him to the hearing aid's approximate location.

My much-relieved husband returned home fewer than fifteen minutes later wearing both of his hearing aids and a huge smile. Together we thanked Jesus for protecting the hearing aid from pedestrians stepping on it, cars driving over it, and the marina's resident geese snatching it. The chances of finding it looked beyond bleak, but even then, Jesus answered our prayers. —Grace Fox

---

Faith Step: *Identify a seemingly bleak situation in your life and surrender it to Jesus, praying, "Even now, I choose to trust You for the best outcome."*

FRIDAY, OCTOBER 9

Do not gloat over me, my enemy! Though I have fallen, I will rise. Though I sit in darkness, the LORD will be my light. Micah 7:8 (NIV)

LAST FALL, MY COLLEGE CLASSMATES and I reunited at our alma mater in Ohio to perform at a highly anticipated concert to celebrate the fiftieth anniversary of the gospel choir we were a part of decades ago. We were all excited, snapping pictures, laughing, and enjoying the last few minutes before going onstage when the power went out. *What in the world?*

I gasped but thought the electricity would come back on soon. We waited and waited. Still no power. I immediately recognized it was a spiritual attack to discourage us, and I silently asked Jesus for help. We could barely see one another. We had no idea what it looked like in the concert hall where the audience was seated. Finally, it was decided that nothing was going to stop us from singing praises to God—we had rehearsed for too long and traveled too far to let anything stop us now.

Cell phone flashlights helped us find our way to the stage, as did some early-evening light that was still coming through the windows. By divine providence, our first selection was a cappella, so there was no need for the electric guitar and keyboard that now stood silent. By the fourth song, the electricity returned. Hallelujahs resounded!

I never discovered what caused the power outage, but I know Jesus, the Light of the World, heard my prayers. He's the One with the real power, and that's certainly something to sing about.
—BARBRANDA LUMPKINS WALLS

FAITH STEP: *Turn out the lights or go into a darkened room. Sing your favorite hymn to Jesus. Feel His power.*

Saturday, October 10

Do not say to your neighbor, "Come back tomorrow and I'll give it to you"—when you already have it with you. Proverbs 3:28 (NIV)

When an unfamiliar brown blanket appeared in my laundry room, I washed it first and asked questions later. Random items of clothing are always left behind by my children's friends, but a blanket like this was a first. I finally discovered its origin when I asked my daughter Adelle. A few weeks earlier, she and my husband had been in a very serious car accident. A few people stopped to help, including a woman who focused entirely on helping my injured daughter until emergency workers arrived. The good Samaritan helped Adelle limp to the guardrail of the freeway so she could lie down, then used the blanket as padding under her head. "She told me to keep it," Adelle said.

The woman was gone before I arrived on the scene, but I had been so grateful to hear that Jesus had sent someone to care for my child when I wasn't there. Now the blanket served as a tangible reminder of this stranger's generosity.

As I folded the clean blanket, I realized that I also wanted to be ready, just as the woman was, to meet a need in the moment. Having a spare blanket in the car could be an easy step to be prepared for an unplanned opportunity. As I placed the brown blanket in the back of my car, I prayed that the person who received it next would feel the love of Jesus and the generosity of His people. —Emily E. Ryan

Faith Step: *Put an extra blanket in your car, and pray for an opportunity to bless someone with it.*

Sunday, October 11

"Why worry about a speck in your friend's eye when you have a log in your own?" Luke 6:41 (NLT)

Cell phones, while a marvelous convenience, are fraught with peril when transported into quiet places. Often, before a program begins, the speaker cautions the audience to silence their phones. My husband, Jeff, and I have marveled at the number of times we've been in quiet gatherings and someone's phone rings, music plays, or Siri makes a random announcement. We have judged the phone's owner. Dear Lord, how we have judged! How could people be so clueless?

Our pastor had paused in his sermon when a strident female voice rang out, "Eleven-fifteen a.m." And it came from right next to me! Siri? I poked Jeff in the ribs. The pastor said, "Thank you for letting me know," and the congregation roared. We both slunk down in the pew. Only after we'd skulked away from church, driven home, and studied the manual for Jeff's new Apple Watch did we discover an unusual feature. When the wearer places two fingers across the face of the watch, there's an oral announcement of the time. Jeff just didn't know. He immediately turned off the function, but the damage had been done.

Jesus, thank you for this lesson in humility and not judging others. Jesus Himself did not judge. In this tough old world, I need to be compassionate rather than judgmental at all times. I bet Siri would agree! —Pat Butler Dyson

Faith Step: *Was there a time when you judged someone and later did the same thing yourself? Ask Jesus to remind you. And if you have a smartwatch, consider silencing this announcement feature!*

Monday, October 12

He who sows sparingly will also reap sparingly and he who sows bountifully will also reap bountifully. 2 Corinthians 9:6 (NKJV)

LAST AUTUMN, MY HUSBAND BOUGHT a few pumpkins to display on a straw bale at the end of our driveway. As winter neared and the pumpkins began collapsing in on themselves, he tossed them toward the back of the garden for the deer to eat. Spring came, and the pumpkins were gone. He tilled the garden a few times and planted all his usual veggies.

Before long, unexpected vines grew behind the corn along the back edge of the plot and sprouted big yellow blossoms. We watched the blossoms turn into pumpkins of all colors and sizes—small ornamental pumpkins, white pumpkins, yellow ones, green ones, and big orange pumpkins. We harvested a wheelbarrow full of our beautiful, unexpected crop!

In the garden, Russ planted seeds that sprouted and some that didn't. However, he didn't realize he had "planted" the pumpkin seeds. And isn't that the way it is when we share Jesus? I can be intentional about modeling Jesus's character traits, and I can be intentional about telling others about Him. Sometimes the seeds I plant grow, and sometimes they don't.

But sometimes a thoughtful action or kind truth may unintentionally touch someone's heart and something beautiful blossoms. Just like our unexpected crop of pumpkins. This persuades me to send those notes of encouragement that come to mind or to text a friend and ask how I can pray for her. Actually, the results of unintentional planting have made me want to be more intentional! —KAREN SARGENT

FAITH STEP: *What kindness has Jesus been prompting you to do for someone? Be intentional and do it today.*

TUESDAY, OCTOBER 13

"The rising sun will come to us from heaven to shine on those living in darkness and in the shadow of death, to guide our feet into the path of peace." Luke 1:78–79 (NIV)

IT WAS ONE OF THOSE nights. I tossed and turned. My mind did the same. Extended sleep stiff-armed me. It would not agree to stay.

Will this night never end? I checked the clock after dozing off and waking again. One a.m. Fifteen minutes since I'd last looked. Maybe if I flipped my pillow over. Two a.m. Then three a.m. I saw every single hour's declaration shining through the clock's not-at-all-comforting LED lights.

Endless night.

But the Bible told me differently. As did a video I recalled viewing just before bed the night before. The video traced the path of the sun as it traveled across earth's time zones—a continuous wave of endless dawn. It is never not dawn somewhere on earth. In the middle of my restless night, someone in some other time zone in the world is greeting the dawn.

If I could just retain that mental image the video presented—dawn crawling across the planet, chasing away the darkness, bringing light and hope as it plowed through to return humanity's view of the sun.

Time zones can foul me up when I'm traveling. But the truth is that God's presence at creation set it all up, including the precise rotation of the earth, so somewhere it would always be the end of darkness and the return of dawn. —CYNTHIA RUCHTI

FAITH STEP: *The next time you struggle with a restless night, remind yourself of two things—God vowed He would always be with us, and it's already dawn somewhere on the planet.*

WEDNESDAY, OCTOBER 14

Keep your roots deep in him, build your lives on him, and become stronger in your faith, as you were taught. And be filled with thanksgiving. Colossians 2:7 (GNT)

DURING A RECENT APPOINTMENT, I ended up in a conversation with the office receptionist about genealogy. She shared her frustration that attempts to research her family on her mother's side had been hampered by the fact that the last name had been changed at some point. No one seemed to know when the change had been made or even exactly what the original name was. When she later discovered a horse thief in her lineage, she decided to stop her research altogether.

We laughed about her shady ancestor, but I'm sure we could all find a few skeletons in our closets if we opened enough doors. Each one of us has sinned; we all fall short of God's standards (Romans 3:23). We may try to label people or classify them into more or less desirable groups, but, thankfully, Jesus doesn't do that. Neither a family history nor a personal "shady" background stands between us and His forgiveness and love. Jesus's arms are open to everyone.

No matter what the branches of my family tree look like, I want to focus on sinking my roots deep in Jesus. That way, I can hopefully leave a legacy that won't be a total source of embarrassment to those who come after me. —DIANNE NEAL MATTHEWS

FAITH STEP: *Take a moment to look at some black-and-white photographs of the generations who came before you. Thank Jesus that each person pictured is part of your family tree (no matter how shady). Pray that your roots go deep in Him.*

Thursday, October 15

> *"'Lord, when did we see you hungry and feed you, or thirsty and give you something to drink?'"* . . . *"The King will reply, 'Truly I tell you, whatever you did for one of the least of these brothers and sisters of mine, you did for me.'" Matthew 25:37, 40* (NIV)

I STARED INTO THE GLASS case at Harry's Café. A pie on the top shelf caught my attention. Banana cream overflowing a flaky deep crust with thick golden swirls of meringue adorning the top. I placed my order and sat on a barstool.

Three seats away, a woman with gray, tangled hair ate the last bite of her cheeseburger. She pulled on a stained jacket and a holey hat and shuffled toward the register, crumpled dollars in hand. I motioned to the server and whispered, "I'd like to pay for her food. Can you add it to my bill?" She smiled and nodded.

The server met the woman at the register and said cheerfully, "You don't owe us a thing. Someone paid for your meal."

"I don't want anyone to pay for my meal!" The woman glared at the employee for what seemed a long time. I felt my face flush as the recipient of my generosity huffed and stomped out the door.

I have two distinct memories from my visit to Harry's Café: banana cream pie and a paying-it-forward experience gone awry. Perhaps the woman felt judged by my actions—I will never know. But I do believe that Jesus nudged me to pay for her meal that day. I hope that as she looks back on the experience, Jesus will comfort her with the love that was intended. —BECKY ALEXANDER

FAITH STEP: *Pray for Jesus to nudge you to be generous. Consider ordering a slice of pie and waiting patiently for an opportunity.*

Friday, October 16

I will give you a new heart and put a new spirit in you; I will remove from you your heart of stone and give you a heart of flesh. Ezekiel 36:26 (NIV)

WHEN PEOPLE ASK ABOUT THE ages of my children and learn that my oldest are in their thirties—despite my being in my early fifties—they often express surprise. "Wait, what did you say? There's no way you can have children that old," they remark. I just laugh and assure them it's quite possible. Though I smile about it now, I was ashamed of my story for years.

In the early days of my faith, I dwelled on the mistakes I made as a teenager, but as I grew closer to Jesus, my perspective shifted. I began to share my story as a teen mom not to focus on my past but to illustrate how Jesus welcomed me when the world thought I'd messed up.

My transformation is a testament to the Lord's kindness. He gave me a new heart and a new spirit, turning my past as a teen mother into a testimony of His grace and redemption.

Wherever you are in your journey, remember that Jesus has a good plan for your life and your story. With all its twists and turns, it's a tool He can use to inspire and encourage others. Trust that your experiences, redeemed by His love, can offer hope and guidance to those who hear them, even if they are surprised. —TRICIA GOYER

FAITH STEP: *Reflect on aspects of your past that you may feel ashamed of or regret. Consider how Jesus has worked in your life, and pray for the courage to share your story with others as a testament to His grace.*

SATURDAY, OCTOBER 17

How good and pleasant it is when God's people live together in unity! Psalm 133:1 (NIV)

OUR THIRTEEN-YEAR-OLD DAUGHTER, JOCELYN, WANTED to go to California with her school orchestra to play violin at Disneyland. As much as I wanted to say yes, we live on the other side of the country in New Hampshire. Plus, I was still trying to save the money we needed to pay for her school trip to Philadelphia. Going on both trips was out of reach.

When it came time for the online fundraiser for the California trip, I felt a nudge and put a post about it on my Facebook page. I was astounded by people's kindness and support. Friends from college, distant relatives, and even my sister's high school friend wanted to participate. Jocelyn had to go back to her teacher twice to request more raffle calendars to meet the demand. My daughter is going to California after all!

I sometimes forget that the body of Christ is a community, and we're meant to work together to help out one another (1 Thessalonians 5:11). All those people who stepped forward on Facebook to participate in Jocelyn's fundraiser created a community that is lifting her up and helping her to fulfill her dream. She may be going to California to play violin in Disney's Magic Kingdom, but her joy in doing so will help Jesus's kingdom shine bright.
—CLAIRE MCGARRY

FAITH STEP: *What activity is out of reach for you, whether financially, physically, or emotionally? Pray about possibilities and ask Jesus to make it happen.*

Sunday, October 18

Therefore I remind you to stir up the gift of God which is in you through the laying on of my hands. For God has not given us a spirit of fear, but of power and of love and of a sound mind. 2 Timothy 1:6–7 (NKJV)

I ATTENDED A MEGACHURCH IN Brooklyn, New York, for years. I was maturing in my faith and looked for opportunities to pray for others. During a Sunday service, a woman walked down to the altar. The worship team was playing softly, and she began sobbing, her shoulders heaving. As she knelt in front of the platform where our pastor stood, I felt a nudge to go forward and kneel by her to offer support, prayer, or even just a shoulder to cry on. But stepping out of the row and walking toward the stage—in front of thousands of people—felt out of my comfort zone.

Since I'd committed myself to Jesus after college, I'd had some practice with noticing when He was prompting me to do something. Over the years, I grew in courage, and I was able to share my faith spontaneously and to pray for others more freely. Still, situations like this one brought back my early inner trembles.

But Jesus calmed my fears. I waited for the right moment, quietly stood, and made my way to the altar. When I reached the woman, I gently placed my hand on her back and whispered comforting words, encouraging her that Jesus cared about whatever she was going through. She stopped sobbing. I sheepishly glanced around. My pastor nodded at me and smiled. All was well. —PAMELA TOUSSAINT HOWARD

FAITH STEP: *Ask Jesus to show you opportunities to comfort others. Don't be afraid to step out of your comfort zone.*

Monday, October 19

The light shines in the darkness, and the darkness has not overcome it. John 1:5 (NIV)

After writing a report on the Middle Ages, my daughter Ana was fascinated with the simplicities and practices of ancient living. She suggested we go electricity-free for a month to experience it ourselves. Instituting a few parameters for cooking, schoolwork, and such, our family decided to give it a try. I'll admit, eating dinner by the flicker of only three pillar candles that first week was a challenge. As was dressing, styling my hair, and applying my makeup in the dimly lit predawn autumn mornings. I couldn't wait for the experiment to end. I missed my modern routines.

However, by mid-month, I felt an unexpected calm follow me out of bed each morning and past the dinner table at night. And I wasn't the only one. By month's end, a complete change had come over my home. Sleepy morning chats. Afterschool puzzles. Nightly card games. Bible reading and group prayer. No longer were we retreating to the solitude of our devices. My family was tuned in to one another, like families of old. And we were tuned in to Jesus. Slowing down to embrace the darkness illuminated us with the joy of His Word. Jesus shone a light on our dark ways and allowed us to rekindle anew. Through being present together, we saw His great Light in our lives. —Gloria Joyce

Faith Step: *Try going electricity-free for a portion of the day for a week. What do you discover about yourself and Jesus?*

Tuesday, October 20

Let each of us please his neighbor for his good, to build him up.
Romans 15:2 (ESV)

When our marina managers replaced our dock, all liveaboards had to relocate for a couple of months. Once the project was complete, we migrated back. The process wasn't as simple as it sounds because some boats had nonfunctioning engines and needed to schedule a tow. Besides that, however, everyone had to consider the tide, currents, and wind conditions as they made their plans to return. If the tide was too low, their vessel's keel could get stuck in the river's bottom mud. If the current and wind were too strong, they would push the vessel away from rather than toward the new dock upon approach.

One of our neighbors considered all the factors and chose to bring his sailboat home at 4 a.m. Then he texted my husband and asked for help. Despite his need for rest after undergoing radiation therapy, Gene said yes without hesitation and set his alarm for 3:45 the next morning. When he woke, he walked a quarter mile to the dock where our neighbor's boat was moored, climbed aboard, and, using a handheld spotlight, helped guide the forty-five-foot vessel through the dark to safe moorage.

Considering Gene's physical limitations, no one would have blamed him for not lending a hand at that hour—it was a difficult task and an inconvenient time. Because my husband follows Jesus, the thought of declining an opportunity to help and show the love of Christ never occurred to him. He loves Jesus and our neighbors too. —Grace Fox

---

Faith Step: *Ask Jesus for an opportunity to show His love in a creative way to one of your neighbors, no matter how difficult or inconvenient the act of service may be.*

WEDNESDAY, OCTOBER 21

He said to me, "My grace is sufficient for you, for my power is made perfect in weakness." Therefore I will boast all the more gladly about my weaknesses, so that Christ's power may rest on me. 2 Corinthians 12:9 (NIV)

I SMELLED LIKE A PUNGENT combination of Vicks VapoRub and Ricola cough drops. My nightstand displayed various half-used packages of cold remedies that had provided me with some amount of relief as I battled the lingering congestion that filled my head.

Wadded-up tissues filled the nearby trash can. With zero energy or motivation to shower for three days, I looked precisely as bad as I felt. The sun came up on day four. My brain felt clearer and my body felt functional, so I returned to work. A coworker stopped by my office to welcome me back and asked how I was feeling. "I'm much better and deeply thankful for God's recent kindness," I said.

Of course, she thought I was talking about my health being restored, but I was actually referring to God's gracious reminder of my ever-present need for Jesus. I've lost count of how many times I've breezed through regular days, strong and healthy, without giving much consideration to my spiritual condition. But when I was weak with this cold, Jesus was always on my mind. *Jesus, I feel so bad. I need You!* was my constant prayer. Between doses of NyQuil, I recognized my frailty and His strength. And finally, thanks to Vicks VapoRub, Ricola, and Jesus, I'm now on the mend. —KRISTEN WEST

FAITH STEP: *What weakness in your life you can surrender to Jesus so He can be your strength? Write 2 Corinthians 12:9 on a note card and put it with your medicines as a reminder.*

Thursday, October 22

> *Peter remembered the words Jesus had spoken: "Before the rooster crows, you will disown me three times." And he went outside and wept bitterly.* Matthew 26:75 (NIV)

PRAYERFULLY TAKING STOCK OF SOME failed friendships a few years ago, I realized I had an awful pattern. I'd get my feelings hurt, neither forgiving my friend nor confronting the issue that was bugging me. Over time, my resentment would harden or some last straw caused me to drop the friendship suddenly, often without explanation. This destructive pattern had been unconscious for many years, an outdated protective mechanism. When the lights came on and I could see it clearly, I was heartbroken, like the Apostle Peter was when he realized he'd denied Jesus just as predicted.

Notably, the pain of remorse didn't drive Peter into hiding even though his denial was a grievous sin Jesus had warned of just a few chapters earlier in Matthew 10:32. In fact, Jesus later thoroughly forgave Peter by asking him a parallel three times if Peter loved Him (John 21:15–17). Despite knowing how Peter would fail Him, Jesus made Peter the rock on which he'd built His church (Matthew 16:18). The Peter we see in Acts is a changed man, bold and fearless—unto death.

Once I clearly saw and fully repented of my sin, I prayed for help changing my ways. Jesus enabled me to mend a few of those friendships and empowered me to be more communicative, tolerant, and forgiving. He also gave me the grace to forgive myself and move on without shame. —ISABELLA CAMPOLATTARO

FAITH STEP: *Are you burdened by recurring guilt about some unconfessed or long-ago sin? Write a detailed letter to Jesus asking for forgiveness. Burn the letter, receive Jesus's complete forgiveness, and make amends if appropriate.*

FRIDAY, OCTOBER 23

Dear children, let us not love with words or speech but with actions and in truth. 1 John 3:18 (NIV)

THAT MORNING, AS I READ my daily devotions, I detected a common theme—kindness. Then, a friend texted me a meme that read "Always be kinder than you feel." Hmm. Jesus, are you trying to tell me something?

Sounds of heavy machinery and truck doors slamming jolted me off the couch. My husband, Jeff, had told me the construction crew would be here at 8:00 a.m. to pour concrete for our new deck, but it was only 7:15. Ugh, Jeff! *Always be kinder than you feel.* I scrambled to the bedroom and threw on some clothes. I needed to work at my computer, but the booms and crashes made it too distracting to concentrate. Grrr. *Always be kinder than you feel.* One of the workers tapped on the door. "Ma'am, could we get some water?" As it turned out, the men needed all the water bottles I'd just bought. I decided to take a tray of cookies I'd made for the grandkids out to them as well. *Always be kinder than you feel.*

I needed to mail a package before the post office closed, but the trucks were in the way. When I asked the foreman when they might be finished, he couldn't tell me and wondered if that was a problem. I assured him it was not. *Always be kinder than you feel.*

When Jeff got home, he apologized for the early arrival of the crews. "No worries," I told him. "I just had the best day!" —PAT BUTLER DYSON

FAITH STEP: *As you go about your day, ask Jesus to remind you always to be kinder than you feel. It will change your outlook and your life.*

SATURDAY, OCTOBER 24

For Your lovingkindness is before my eyes, and I have walked in Your truth. Psalm 26:3 (NKJV)

WHEN MY KIDS WERE YOUNG, I took them on day trips to create special memories. Now I enjoy replicating such days with my grandchildren.

This October day, I took my three-year-old and eighteen-month-old grandsons to a pumpkin farm near their home in Alexandria, Indiana, also the hometown of Christian recording artists Bill and Gloria Gaither. Our adventure started with donuts at the Gaithers' bakery. Then, the boys played in a gazebo by the parking lot before we left.

As we approached our car, a woman exited her car and greeted the boys. Her face looked familiar as she asked me their ages. *Could she be Gloria Gaither?* I sheepishly asked if she was Miss Gloria. I was tongue-tied when she answered yes.

The moment felt sacred in a way I couldn't describe. The experience lingered with me for days. The following Sunday, our congregation sang one of the Gaithers' songs, and I understood the awe of the parking lot encounter. Many of the Gaithers' songs have ministered to me through the years, especially in hard times. Encountering Mrs. Gaither and her being so engaging and kind felt like a personal conversation with Jesus.

While I made special memories with my grandsons, Jesus created a special memory for me. Like Gloria Gaither, Jesus saw me. The brief conversation held such personal meaning only He could know. Jesus revealed how deeply He loves me through that divine autumn encounter. —BRENDA L. YODER

FAITH STEP: *Reflect on Psalm 26:3 and journal about a particular moment that seemed ordinary but felt sacred. Write the date and store it in the pages of your Bible as an encounter of Jesus's love.*

Sunday, October 25

Restore to me the joy of your salvation and grant me a willing spirit, to sustain me. Psalm 51:12 (NIV)

A PETITE SEVEN-YEAR-OLD GIRL WAS baptized at church last week. One of our pastors waded into the baptistry first and held his hand out for her to enter. She grabbed it eagerly, then relied on his arm as she inched to the middle of the water. She was so small, it appeared she must be tiptoeing. The pastor placed her feet on a riser at the bottom of the pool to raise her up, and she flashed a huge smile to the congregation, causing a muffled giggle to spread throughout the auditorium.

Before baptizing her, the pastor introduced the girl and told us how she learned about Jesus through lessons at church and chose to follow Him after a conversation with her parents. After she prayed and placed her faith in Jesus, she was so happy she jumped up and started turning cartwheels all over the house.

I remember what it was like to have childlike joy so strong it had to explode from my body through jumps, turns, flips, and spins, but it's been years now since I've attempted a cartwheel. The little girl's story inspired me—not to return to my gymnastics days but to return to my own childlike enthusiasm for Jesus. I bowed my head and prayed the words of King David, asking Jesus to restore to me the joy of my salvation. Then I jumped up and did a cartwheel in the aisle. (Just kidding. But I did smile!) —EMILY E. RYAN

FAITH STEP: *If you've lost the joy of your salvation, pray that the Lord will restore it to you. Spend time with children or do something childlike to ignite your joy.*

Monday, October 26

The LORD is trustworthy in all he promises and faithful in all he does. Psalm 145:13 (NIV)

WHO HAS STRUGGLED AS MUCH as I have with putting together a weekly meal plan? It worked, somehow, when my kids were little. But now? How can I slot tuna salad for next Wednesday if I have no idea how I'll feel about tuna a week from now?

I'm not a mood-eater in the sense of eating my feelings, as they say. But I am a mood-eater about the uncertainty over whether I'll be in the mood for meatloaf or pork roast two or three days from now. Or even tomorrow.

It occurs to me how curious it is for me to say, "I have no idea how I'll feel about tuna." As if feelings are great deciders. As if feelings matter more than wisdom. As if feelings should get the final say in anything in life.

Go to school? I don't feel like it. Oh, OK.

Show up for work? Don't feel like it. Fine, then.

Follow Jesus's instructions about how to treat a neighbor? But I don't feel like…

My feelings should never be allowed to sit in the driver's seat of my life. They may lead me down a path that feels right, but feelings are often blind to consequences and long-term effects.

These days, I'm asking myself, "Are you following Jesus or your feelings? Which is more trustworthy?"

It sure simplifies life. And, yes, tuna is on the menu for tonight.
—CYNTHIA RUCHTI

FAITH STEP: *Create a side-by-side comparison of what feelings often tell us versus what Jesus says. Keep it close when you need to make a decision.*

Tuesday, October 27

Therefore humble yourselves under the mighty hand of God, that He may exalt you in due time, casting all your care upon Him, for He cares for you. 1 Peter 5:6–7 (NKJV)

My husband, Larry, and I made a trip to our local landfill recently. As we approached the dumping area, I was amazed at the number of trucks that had lined up with tons of garbage and debris, waiting their turn to unload. Truck after truck pulled in, emptied their trash, and drove away. Immediately, men in massive dozers drove in and pushed the junk into a huge pile of sludge and dirt. This process was done over and over in the twenty minutes we were there.

As I watched out of my truck window, I began to realize how much I could associate my Christian walk with this process. I sometimes carry a burden so great that it feels like a heavy load. If I don't give it to Jesus and let Him discard it for me, it piles up and becomes too big to carry. My attitude and disposition are affected, and at times I even go quiet when it gets to be too much. Through the window of my heart, I can see Jesus waiting for me to come to Him and dump it all. I know I can unload my cares on Jesus, all my junk and trash, for Him to take away. —Renee Mitchell

Faith Step: *Write down everything you are mentally carrying today and take it to Jesus. Make sure you include all your doubts and fears. Let Him take it away for good.*

WEDNESDAY, OCTOBER 28

Now to him who is able to do immeasurably more than all we ask or imagine, according to his power that is at work within us. Ephesians 3:20 (NIV)

ON A TRIP TO GREECE with girlfriends, four of us took a taxi from our villa on the island of Tinos to catch a ferry. I asked our taxi driver if he had ever been to the United States, and he said no. Then I asked where in the U.S. he would like to go. He said, "Walnut Grove." I thought California, but he meant Minnesota. Baffled, I probed. Turns out he was obsessed with the book and TV series *Little House on the Prairie*. Walnut Grove is the setting for this series. He even named his children after characters in the book.

On the ferry, my friends and I talked about our taxi driver's dream to visit Walnut Grove. His imagination of what he could experience in the U.S. seemed so limited. This made me wonder if I, too, had starved my God-given gift of imagination. When Jesus encountered people, He did more than they asked or imagined. His thoughts and ways are so far beyond our own (Isaiah 55:8–9).

Talking with this taxi driver and my friends inspired me to open up my imagination. I began to dream about what Jesus could do with me. I imagined helping children around the world learn photography with a friend who does this, or hosting home worship concerts, or buying a villa in Greece to minister to burned-out missionaries. It's fun to dream and believe that with Jesus I can do immeasurably more than I can ever envision. —JEANNIE BLACKMER

FAITH STEP: *Write about a dream you can entrust to Jesus. Pray that He will show you how to achieve it.*

THURSDAY, OCTOBER 29

"I have come that they may have life, and that they may have it more abundantly." John 10:10 (NKJV)

TODAY I PLAYED RACQUETBALL AT the gym, did laundry, baked bread, and enjoyed ham and bean soup from the slow cooker with my husband, David. We strolled the neighborhood in the evening, enjoying the lingering warmth of the sun on our skin. It was just an ordinary day—nothing more.

But while playing this morning, my racket's "sweet spot" buzzed repeatedly as I hit the ball, a rare and coveted experience for me. As for the laundry, well, it's my favorite household chore. I love tossing things into the washer dirty, only to exit the dryer smelling fresh and clean. The French bread I baked tasted every bit as good as it smelled. Slow-cooker meals always remind me of soul food, nurturing both the body and the soul. And walks with my husband through our neighborhood feed my inquisitive mind. As we encounter new friends, whether two- or four-legged, my spirits rise.

Maybe it wasn't ordinary after all. It was filled with blessings, one after the other, awash in the everyday miracles Jesus gifted me with. The greatest blessing of all is the knowledge this day is only one among countless others of the abundant life He gives. An extraordinary day from an extraordinary Savior. The abundant life Jesus died to give me. —HEIDI GAUL

FAITH STEP: *Circle back this evening and list the everyday miracles and not-so-ordinary blessings Jesus gave you throughout the day. Thank Him for your abundant life.*

Friday, October 30

"My command is this: Love each other as I have loved you."
John 15:12 (NIV)

My one-year-old granddaughter, Olivia, sits on the living room floor across from Della, my daughter's friend's baby, who is a few months younger. The little ones watch each other curiously, sometimes smiling, often reaching out to touch the other or to snatch a toy.

I listen as my daughter Kelli and her childhood friend Anna discuss baby milestones and lack of sleep, their eyes filled with delight at the budding friendship of their young daughters. Kelli and Anna's love for each other is moving into the next generation. My heart spills over with joy.

This must be how Jesus feels when he watches us love each other. Surely, He delights in new relationships developing between His children and enjoys watching old friends share the blessings and trials of life in the same way I am filled by watching these two new mommas and their babies.

The older I get, the more I understand what it means to be made in His image (Genesis 1:27). I wonder if the emotion I feel reflects the emotion He feels (Hebrews 4:15). I know what it means to love intensely and unconditionally and how a child's disobedience can break my heart. Parenting and grandparenting have allowed me to accept Jesus's love on a deeper level. As much as I love my children and grandchildren, I know He loves them, and me, even more. —Karen Sargent

Faith Step: *Pull out some pretty stationery and take a moment to write an old-school love note to someone today. Remind that person how much he or she is loved by you and by Jesus.*

SATURDAY, OCTOBER 31

"Because he loves me," says the LORD, "I will rescue him; I will protect him, for he acknowledges my name." Psalm 91:14 (NIV)

I WORK PART-TIME FOR SOME local Realtors. Recently, an agent asked me to deliver plants to her clients to express her gratitude for their business.

My decades-old GPS was able to locate thirteen of the fourteen addresses. For hours, I drove from one home to another, listening to a podcast to keep me entertained. I couldn't find the last address, so I switched to the Waze app for up-to-date navigation and live traffic conditions. I could barely see the roads on the small screen of my phone. So I turned off my podcast and fully focused on the voice directing me. That's how I heard it say: "Object in right lane, one mile ahead." Traveling at 65 mph, I quickly switched to the left lane. Less than a minute later, I rounded the bend to see a fifteen-foot ladder in the right lane. Goodness knows what would have happened if I'd been using my old GPS, with no capability to detect debris in the road or warn me about it.

Some might say it was luck that forced me to switch to the more sophisticated app for that last house. I know it was no coincidence at all. Jesus uses whatever method He wants to send the messages we need. In this case, Jesus spoke through my app, warning me about the upcoming danger. Yes, the voice may have sounded robot-like, but I still recognized it as His. —CLAIRE MCGARRY

FAITH STEP: *Make a list of the ways you've heard Jesus's voice—be it through technology, a conversation with a friend, or even the lyrics of a song. Thank Him for speaking to you.*

SUNDAY, NOVEMBER 1

God created humans in his image, in the image of God he created them; male and female he created them. Genesis 1:27 (NRSVUE)

YESTERDAY, I WENT TO MY mailbox and found the fourth children's book I'd written inside. I couldn't wait to open it. It is newly released and wrapped in a colorful bubble mailer. I get a little weepy just thinking about it. It still seems unbelievable to me that I get to live out my dream of writing for kids.

Last year, I began working with a nonprofit to write their monthly blogs. Over the course of the year, my position morphed, and I joined their curriculum team. They needed a children's book to accompany each curriculum unit. I jumped at the chance to help write these fun, uplifting books. I love creating with words. Writing these books has unleashed a new creative passion: rhyming. While in a meeting the other day, a coworker mentioned the word *mellow*. All I could think was *Mellow rhymes perfectly with yellow*. Who knew rhyming could bring so much joy?

I'm at my best when I am creating. I feel energized and fulfilled. I think it's because I'm made in God's image—and He is the most creative of all. He spoke the world into existence and breathed life into humanity (Genesis 1–2). His creativity is revealed daily in the beauty of nature and His people. When I am creative, I honor God and the gifts He has given me. —SUSANNA FOTH AUGHTMON

FAITH STEP: *Plan to do something creative today—write in a journal, paint or color, sew or crochet, or write a rhyming poem. Whatever you do, spend time nurturing the creative gifts God has given you.*

MONDAY, NOVEMBER 2

I love those who love me, and those who seek me find me.
Proverbs 8:17 (NIV)

MY HUSBAND AND I HAVE had date nights every Tuesday evening since we met twenty-five years ago. Before kids, it entailed all kinds of fun activities. Since kids, it's been watered down to sitting on the couch together watching TV. Now that our kids are older and more independent, I wanted to breathe new life into our tradition. So I signed us up for guitar lessons. I played years ago, but John never did. Our instructor structured the class to bring John up to speed, while still challenging me.

Lo and behold, John progressed by leaps and bounds. Unfortunately, I did not. John practiced two or three times a week, while I only picked up my guitar during lessons. Talent and skill certainly play a part, but it's clear to me now that improvement comes with time, effort, and consistency.

The same holds true with my spiritual life. When I get lazy and skip my prayer time with Jesus, my faith life can remain at a standstill. Jesus feels distant—not because He moved but because I did. It all comes down to time, effort, and consistency.

Our date night goal is to grow closer as a couple, so if I don't practice or improve at guitar it's no big deal. But if my goal is to continuously grow closer to Jesus, and I don't want my faith to fall flat, I need to put action behind my desire to make beautiful music with Him. —CLAIRE MCGARRY

FAITH STEP: *How close do you feel to Jesus? Consider making a daily date with Him and invest time, effort, and consistency.*

Tuesday, November 3

So it is with you. When you heard the true teaching—the Good News about your salvation—you believed in Christ. And in Christ, God put his special mark of ownership on you by giving you the Holy Spirit that he had promised. Ephesians 1:13 (NCV)

ONE RECENT RAINY MORNING, MY husband and I made our way to the neighborhood elementary school to vote in a primary election. There were very few people, so the election workers were glad to see us come in. They cheerfully and quickly checked us in and handed each of us a ballot.

After I submitted my ballot, as usual an election worker thanked me for coming and handed me an "I Voted" sticker, signifying that I had been to the polls and performed my civic duty. I smiled and pressed it on my jacket, hoping that anyone who saw the sticker as I went about my day would be prompted to follow my example and vote.

I glanced down at the sticker and was reminded of scriptures that mention being marked as followers of God (Revelation 7:3, 14:1). I then thought about how I already wear a sticker of sorts that's invisible and will never come off—the seal as a child of God. That sacred sign helps me to love others, be kind, and reflect Jesus to those around me. Without Him and the Holy Spirit, I could do none of those things. I am among those who elected to be a disciple of Jesus. I cast my vote for Him because Jesus is the clear winner.
—BARBRANDA LUMPKINS WALLS

FAITH STEP: *As a follower of Jesus, you are a marked woman. Consider writing something on your palm to remind you that you belong to Him.*

WEDNESDAY, NOVEMBER 4

When Jesus reached the spot, he looked up and said to him, "Zacchaeus, come down immediately. I must stay at your house today." So he came down at once and welcomed him gladly. Luke 19:5–6 (NIV)

I RECENTLY VOLUNTEERED AT MY son Pierce's high school baseball game snack bar with a mom I didn't know. After I introduced myself, her eyes warmed, and she told me how much she appreciated Pierce—his manners, his maturity, but mostly, how kind he'd been to her son. She got teary-eyed as she explained that Pierce had welcomed her son into the friend group and included him in activities after they'd moved from a neighboring city.

Of course, as a mom, I was very proud to hear Pierce was being kind to a newcomer, though I was surprised at how emotional the mom had been. I made a point of passing along the compliment to Pierce and asked him if something would account for the mom's depth of feeling. It turns out that the young man had had some issues at his former school. Moving to a new high school sophomore year and joining a new, closely knit friend group were extra tough.

Now, I was doubly proud that Pierce gave his buddy warm encouragement. I've taught Pierce to be welcoming and inclusive, especially with outsiders and outliers. Jesus not only warmly greeted the reviled and rejected Zacchaeus but also invited Himself over for dinner. Jesus embraces the newcomer, the outcast, and all of us with open arms. —ISABELLA CAMPOLATTARO

FAITH STEP: *Next time you're at church or a social gathering, seek someone who looks left out and welcome them with enthusiasm.*

THURSDAY, NOVEMBER 5

In all my prayers for all of you, I always pray with joy because of your partnership in the gospel from the first day until now, being confident of this, that he who began a good work in you will carry it on to completion until the day of Christ Jesus. Philippians 1:4–6 (NIV)

ONE OF THE GREATEST CHALLENGES of being a homeschooling mom is the constant worry that you're not doing enough. Over the years, I often didn't finish the entire curriculum, and while I excelled at teaching writing, math was a struggle. Despite these concerns, I felt a strong divine nudge to educate my children at home, trusting that if Jesus called me to this task, He wouldn't let me fail them.

This trust was rewarded beyond my expectations. Imagine my joy when my son Nathan became a published author a decade after graduating high school. Even more thrilling, we recently coauthored a historical fantasy novel together. During our collaboration, as Nathan and I delved into plot structures and researched World War II, I realized he was still learning.

Homeschooling may not have prepared Nathan for advanced college math, but it nurtured our relationship and allowed us the opportunity to become coauthors. More importantly, it gave Nathan a solid foundation in a career he is passionate about pursuing. Jesus's grace filled in the gaps of my homeschooling limitations. He didn't let me fail my children, nor did He fail me. —TRICIA GOYER

FAITH STEP: *Write a prayer for continued faith and trust in a situation you feel inadequate. Put it in a place you can discover it in the future to see how Jesus didn't fail you.*

Friday, November 6

This is all that I have learned: God made us plain and simple, but we have made ourselves very complicated. Ecclesiastes 7:29 (GNT)

"Rats," I groaned, when I discovered I had only one egg when I needed two for the banana bread I was baking for a sick friend. I was delighted when my husband, Jeff, on his way out the door to work, offered to grab some eggs to save me a trip.

"Great!" I said. "You can get either brown or white, but buy large, not jumbo or medium. Lift each egg to be sure it's not cracked at the bottom. Check the use-by date at the end of the carton, and pick the one that's farthest away. Oh, and if they don't have eggs at Dollar General, you'll need to go to Market Basket." Jeff didn't say a word, but the look on his face communicated volumes. An hour later when he returned with the eggs, something told me it might be a while before he volunteered to shop for me again.

I'll bet Jesus wouldn't have squeezed the bread for freshness or checked the use-by date on the olive oil. He lived a simple life and encouraged his followers to do the same. He cautioned against worrying about one's life, what to eat or drink or what to wear (Matthew 6:25). He warned against collecting material things (Matthew 6:19). He concentrated on doing the will of His Father (John 6:38). How much easier would life be if we lived simply, like Jesus? —Pat Butler Dyson

Faith Step: *Make a list of three things you could do to simplify your life. Then do them!*

SATURDAY, NOVEMBER 7

"While he was still a long way off, his father saw him and was filled with compassion for him; he ran to his son, threw his arms around him and kissed him." Luke 15:20 (NIV)

I WAS ON A SKI bus taking me to the outlying parking lot at the end of a ski day. I noticed a boy, maybe twelve years old, with Down syndrome, looking intently out the window. At each stop, more people departed until we reached the final stop where I had parked. The only other person on the bus was this boy. I knew he must have been separated from his family. I asked him if he was lost, and he said he was. He explained he was trying to find his car because his dad would be there. I asked him if he knew his dad's phone number, and, thankfully, he did.

I called his dad and told him I was with his son in the parking lot and would stay with him until he could get there and pick him up. Then I handed my phone to the boy, and he proudly told his father how he had ridden the bus by himself. When his father arrived, he jumped out of his car and hugged his son, lifting him into the air.

Seeing their joy at being reunited reinforced how much our heavenly Father loves us. Even if we wander off the path a bit, when we turn back to Him, He doesn't scold us but instead hugs us tightly.
—JEANNIE BLACKMER

FAITH STEP: *Are you headed in the wrong direction in an area of your life? Call a trusted friend today, and tell them about it. Be assured Jesus will welcome you with open arms.*

SUNDAY, NOVEMBER 8

He shall be to you a restorer of life and a nourisher of your old age.
Ruth 4:15 (ESV)

MOST LIKELY I'M PAST THE halfway mark of my life on earth. Never thought I'd write that. Aging is for everyone else, right? At least it seemed that way when I was younger than, well, this age I am now. Approaching midlife and being a woman of a certain age, I see the way my body has shifted and changed. I can't help but wonder if my best days are behind me.

Ruth's first mother-in-law, Naomi, thought her best days were behind her, too, and grieved deeply. But a grandson, who was not of her blood but was a direct ancestor in the bloodline of Jesus, restored her. Jesus's ancestor, tiny baby Obed, proclaimed a new truth through his wrinkled, squinty-eyed newborn arrival: The best days of Naomi's past would be bested by the days of her menopausal old age. Hallelujah, amen to that!

As I'm studying up on the age-old, time-of-life changes we women face, this verse takes on a fresh level of meaning. Like Naomi, some dreams of mine have worked out, and others have shifted for Jesus's better plans. And through it all, I'm reminded to look for His face and listen to His voice saying the best is yet to come. Jesus gives me nourishment and refreshment for each day, including this one.

The best is yet to come. That is eternal heavenly truth for Jesus's followers. Naomi's and baby Obed's lives testified to it, and yours and mine will too. —ERIN KEELEY MARSHALL

FAITH STEP: *Using a dry-erase marker, write this on your bathroom mirror: "The best is yet to come." As you gaze at your reflection, ask Jesus to reflect His eternal truth. Keep the words there until you believe them.*

Monday, November 9

People brought little children to Jesus for him to place his hands on them and pray for them. But the disciples rebuked them. Jesus said, "Let the little children come to me, and do not hinder them, for the kingdom of heaven belongs to such as these." Matthew 19:13–14 (NIV)

"I'm wearing blue for kindness," Sadie said. "It's Kindness Week." My eight-year-old granddaughter calls me every morning on the drive to school. Her sweet voice begins my day with a bright blessing.

"Tell me about Kindness Week," I said. "That sounds like something I'd love."

"Today is Manners Monday. We're supposed to say 'please' and 'excuse me' a lot. Tomorrow is Thank You Tuesday. I'm going to write notes for the janitors and the lunchroom ladies." Sadie told me all the details of What Can I Do to Help Wednesday, Thoughtful Thursday, and Family Friday.

I'm happy Sadie is learning about kindness at school, but the best example of kindness is Jesus. When a group of men were ready to stone an adulterous woman, Jesus spoke gently to her and forgave her (John 8:3–11). He offered the criminal on the cross beside Him love and the hope of heaven (Luke 23:39–43). And though His disciples tried to stop some little children from approaching Him, Jesus welcomed them with open arms (Matthew 19:13–15).

Sadie's enthusiasm for goodwill is contagious. I may be a grandmother, but I think I'll participate in Kindness Week too. Will you?
—Becky Alexander

Faith Step: *Follow Sadie and her school's lead to celebrate Kindness Week. If possible, wear the color blue.*

TUESDAY, NOVEMBER 10

The LORD is close to the brokenhearted and saves those who are crushed in spirit. Psalm 34:18 (NIV)

ALL THREE OF MY BOYS have broken their front two teeth. Gideon fell off his bike when he was eight and chipped a small corner off both teeth, right in the middle. Solomon was running on the basketball court in elementary school and tripped. His breaks were more prominent and created a triangular void in his smile. In high school, Canaan and a friend were roughhousing at a church retreat when he collided with a plastic baseball bat and ended up with a busted lip and a snaggletoothed smile.

In each case, my heart dropped into the pit of my stomach when I heard the news, and I wasn't always successful in holding back my tears. Logically, I knew the injuries were easily fixable—teeth can be repaired in a single dentist visit and often end up looking better than before. But emotionally, the injuries were too much for my heart to handle. The losses, as minor as they were, left me feeling disappointed and crushed in spirit.

Each time, I felt silly for being sad over such superficial problems when I knew others have much bigger setbacks to navigate. But every time I prayed about my feelings, I felt the nearness of Jesus. He holds me close when I am brokenhearted, but He also holds me close when I am simply sad and melancholy from processing minor disappointments. Now, when my boys smile with their like-new smiles, I smile too, remembering that Jesus cares. —EMILY E. RYAN

FAITH STEP: *Talk to Jesus about the disappointments you are feeling. Listen and wait for Him to lift your spirits as you feel Him near.*

Veterans Day, Wednesday, November 11

Remember the days of old; consider the generations long past. Ask your father and he will tell you, your elders, and they will explain to you. Deuteronomy 32:7 (NIV)

My principal and I discussed the inability to teach civics and history to our elementary students due to testing demands. Students' reading, writing, and math proficiency often crowded out social studies lessons. Currently, I serve as the school counselor, but as a former US history teacher, this frustrated me.

As we brainstormed ways to incorporate civics awareness into our school year, I mentioned how I used to host veterans in my school classroom on Veterans Day. The experiences seemed sacred not only to a history buff like me but also to my students.

"One year, we had a woman fighter pilot who served during World War II," I said, admitting it was a role I didn't know existed, even though I had a history degree. I recounted how a Vietnam veteran told students about each Purple Heart he received, describing one combat story that left several of us in tears. Another year, a nurse who served in Europe during World War II shared about being in the Battle of the Bulge and working alongside General Dwight D. Eisenhower.

My principal liked and acted on the idea. On Veterans Day, many veterans visited our elementary classrooms and ate lunch with the students. It was delightful watching young children and veterans interact and learn from one another—life lessons that were just as powerful, if not more so, than the required academic assessments.
—Brenda L. Yoder

Faith Step: *If you're a veteran, volunteer to speak to local schools about your experiences. If you know a veteran, ask them about their service. You'll be surprised by the reciprocal blessing.*

THURSDAY, NOVEMBER 12

Jesus Christ is the same yesterday and today and forever. Hebrews 13:8 (NIV)

I AM FIFTY-TWO YEARS OLD, and most days I wonder where the time has gone. I have a daughter who just yesterday, it seems, learned how to read her first words, and now she is graduating from law school. My son, who used to stand on my shoulders to look for lizards under our shutters, now stands much taller than I and is engaged. Another daughter, who still should be pushing our cat around the house in a doll stroller, now drives her own car to school. And then the baby of our family is in the sixth grade.

I never planned for my kids to get older. I dreamed of becoming a mother, doting on my babies, and nurturing them through childhood. I no more prepared myself for their growing up and leaving the nest than I imagined my parents aging and slowing down, or myself with crow's feet. Life just happens. People change, the world changes, and there is not one thing I can do to stop it.

Even so, I'm comforted that in every season I can count on Jesus to remain the same. He is there, steady and secure, never wavering in His love for me. Though I may be blindsided by unexpected changes, nothing ever takes Jesus by surprise. He is always prepared for whatever I face. Though everything around me changes, Jesus does not. —GWEN FORD FAULKENBERRY

FAITH STEP: *Ponder how your life has changed through the years. Thank Jesus that you can count on Him never to change.*

Friday, November 13

We have thought, O God, on Your lovingkindness, in the midst of Your temple. Psalm 48:9 (NKJV)

I'D HAD A FULL SCHOOL day of helping elementary students with various emotional and behavioral issues. Several administrative and programming tasks still needed to be done, including creating a paper quilt displaying acts of kindness written by second graders for Random Acts of Kindness Week. Ugh! The students had gone home, and I wanted to do the same.

I trudged to the teachers' workroom and dug out a sheet of blue poster paper. Laying it on a table, I arranged and taped more than one hundred three-inch squares containing the students' handwriting and drawings. My tired mind focused on each colorful square. One drawing was of a stick figure helping another one. Another square had a sentence saying, "Kindness is getting a toy for my brother." Another child wrote about inviting a new student to sit with her at lunch.

As the squares came together, gratitude energized my tired body. I thanked Jesus for my job as the school counselor and for the opportunity to teach students about kindness. What a blessing to witness how they were learning how to be kind.

A task I thought I was too tired to do gave me a perspective I didn't know I needed. Late that afternoon, I was the one who received the lesson by piecing together a beautiful quilt of kindness, thanks to a bunch of second graders and Jesus. —BRENDA L. YODER

FAITH STEP: *No matter how busy you are, take a moment to thank Jesus for His kindness to you. Ask Him to inspire you to share kindness with someone this week. Perhaps sketch a paper quilt or another creative display of your kind acts.*

SATURDAY, NOVEMBER 14

"You have left the love you had in the beginning. So remember where you were before you fell. Change your hearts and do what you did at first."
Revelation 2:4–5 (NCV)

GO BACK TO THE ACTIVITIES *you did when you started dating. Revisit the same places. Listen to music from that time period.* I often see this advice given to couples seeking help. After years of marriage, it's easy to slip gradually into a rut, going through the motions of our daily routine while taking each other for granted. Demands of work, family, and other responsibilities can make us forget those days when our love was new, exciting, and openly expressed—with spouses and Jesus.

The Apostle John wrote to a church in Ephesus whose members had fallen into this pattern (Revelation 2:1–6). He commended them for holding on to correct doctrine, guarding against false teachers, and working diligently to serve the community. But he noted that their love for Jesus and for each other had cooled. The church members were doing the right things, but love was no longer their primary motivation.

I decided to take some steps of my own. I reread Romans 10:9, the verse that made the familiar gospel message apply to me personally. I meditated on Psalm 42:5, the first verse I memorized after accepting Jesus. I listened to music played on the radio at that time and sang a hymn I'd learned in the church where I opened my heart to Him. And I remembered anew why Jesus will always be my first love. —DIANNE NEAL MATTHEWS

FAITH STEP: *Spend some time remembering when your relationship with Jesus was new. Jot down ideas to renew your love and gratitude that He chose you to be His.*

Sunday, November 15

Having risen a long while before daylight, [Jesus] went out and departed to a solitary place; and there He prayed. Mark 1:35 (NKJV)

As I watch my daughter in her first year of motherhood, I kind of wish for a do-over. Kelli has so much information available to her that I didn't have as a new mom nearly thirty years ago. I admire the choices she makes about the products she uses and the food she feeds her little one, some of which are different from the choices I made.

But when I watch Kelli juggle motherhood, the last thing I desire is to live that season over. While her husband runs their business, Kelli runs the household. She wakes up early with the baby, makes doctor and vet appointments, orders the Walmart pickup, gets the oil changed in her car, and the list goes on. Observing her life exhausts me. How does she do it? How did I do it? Oh, to have that energy again!

When my daughters were toddlers, I asked my husband for a weekend of solitude. I was ridden with guilt over being so exhausted. Time alone seemed like a selfish luxury.

But even Jesus needed solitude. He often disappeared from the crowds and those closest to Him. Solitude gave Him space to pray to the Father. Solitude restored Him so He could continue meeting the demands of everyone who needed something from him (Luke 5:15–16). He chose His twelve disciples after a night of solitude on the mountain (Luke 6:12–13). Yet Jesus never apologized or expressed guilt because he needed time alone.

I can't have a do-over, but I can offer my daughter the gift of solitude so she can connect with Jesus and refuel. After all, what are grandmas for? —Karen Sargent

Faith Step: *Offer to babysit to give a busy mom a break.*

Monday, November 16

Let no one deceive you with empty words, for because of such things God's wrath comes on those who are disobedient. Ephesians 5:6 (NIV)

A LARGE PART OF MY workday is spent evaluating words for other writers. How does this sentence communicate what the author intends? What about this paragraph makes it feel repetitive? Does this chapter move the story forward, or is it wasted space?

I'm on the lookout for empty words. If unnecessary, if they accomplish nothing or mislead, they get deleted. In the absence of hollowness, the work and message are stronger.

Jesus was concerned, too, about unnecessary or empty words. One of His followers, Paul, wrote to the church at Ephesus, cautioning them against the deception of empty words. That might have meant false claims, spiritual trickery, flattery, words that sound good but like an empty eggshell prove to be hollow, lifeless.

Where is that concept a danger in my life? Like empty calories, empty words take up space that could have been filled with something nutritious for body, mind, or spirit. I may not be listening to a false teacher's deceptive words, but am I chewing on empty thoughts of no value? Am I letting my mind wander to space-fillers, time-fillers, rather than soul-fillers?

I can listen to chatter online or delete that and turn to the always precise, always rich, always meaningful, always life-giving words of Jesus. —CYNTHIA RUCHTI

FAITH STEP: *Pay attention to the words you speak today. Are you effectively communicating in a manner that glorifies Jesus? If not, edit yourself.*

Tuesday, November 17

God said, "Let there be light," and there was light. God saw that the light was good, and he separated the light from the darkness. God called the light "day," and the darkness he called "night." Genesis 1:3–5 (NIV)

My kids and friends often tease me about my fondness for type A organizational strategies. I have bins in the fridge with food categories noted in permanent marker. I have baskets in my office credenza with pens, pencils, markers, scissors, ink cartridges, tape, and glue neatly sorted. I have shoeboxes with greeting cards sorted by handmade dividers noting every occasion. The clothes in my closet and bedroom dresser are color-coded. My motto is this: A place for everything and everything in its place.

Other people can laugh and tease all they want. When they want or need something at my house, they know just where to look! I'm vindicated. After all, Jesus, Word with God from the very beginning (John 1:1), created a supremely ordered world.

Genesis details how light, darkness, water, sky, and land were all thoughtfully separated to produce the well-ordered world we enjoy today. Likewise, vegetation, plants, and trees were all distinguished "according to their various kinds" (Genesis 1:11, NIV). Finally, man was set apart from a vast assortment of other living creatures and then was thoughtfully provided a separate companion woman (Genesis 1:27).

Our divinely tidy world continues to dazzle us. Every day, scientists discover more evidence of the incredibly intricate organization of creation—a place for everything and everything in its place!
—Isabella Campolattaro

Faith Step: *Is there something in your home that is begging to be organized? Read Genesis 1 as inspiration, and hop to it!*

WEDNESDAY, NOVEMBER 18

We must continue to hold firmly to our declaration of faith. The one who made the promise is faithful. Hebrews 10:23 (GW)

A POSTER OF A KITTEN dangling from a tree branch, holding on for dear life with the encouraging caption "Hang in There!" was popular during my childhood. Today, something outside my office window calls to mind that sentiment. A lone dry brown leaf dangles, twisting and turning, hanging on by a thread, from a branch of a giant oak tree. Mesmerized by its tenacity, I can't tear my gaze away. How is it possible that against all odds, a single leaf has held steadfast through all the gusty, blustery winds, rains, and snowstorms of fall and winter?

Some people have faith like that. People enduring tragic loss or facing catastrophic medical diagnoses, still praising God. People in seemingly hopeless situations, steadfastly believing that God is in control. I want that kind of faith. I want to be a believer who hangs in there, never gives up, clutches on for dear life as I hold firmly to my faith in the One who never lets me go, no matter what. Scripture is full of real-life accounts of people who never gave up in their pursuit of Jesus and His miraculous healing power. And I'm so thankful Jesus never gives up on me. —CASSANDRA TIERSMA

FAITH STEP: *Go outside and pull a dried leaf off a branch. Spend a moment with Jesus, thanking Him for holding on to you through all the seasons of life. Bring the leaf inside and let it remind you to hang in there with Him.*

Thursday, November 19

"Call upon Me in the day of trouble; I will deliver you, and you shall glorify Me." Psalm 50:15 (NKJV)

There he was, that vicious yellow dog that had bitten me 3 years ago, running up and down inside his fence, snarling and barking. At the time he bit me, his owner had said she would do something about him. I was hoping for banishment to Siberia, but her solution had been to keep him inside the fence. After my bite had healed, I resumed my route on *his* street, secure that he was contained. I may have called him a wretched cur and wished him a flea infestation.

Recently, as I walked down the left side of the street, Old Yeller snarled and ran the fence as was his habit. When I made the turn and began walking down the right side of the street, I noticed he was strangely silent. As I got closer, I saw the reason. He was *outside* the fence, sitting on the driveway, smiling as he licked his chops, anticipating another bite of me.

Jesus, help! Fear seized my very soul as I begged for guidance on what to do. I was pretty sure I couldn't outrun him. I knew not to look in his eyes. Scared as I was, I felt Jesus's calming whisper, *Keep moving.* So I did. I maintained my usual vigorous pace, looking straight ahead and praying fervently. When I reached the corner, I glanced back and saw that he had moved but not much. Then I ran and didn't stop until I got to my street. And I thanked Jesus for His direction and protection. —Pat Butler Dyson

---

Faith Step: *In a dangerous situation, call out to Jesus. He will show you what to do.*

Friday, November 20

Blessed are those who find wisdom, those who gain understanding.
Proverbs 3:13 (NIV)

Each morning, I wake, greet Jesus, and do some basic warming stretches at my bedside before dressing. Then, I head to the kitchen for my morning tea. However, after another restless night of sleep, I opted to forgo my hot cuppa for a cold glass of orange juice instead. Drinking it at the sink, I was miserable. So much of my routine was changing to accommodate my aging female body. New diet. Mood swings. Unexpectedly warm moments at the worst times. It seemed like each day, a new symptom of menopause emerged.

Frustrated, I flopped down at the table as my phone rang. It was my sister, Kris. She was ecstatic from learning that her daughter was pregnant. Her first grandchild. Thrilled, I jumped from my seat and danced around the kitchen. Clicking off the quick call, I bowed my head in prayer. I thanked Jesus, asking Him to bless my niece and her baby.

Making peace amid raging hormones is difficult. Yet the very same body that keeps me up at night with insomnia or hot flashes nowadays is the one that transformed to bless me with two daughters almost twenty years ago. By giving our family a new baby, Jesus reminded me of how awesome it is to be a woman (Proverbs 31:10–31). Each miraculous change my body experiences holds a greater purpose. And while some of those changes are unpleasant, I know they are beautifully joyful too. Especially the little giggly ones. —Gloria Joyce

Faith Step: *Offer a prayer of thanksgiving today for all the pregnant mothers around the world. Praise Jesus for the gift they each carry within their womb.*

Saturday, November 21

We all, who with unveiled faces contemplate the Lord's glory, are being transformed into his image with ever-increasing glory, which comes from the Lord, who is the Spirit. 2 Corinthians 3:18 (NIV)

"Excuse me, are you Barbara Wallace?" I glanced up from washing my hands in the airport restroom and looked at the woman I'd never seen before. Although my name is very similar, it's not what the woman said. It turned out that I looked just like someone the lady knew but hadn't seen in a while. She apologized and said she couldn't believe how much I resembled her friend.

That seems to happen to me quite often. People have stopped me on the street or in restaurants to ask if I am related to someone they know. They tell me that I'm the spitting image of a family member or friend. I've even been told that I look like various celebrities and, more than once, a presidential cabinet member. I never can see the resemblance, but somehow strangers believe they can.

Although I may have doppelgängers roaming around, the only one I really want to look like is Jesus. I pray every day that He will make me a little more like Him—more patient, loving, kind, compassionate, selfless, obedient, and forgiving. He is changing me in His own time and way, but sometimes I wish He would speed up the process. However, I know transformation doesn't happen overnight. It comes little by little.

I hope one day somebody will stop me and say that I resemble Jesus. That will be the ultimate compliment. —Barbranda Lumpkins Walls

Faith Step: *Think about how you can look more like Jesus. Picture His face in your mind as you show His love and compassion to others today.*

Sunday, November 22

Just as a body, though one, has many parts, but all its many parts form one body, so it is with Christ.... Now you are the body of Christ, and each one of you is a part of it. 1 Corinthians 12:12, 27 (NIV)

OUR MINISTRY RECENTLY HOSTED AN evening to celebrate the work Christ is doing through our missionaries worldwide. Teamwork made the event an overwhelming success.

Our administrative assistant used her online purchasing skills to buy tablecloths, dishes, and decorations at bargain prices, and she applied her artsy skills to assemble centerpieces. Her labor created a welcoming atmosphere for our guests. Her brother and another fellow lent muscle to set up tables and chairs. One of my dear friends has worked as a caterer, so she volunteered to cook and serve a Mediterranean-style meal. She prepared kebabs, pita bread, couscous, and veggie dishes that impressed and satisfied the crowd. A member of our church donated his technical expertise to run the sound system and visual slides. My hubby and I organized the program and led the presentation.

How might the event have turned out if every team member could hoist tables and chairs but were clueless about microphones and PowerPoint? What if everyone cooked like a professional chef but lacked bargain-hunting prowess? What if everyone could decorate a room to resemble a magazine photo shoot but could neither organize nor deliver the program?

As individual members of Christ's body, each of us contributed a necessary and unique skill. We rejected any temptation to compete or compare, and we worked cooperatively to produce a lovely event that truly celebrated Jesus and His kingdom. —GRACE FOX

FAITH STEP: *Identify your God-given skills and three ways you can use them to build Christ's kingdom.*

Monday, November 23

Neither the one who plants nor the one who waters is anything, but only God, who makes things grow. 1 Corinthians 3:7 (NIV)

PART OF MY JOB AS an elementary school counselor is presenting class lessons on various topics. One lesson I teach is about how our words impact others. I taught the fourth-grade lesson through the lens of being a social media influencer, a person who endorses products and has the ability to sway opinions. "You can be a good or negative influence," I said.

Cooper raised his hand. "Why did you use the word *negative* instead of *bad*?" The question made me pause. Cooper came from a difficult home environment. His question was an invitation for an important seed to be planted in his life and that of his classmates. "I used the word *negative* because *bad* makes us think we are bad," I said. I told the kids that no one is bad—our actions or words may have negative consequences, but we are separate from what we do. Though we may do something hurtful, those actions aren't who we are.

I looked across the classroom of kids who may often be cursed at, dismissed, or told they are bad. I can't share the gospel in a public school, but I gave them God's truth in that moment, which I hoped went deep down into their soul. As I finished the lesson, I prayed that Jesus would grow that message in the children's minds and hearts—that I could be a Jesus influencer, teaching positive lessons that model Him while encouraging students. —BRENDA L. YODER

FAITH STEP: *Whom do you influence? Make a list of names, then pray for ways you can plant seeds that will grow Jesus's love in others.*

TUESDAY, NOVEMBER 24

Keep your lives free from the love of money and be content with what you have, because God has said, "Never will I leave you; never will I forsake you." Hebrews 13:5 (NIV)

As I survey the chaotic scene spread throughout the living room, I smile. Several boxes perch on the sofa, chairs, and across the floor. They're full of clothes, kitchen gadgets, books, and what-have-you. This collection of odds and ends represents things I thought I needed until I realized I didn't. It also represents something more important. I'm letting go.

This is an annual ritual in my household. Coming from a history of financial struggles, it's a pledge of trust. I have learned over the years that just when our money situation seems at its worst, Jesus steps in with some sort of relief. His power to solve the problems I've faced, even the ones I've deemed impossible, reassures me that I don't need to fret over my needs. As a tangible show of my faith, I often include something that perhaps I hold too dear, an item that distracts me from my goals or impedes my faith walk. My donation is tangible proof that I trust in Jesus's provision.

Seeing this excess in my living room makes it real. Not only do I have enough; I have too much. Jesus knows my needs, wants, and desires. I can place my trust in Him to provide. It's time to let go.
—Heidi Gaul

Faith Step: *Fill boxes for donation. Include one item that is a little hard to let go of, trusting Jesus to provide.*

WEDNESDAY, NOVEMBER 25

It is God who works in you to will and to act in order to fulfill his good purpose. Do everything without grumbling or arguing, so that you may become blameless and pure. . . . Then you will shine among them like stars in the sky. Philippians 2:13–15 (NIV)

RECENTLY, AS I'VE BEEN COMPLETING some real estate continuing education, I've had the mixed joy of driving on Indianapolis highways through road construction.

Let's be real. "Mixed joy" is gracious. Traffic and roadwork are no fun. However, I do like passing by the multistory business buildings on my commute. It may sound odd, but I see beauty in them, especially at dusk. It's as if the city planners and architects designed them with plenty of windows to create a mirrorlike palette for the sun to reflect.

As the sky glows with gorgeous sunsets, the buildings' facades turn into a Technicolor, museum-worthy display of reflected sunrays. It's unexpectedly gorgeous and even calming.

On a larger scale, I wonder how I reflect the "Son light" of Jesus when life heats up. Is the purity of Jesus's work in me such that I shine His light among my family, friends, and neighbors?

Granted, I'm not Him. I'm His follower but not perfect as He is. Yet He gives me power through His Spirit to become more like Him, even through difficult times. When His light shines on me like a mirror, what does He see? Do others see the light of His love reflected in me? —ERIN KEELEY MARSHALL

FAITH STEP: *Today on your commute, as you're driving, or as you look out your window, look for reflections of light. Each time you see one, ask Jesus to keep you aware of opportunities to let His light shine through you for someone else's benefit.*

Thanksgiving Day, Thursday, November 26

Give thanks to the LORD, for he is good; his love endures forever.
Psalm 107:1 (NIV)

WANTING TO BRUSH OFF THE cobwebs on my Spanish, I'm taking a night class at a local high school. After all, it's been thirty years since I lived in Guatemala and spoke the language. It's amazing how studying another language makes me more aware of the grammar and word construction of my own.

Years ago, when I was young, naïve, and in training for a mission trip to Guatemala, a discussion about giving thanks to Jesus came up. "Isn't it enough that Jesus knows I'm grateful when I stop and appreciate all He's given me?" I asked. The resounding answer from the group was NO! They explained that appreciating something is keeping the sentiment to myself. True gratitude completes the giving cycle by expressing the emotion back, full circle, to the giver.

That conversation and my renewed awareness of word construction from my Spanish class make me mindful of what today is really about. *Thanksgiving* is a compound word made up of two words: *thanks* and *giving*. If I just declare the blessings I'm grateful for to my family before we eat our turkey dinner, I'm not living out the full meaning of the word. I have to *give thanks* to the actual Giver. It isn't fate that blesses me with all I have, nor karma, nor serendipity. It is Jesus, the One True Giver, who deserves to hear my sincere gratitude today and every day, in all languages. —CLAIRE MCGARRY

FAITH STEP: *Before telling anyone else what you're grateful for today, take a quiet moment to give thanks to Jesus for all your blessings.*

Friday, November 27

The LORD is compassionate and gracious, slow to anger, abounding in love. Psalm 103:8 (NIV)

Parenting often seems most challenging during the baby and toddler years, yet launching young adults into the world presents unique trials. For instance, one of my daughters moved to Europe at twenty-one to work with a church, while her sister, at the same age, hasn't yet gotten her driver's license despite having a good job and her own apartment. She prefers spending her evenings at our home, even though she has her own place. As a mom who has launched six children so far, I've realized that my expectations for their achievements by certain ages were often unrealistic. It's more constructive to consider what's best for each child individually, rather than comparing, and support them toward their next steps in loving ways.

This approach mirrors my relationship with Jesus. I recognize that I need a lot of help in my spiritual walk and that there are many areas in which I need to mature. Fortunately, Jesus is infinitely kind and patient. He doesn't compare me to others (Galatians 6:4–5) or focus on my shortcomings (2 Corinthians 12:9). This realization has impacted how I parent my adult children, teaching me to guide them with the same patience and kindness Jesus shows me. The Lord's enduring patience and deep love are qualities that I as a parent, daughter, granddaughter, wife, and friend strive to embody. —Tricia Goyer

Faith Step: *Write a note to a family member to apologize for unrealistic expectations you have had. Pray for wisdom and grace to guide your actions and relationships, remembering Jesus's way of gentle, loving guidance can lead to greater peace and fulfillment.*

SATURDAY, NOVEMBER 28

Surely I have calmed and quieted my soul. Psalm 131:2 (NKJV)

A FIVE-HOUR LAYOVER IN AN airport may seem excessive, but it afforded me the opportunity to notice more than if I had been rushing to my next gate, hoping the plane was delayed just long enough for me to arrive before the door closed. The door closing was last week's experience. This week, I had time to linger and loiter, in a good way.

I stopped at a spinner rack of books and allowed myself the privilege of reading all the titles. Many were devotionals. Several were guides to a meaningful quiet time with Jesus.

But I misread one title. At first glance, I saw *Quieted Time* rather than *Quiet Time*. I wish someone would have written a book about that.

Isn't it a more accurate depiction of what the world most needs—quieted time? To get a quiet time alone with Jesus, we need to quiet the time we have. Cancel the noise. Hush the other voices calling us to watch the clock, the ones insisting we have responsibilities to attend to.

Today, I told the clamor to "Hush!" I had business of the utmost importance to attend to—sitting in the quiet with Jesus. At first, I was aware of the white noise, the furnace motor, clothes tumbling in the dryer, traffic on the road beyond the window. But soon, because I told my brain, "Quiet down," it did. It noticed nothing but the sweet, calm, presence of Jesus.

I had His attention. And He had mine. —CYNTHIA RUCHTI

FAITH STEP: *If you have trouble finding quieted time alone with Jesus, consider wearing noise-canceling headphones.*

First Sunday of Advent, November 29

In him was life, and that life was the light of all mankind. The light shines in the darkness, and the darkness has not overcome it. John 1:4–5 (NIV)

IN EARLY DECEMBER, OUR NEXT-DOOR neighbors put a display on their lawn with life-sized figures of Baby Jesus, Mary, and Joseph that glowed from within. I loved seeing the radiant scene each time we drove by. I could also see it from my bedroom window, shining in the darkness of the cold night.

When I walked into the bedroom to change my clothes after work or to go to sleep, I gazed at the trio. I smiled every time, a sense of hope blanketing my soul. My health issues, family worries, and world problems seemed smaller when I glimpsed those lights glowing in the darkness.

Around December 20, I noticed the light inside of the Joseph figure had gone out. "Uh-oh," I told my husband, Kevin. "Joseph lost his light." We laughed about that. A few days later, Mary's light disappeared. The only figure that remained radiant was Baby Jesus. I knew it was just an outdoor decoration, but a two-thirds dark nativity scene didn't seem very hopeful.

Then it dawned on me. *Of course! God wants me to focus on Jesus alone. In Him is my hope. He is the reason for Christmas.* Everything else dims in comparison to Him because Jesus is the Light of the world. —JEANETTE LEVELLIE

FAITH STEP: *Take a flashlight into a dark room or closet. Switch it on and note how it illuminates everything around it. Thank Jesus for being the Light of the world and the Light of your life.*

Monday, November 30

Taking the five loaves and the two fish and looking up to heaven, he gave thanks and broke the loaves. Then he gave them to the disciples, and the disciples gave them to the people. . . . The number of those who ate was about five thousand men, besides women and children. Matthew 14:19, 21 (NIV)

I STOPPED ON THE SIDEWALK to read a large sign in the restaurant window. "For those who must go through the garbage to find food, please don't do that. You are human beings and deserve love and respect. Come inside, and we will be happy to give you a bite to eat. No questions asked."

Hyman's Seafood was already one of my favorite lunch spots in Charleston. I took tour groups there often for boiled peanuts, fried green tomatoes over grits, sweet potato soufflé, and the catch of the day. Eli Hyman, the fourth-generation owner, greeted us with a smile and a personal story about his family's business. Everyone enjoyed the Southern atmosphere and some of the best seafood in the city.

But now, reading the sign through teary eyes, I raised Hyman's to the top of my favorites list. The owners were using their skills and resources to feed the hungry. I considered my own assets, though I'm not in the food industry. I felt challenged to find a way to help because compassion for hungry people mirrors the compassion of my Savior.

Next week, I'll be in Charleston again. I'll walk my tour group to Hyman's Seafood for lunch, being sure to point out the extra-special message in the window. —BECKY ALEXANDER

FAITH STEP: *Jesus fed hungry people with fish too. Read about it in Matthew 14:13–21. Consider the examples set by Jesus and by Hyman's. How can you help to alleviate hunger?*

Tuesday, December 1

News of this reached the church in Jerusalem, and they sent Barnabas to Antioch. When he arrived and saw what the grace of God had done, he was glad and encouraged them all to remain true to the Lord with all their hearts. Acts 11:22–23 (NIV)

I CALL MY FRIEND SARAH my little Barnabas, which means "son of encouragement." Sarah and I had known each other for years, but during the pandemic and the upheaval following my divorce, we became much closer. Sarah was—and is—my rock.

I took a difficult, long-term substitute teaching position at a public high school, my first full-time job in twenty-five years. Soon after the assignment ended, I accepted a thorny part-time job while juggling several spiritually demanding writing projects. I became burned out and heavy-burdened, sinking into a deep place of discouragement that no amount of prayer and fasting penetrated. Sarah was there for me.

Sarah listened patiently to my exhausted rants about my toxic workplace. She was a devoted prayer partner and diligently shared my requests with her Friday night prayer group. She was usually the first to read, like, and share my *Mornings with Jesus* devotionals and other writings online. She sent me Bible verse memes, encouraging notes, and little gifts to lift my spirits. She pointed me to Jesus when I struggled to look up and see Him.

Perpetuating the spirit of loving service Jesus embodied and taught, Barnabas was a great help to Paul and a dedicated supporter of the beleaguered early believers. I want to be more like Barnabas and my friend Sarah, providing the valuable gift of encouragement to others. —ISABELLA CAMPOLATTARO

FAITH STEP: *Think of someone for whom you can be a Barnabas or Sarah today. Ask Jesus how you may be an encouragement.*

Wednesday, December 2

"Let your 'Yes' be 'Yes,' and your 'No,' 'No.' For whatever is more than these is from the evil one." Matthew 5:37 (NKJV)

I WAS MAKING INTERIOR DESIGN decisions for our new house. Our son Josh is an avid elk hunter and suggested an elk head above the fireplace. I emphatically said, "No!" In the past, saying no was difficult for me. Saying yes was a method for me to avoid the discomfort of disappointing others.

Jesus said, "Let your 'Yes' be 'Yes,' and your 'No,' 'No.'" I know He wasn't talking about decorating decisions but rather being a person of integrity and true to your word. Jesus, in His Sermon on the Mount, encourages believers to be honest and be people who mean what we say and do what we say. Over time, I've learned to say no more often, but I still find it uncomfortable. For example, a friend asked if I would help her host a bridal shower. I almost said yes, but in my spirit, I felt panicked by adding another commitment to my already overwhelmed schedule. I paused and said no. She expressed disappointment, but I felt relief.

I'm better at saying yes to some things and no to others. I also understand Jesus's desire for honesty and keeping my word. So, although I support Josh's hunting hobby, I knew if I agreed with his suggestion, I would have to do it. And honestly, the last thing I wanted over my fireplace was an elk head. I have no regrets for saying no to that request. —JEANNIE BLACKMER

FAITH STEP: *On an index card, write about a recent time you said yes but wished you had said no. Place it in your Bible near Jesus's Sermon on the Mount as a reminder it's OK to say no sometimes.*

Thursday, December 3

Have mercy on me, Lord, for I am faint; heal me, Lord, for my bones are in agony. Psalm 6:2 (NIV)

SITTING BY MOM'S BED IN the rehab center, I never felt farther away from her. I thought about the difficult cycle of the past five months while she slept. Fall. Rehab. Repeat. I knew this time would be no different. As soon as Mom was discharged, she'd stop exercising, and she'd be here again.

Mom and I share similar family traits and are physically so much alike. Prone to inactivity, we were both diagnosed with osteoarthritis in both knees by midlife. Over the years, Mom's pain and fear of falling made her more sedentary. But my fear of immobility recently prompted me to add exercise to my daily routine. At fifty-two, my body was finally coming to life as Mom was becoming increasingly trapped within hers. I attempted positive reinforcement, attended her therapy sessions, and even shared my new habits. But nothing worked. I feared her next fall might make her bedridden permanently.

Dropping my head, I prayed, "Lord, how do I reach her?" The sunlight glinted off the crucifix dangling from my bracelet, and Psalm 6:2 came to mind. It was one I repeated many times in the beginning of my difficult journey back to health.

My mother has a long road ahead, but with Jesus's help and mercy, I trust that the ability to change is also one of our family traits. If I did it, so can she. —GLORIA JOYCE

FAITH STEP: *Are you struggling to make a change in your life? Memorize Psalm 6:2, and repeat it often. Ask a friend or family member to pray it for you.*

Friday, December 4

Then, because so many people were coming and going that they did not even have a chance to eat, he said to them, "Come with me by yourselves to a quiet place and get some rest." Mark 6:31 (NIV)

I WENT TO MY FIRST Christmas cookie swap at the home of my friend Katy and was blown away by all the holiday treats brought by the guests. Every cookie imaginable filled the tables and sideboards—chocolate chip, snickerdoodles, oatmeal raisin, Mexican wedding cookies, rugelach, red velvet, and more. But what really caught my attention was the decoration hanging over Katy's laden dining room table.

I marveled at the dozens of little elf dolls wrapped around the chandelier. Some were hanging upside down, while others were precariously dangling from other elves. The whole scene made me smile but at the same time represented how I was feeling—hanging on by a thread. I felt burdened by holiday shopping, shipping gifts to family and friends, preparing for cross-country travel to spend Christmas with our children, and looming deadlines to meet before we left.

As I stood there pondering the helter-skelter elves, the thought came to me that I needed to take a deep breath, pray for strength, and stop worrying whether various tasks that I deemed important were completed. What was important was to slow down and be grateful for the blessings of the season. Jesus doesn't require me to run around imitating a busy little elf. Instead, He would rather I find a quiet place to rest and spend time with Him. Being with Jesus is a sweet treat, indeed! —BARBRANDA LUMPKINS WALLS

FAITH STEP: *Take a break from the holiday hoopla. Grab a cookie and sit quietly with Jesus. Thank Him for the blessings of this season.*

SATURDAY, DECEMBER 5

[Mary] brought forth her firstborn Son, and wrapped Him in swaddling cloths, and laid Him in a manger, because there was no room for them in the inn. Luke 2:7 (NKJV)

GIANT ILLUMINATED SNOWFLAKES HANG FROM each streetlight. The holiday window-dressing contest held by downtown shopkeepers has selected a winner. The Twice-Around-Town parade, complete with Santa, has circled past cheering crowds the designated two times. The Christmas tree has been lit in the square, and we've sung carols at its base. Christmastime hoopla is in full swing.

But tonight, I'm walking my quiet lane, seeking a deeper meaning to this season. In the chill air, I hear laughter and glance at a neighbor's window to see their young boys decorating the living room, kid-style. I notice a dad in his front yard, holding a wilted inflatable snowman's hand, his toddler clutching a flashlight. I smell the scents of the season, both sweet and savory, emanating from one home after another.

When I reach my front door, I'm still searching. On my stroll, I sensed joy and love, and my heart was warmed. But it's something else I'm hunting for. I head to the rocker and pick up my Bible. I open it and read. The mystery and wonder of the birth of Jesus is revealed to me, the incredible miracle only God could perform. I glimpse the profound love and wisdom of the Creator sending His Son into our world. And I am awash in the peace that comes from knowing both the Father and the Son are family.

I close my eyes in prayer. I can stop searching. I am filled.
—HEIDI GAUL

FAITH STEP: *Set aside time this season to find a quiet place and read the story of Jesus's birth in Luke 2:1–20. Rejoice!*

Second Sunday of Advent, December 6

"I am the Lord's servant," Mary answered. "May your word to me be fulfilled." Luke 1:38 (NIV)

I HAVE A LAVENDER WEEKLY planner on my desk at my day job. And another planner on my dining table with watercolors of flowers and birds by my favorite nature artist, Marjolein Bastin. Planning makes me feel secure and at peace. In control.

Which is the opposite attitude that Jesus's mother displayed when the angel Gabriel appeared to her. Gabriel told Mary that God had chosen her to birth the Son of the Most High.

Although Mary was devout and dedicated to God, I have a feeling she didn't plan to become Jesus's mom. She didn't reply to Gabriel's message, "Give me a minute while I look at my weekly planner" or "Whoa there! I can't instantly change my life's plans and have a baby. I'm engaged to marry Joseph." Mary simply said yes.

Oh, to have the soft, obedient heart of Mary. When the Holy Spirit nudges me to speak up and share Jesus's love with someone or to shut up when I feel like losing my temper, I would love to respond by simply doing what is asked of me.

The times I've abandoned my desire to be in charge and obeyed as Mary did, I've sensed Jesus's hand on my shoulder. It didn't matter that I wasn't in charge. No consulting my planner. No second-guessing the Most High. No arguments. Just yes.
—JEANETTE LEVELLIE

FAITH STEP: *Read Luke 1:26–38 and ponder Mary's quick obedience. Ask Jesus to give you the same kind of willing heart that His mother had. The next time He asks, simply say yes.*

Monday, December 7

He stood up to read, and the scroll of the prophet Isaiah was handed to him. Unrolling it, he found the place where it is written: "The Spirit of the Lord is on me. . . ." Luke 4:16–18 (NIV)

THE FIRST BIBLE MEGAN GAVE me was lavender with deep purple vines imprinted on the leather cover. Its colors matched the bridesmaids' dresses in her wedding. An inscription inside read, "I am so proud to have you as our officiant. You have always played a special part in my life, and I know you will in my future also." During Megan's marriage ceremony, I opened the pretty Bible and shared scriptures about love, patience, kindness, and commitment.

Ten years later, Megan brought me a box wrapped in floral paper. "I've been working on this for a while," she said. "I hope you like it."

The box contained the most beautiful Bible I'd ever seen. Megan had coated the linen cover with a turquoise base. She hand-painted a border of golden sunflowers, white daisies, pink roses, and orange lilies around the words *The Holy Bible*. She even brushed my name onto the spine.

Megan chose the two unique presents because of my love for the words of Jesus. Within the lavender leather, I found a message of inspiration to offer her and her new husband at their wedding. And now on the pages beneath the garden of flowers, I meet with Jesus each morning, soaking in the encouragement and direction I need for another day.

God's Word is such a special gift—no matter how it is packaged.
—BECKY ALEXANDER

FAITH STEP: *Read the powerful message of Luke 4:16–18 in your favorite Bible. Draw a flower on the edge of the page.*

Tuesday, December 8

We know also that the Son of God has come and has given us understanding, so that we may know him who is true. And we are in him who is true by being in his Son Jesus Christ. He is the true God and eternal life. 1 John 5:20 (NIV)

I've always wanted to write a book called *Falling Apart at the Seems*, intentionally altering the spelling and meaning of seams that bind garments together. As I improved my sewing skills years ago, I learned the importance of strong seams. No garment is worth much if it falls apart at the seams.

My life suffers if I fall apart at all the *seems* I encounter. This task seems impossible. This crisis seems like the worst that could happen. That relationship seems to be in serious trouble. It seems as if no one appreciates my efforts. I'd make that attitude adjustment, but it seems beyond me.

Life itself can unravel at all those seems.

I can't afford to lean on the "appears to" or "feels like" or "seems as if" emotions when they present themselves. No matter how certain they look, they're illusions. What I can count on is the One who is true (John 1:9). No *seems* to unravel. He is. And always will be. Jesus never changes (Hebrews 13:8). In the most beautiful sense, what we see is what we get. What He said is who He is, now and forever. He is the True One who holds my seams together and banishes seems with truth. —Cynthia Ruchti

Faith Step: *Notice a solid seam on a favorite garment, and let it remind you of the difference between how things seem and the Jesus reality in your life.*

WEDNESDAY, DECEMBER 9

Every good and perfect gift is from above, coming down from the Father of the heavenly lights, who does not change like shifting shadows. James 1:17 (NIV)

CHRISTMAS STOCKINGS ARE ONE OF my favorite traditions. Our sons, Jack, Will, and Addison, have blue, green, and white knit stockings. My husband, Scott, has a plaid one. Mine has multicolored pompons. I also added a new stocking this year for our soon-to-be daughter-in-law, Emmalyn. Getting to fill her tasseled stocking was an added delight.

I love picking out little treats for my people. I spent hours wandering store aisles trying to find different gifts that would bring them joy. This Christmas, I added a new tradition of getting each person a small board game. Scott fills my stocking. He knows that he can always thrill me with dark chocolate and gardening magazines.

Christmas stockings may seem like the least important part of the holiday, but as a gift giver, I enjoy filling them as a way to shower my family with even more goodness. I want them to know that I am tuned in to their wants and needs. I hope each little gift shows them how much I love and care for them.

Jesus is the best gift giver of all. He is constantly looking for ways to meet my wants and needs (Philippians 4:19). He knows every detail of my life and showers me with His blessings (Numbers 6:24–26). Each provision, each moment of grace, each act of goodness lets me know how much He loves and cares for me. —SUSANNA FOTH AUGHTMON

FAITH STEP: *Write down ways Jesus has met your needs and has delighted you, then put the page in your stocking. On Christmas morning, take it out and thank Him for His good and perfect gifts.*

Thursday, December 10

A friendly smile makes you happy, and good news makes you feel strong. Proverbs 15:30 (CEV)

While driving last week, I heard a song on the oldies station that really took me back: "Make Me Smile" by Chicago, a favorite band from my college years. I started thinking about all the people who make me smile and why: beloved family members, close friends, acquaintances who have a warm personality or delightful sense of humor. Suddenly, I realized that the One who makes me smile the most is Jesus for a multitude of reasons.

That evening, I decided to do a little research on what behavioral psychologists say about smiling. Studies show that this simple act can elevate our mood, relieve stress, reduce pain, lower blood pressure, and maybe even increase our life span. A 2010 study of baseball players found that those who smiled in their photos on baseball cards lived an average of seven years longer. Believe it or not, some researchers say that smiling creates more joy in our brain than consuming chocolate does.

In light of these potential physical and mental benefits, I have even more reason to keep my thoughts focused on Jesus. When I read in the Bible about the miracles He performed or the way He treated hurting people so tenderly, I smile. As I reflect on His faithfulness and mercy to me in the past and His promises for my future, I smile, although sometimes with tears of gratitude in my eyes. Thinking about my Savior makes me feel closer to Him, plus it improves my health. And that's something to smile about.
—Dianne Neal Matthews

Faith Step: *On a sticky note, write all the ways Jesus makes you smile and place it on a mirror. Then offer Him your prettiest smile.*

FRIDAY, DECEMBER 11

Whether you turn to the right or to the left, your ears will hear a voice behind you, saying, "This is the way; walk in it." Isaiah 30:21 (NIV)

RECENTLY, I WAS ASKED TO speak to a group of young writers. With my husband, three minor children, and my grandmother at home to care for, I planned to fly in one day, speak, and fly home. Yet deep down, I felt that I needed to stay longer—that Jesus wanted to use me to be available to do more.

As I waited and prayed, my husband had a work trip come up. Then two of my children were invited on vacation with my mom. I easily found someone to help care for my remaining teen and grandmother and was able to attend the entire conference.

The first day after arriving, I understood the purpose of my extended stay. The keynote speaker was sick, and the conference director asked if I could fill in. What could have been a stressful situation for him turned into an easy fix. Jesus inspired me with a keynote message, and afterward, a surprisingly long line of people wanted to talk to me. Many said my words were the encouragement they needed.

My experience at the writers' conference reaffirmed that sometimes, a minor change in plans can lead to a significant impact. So, when you hear His quiet voice guiding you, don't hesitate—walk in it, for Jesus has a purpose in mind. —TRICIA GOYER

FAITH STEP: *Take a moment to pray and listen for Jesus's guidance in your decisions. Trust in His direction, and act on what He is telling you, even if it means changing your plans or stepping out of your comfort zone.*

Saturday, December 12

Jesus grew in wisdom and stature, and in favor with God and man. Luke 2:52 (NIV)

My son Pierce's birthday is December 12, and our family loves how the festive Christmas season maximizes his yearly celebration. When we moved to Florida, we started a tradition of taking Pierce and a carload of buddies to see Christmas lights after his birthday party, a novelty after living in the dimly lit countryside.

One year, we piled a potentially illegal number of giant teenage boys into my minivan to one such neighborhood. My younger son, Isaac, was thrilled to play DJ, blasting Christmas carols on the radio as the carload sang along, while marveling at the amazing lights. My car was brimming with boisterous life. As I caught a glimpse of my firstborn in the rearview mirror, a wave of nostalgia hit me. This perfect baby boy was becoming a man right before my eyes. I got teary-eyed, treasuring the fleeting moments. The very next year, Pierce got his driver's license, and my chauffeur duties came to an end I didn't anticipate.

Surely Mary, the mother of Jesus, had these same thoughts as she watched her heaven-sent bundle of joy who was perfect in every way. The Bible mentions Mary "pondered" the events around the Messiah's birth (Luke 2:19, NIV), and I feel a kinship to her in this introspection. Though Jesus was Savior of the world, he was also Mary's beloved son, whom she raised and treasured like any mama. And like other moms, she probably never fully anticipated how her Son's life would turn out.

Like Mary, I want to love and be present for my children and embrace their futures. I'm also soaking up every moment, perhaps pondering in my heart too. —Isabella Campolattaro

Faith Step: *If you're not already, schedule a regular monthly lunch or special visit with each of your children or grandkids. Treasure the moments!*

Third Sunday of Advent, December 13

When the fullness of time had come, God sent his Son, born of a woman, born under the law, in order to redeem those who were under the law, so that we might receive adoption as children. Galatians 4:4–5 (NRSVUE)

IN OUR MIDWESTERN TOWN OF Paris, Illinois, weather conditions vary. Or maybe I should say swing to extremes—cruelly cold in winter or inhumanely hot in summer. Rarely just right. But every few years we have a phenomenon of nature that resembles diamonds glittering on the grass. That happened this morning. As I gazed at the frost's captivating beauty, I thought of Jesus.

Whether Jesus was born in a barn, a cave, or the ground floor of a house where animals lived (Bible scholars differ), He came in humility. Instead of a nobleman born in a palace, expecting honor, Jesus was born as a helpless infant and became a servant. Jesus's birth was ordinary and lowly. He was a diamond in the dust. Coming to the dust of earth, this sparkling, magnificent manifestation of God willingly and lovingly entered a body created of dust to serve those who would one day reign with Him (2 Timothy 2:12). That thought fills me with joy—shimmering, diamond-like joy.

Despite his humble existence, Jesus didn't demand worship when He walked in the dust of earth. But the brilliant King of kings and Lord of lords (Revelation 17:14) deserves our worship.
—JEANETTE LEVELLIE

FAITH STEP: *If you own anything containing a diamond, hold it in the sunlight until you can see it sparkle. Ponder how Jesus laid aside His glory to come to the dust of earth.*

Monday, December 14

"Peace I leave with you; my peace I give you. I do not give to you as the world gives. Do not let your hearts be troubled and do not be afraid." John 14:27 (NIV)

I WAS AT SCHOOL WHEN my husband texted that my elderly mother called him from her doctor's office. She needed to go to the hospital immediately for a spreading skin infection. He'd pick her up and wanted me to meet them at the emergency department.

Ron and I are the primary caregivers for my parents. This involved attending to their needs during the pandemic, including when my father died from COVID-related complications. I easily get worried now when Mom gets sick, and anxiety rose up in my chest as I drove to the emergency room. I knew I needed to be calm for my mom. I quickly asked Jesus to help me.

We spent several hours in the ER until she went into surgery for the high-risk infection. While I waited in the hospital lounge, one of my sisters texted: "Thanks for being in the ER again. I'm sure it's scary."

Her kind words prompted me to reflect. While I was worried, I realized I wasn't scared. I wasn't alone in these uncertain experiences caring for aging parents. Jesus was with me. His presence calmed me so I could be a peaceful presence for Mom. I took a deep breath of gratitude, thanking my sister for her concern and thanking Jesus for the supernatural way He sustains me in unpredictable situations.
—BRENDA L. YODER

FAITH STEP: *Picture a time when Jesus was with you in an uncertain or frightening moment. Thank Him for His caregiving for you, even if you didn't recognize it then.*

TUESDAY, DECEMBER 15

I can do all this through him who gives me strength. Philippians 4:13 (NIV)

I'M EXCITED. MY OLD COMPUTER needed replacing, so I ordered a new laptop. It arrived five days ago. Today, I'm taking it out of the box.

Why the wait? It's simple. I've avoided starting up this new computer because electronics confound me, though I'm certain that within days I'll be comfortable—even happy—with it. I've procrastinated on accepting what will certainly become a blessing because I allowed fear to outweigh my enthusiasm.

This brings to mind other situations I've postponed or tried to avoid altogether, opportunities Jesus offered that stretched my abilities and made me stronger. Speaking engagements at Christian women's retreats, teaching opportunities at writers' conferences, leadership roles at church.

Jesus lived a life of courage, humility, and love. He faced His challenges—considerably larger than tackling a new computer—with patience and profound wisdom. He gave the Sermon on the Mount (Matthew 5–7) and spoke before thousands with no concern over volume control or eating arrangements. He simply followed God's call on His life and moved forward.

How can I make myself more like Jesus?

I can and will master this new laptop and any other blessing I'm offered. When Jesus tells me I can do all things through Him, I'll believe His promise. Sometimes things will run smoothly. Other times, I might fail, but hopefully I'll become stronger and wiser. Either way, it's a win because it will grow my faith. Now, where's that computer? —HEIDI GAUL

FAITH STEP: *What project do you need to tackle but have been avoiding? Write a list of Bible verses (Philippians 4:13, Joshua 1:9, John 16:33, Isaiah 40:29, 2 Timothy 1:7) on being strong in Jesus, and move forward with His strength.*

WEDNESDAY, DECEMBER 16

Now, dear brothers and sisters, one final thing. Fix your thoughts on what is true, and honorable, and right, and pure, and lovely, and admirable. Think about things that are excellent and worthy of praise. Philippians 4:8 (NLT)

WHEN I WAS SINGLE, I often found myself in conversations with other women about how there were no good men left on the planet, especially tall, dark, holy, and handsome ones. It was enticing to join the crowd and endlessly rehash the details of every bad experience we had with guys we dated. Even as believers, we participated in regular complaint sessions where we attempted to figure out life's challenges—not thinking to invite Jesus into our conversation. Without realizing it, my words became about everything going wrong around me—and even my dissatisfaction with myself became amplified by default. I would renew my mind by talking with Jesus and reading His Word but then be tempted back down in the dumps by the uninspiring conversations I participated in all too often.

Finally fed up with my own negativity, I decided I didn't want to be an upbeat, faith-filled Christian on Sunday and talk like I had no hope in Jesus the rest of the week. It was a daily fight to stay positive but well worth it. —PAMELA TOUSSAINT HOWARD

FAITH STEP: *Has negativity gotten the better of you? Underline Philippians 4:8 in your Bible, then make a list of what is positive in your life. Be the person who finds what is worthy of praise and exits conversations that don't honor Jesus.*

Thursday, December 17

He canceled the record of the charges against us and took it away by nailing it to the cross. Colossians 2:14 (NLT)

YESTERDAY MY HUSBAND RECEIVED A letter saying that a medical bill from thirteen years ago was recently paid. This surprised me. I didn't even know we had any outstanding debt. Over the last 13 years, we've relocated to another state, started other jobs, created new life experiences, including other medical bills acquired and paid off. Nevertheless, the fine print on the statement assured me the erased medical debt has been canceled as "a no-strings-attached gift."

Naturally skeptical, I looked into the charity claiming to have paid off this long-forgotten debt. I learned that this nonprofit national charity dedicated to abolishing medical debt is indeed legitimate and has already paid off billions of dollars in medical debt for millions of families. Amazing! It's wonderful so many have been relieved of the burden of medical debt.

I'm grateful this debt I didn't even know we had has been taken care of. But this type of debt forgiveness is nothing compared to the sin debt relief provided to me by my Lord and Savior Jesus. Jesus is dedicated to abolishing sin debt for humankind. He's legitimate. And He's already paid for the sin of humanity with His life, death, and resurrection. There was a time when I wasn't even aware I had a debt of sin that needed to be forgiven. Now I'm so relieved and grateful to be unburdened by it.

What a blessing that everyone can receive this "no-strings-attached gift." —CASSANDRA TIERSMA

FAITH STEP: *On an envelope from a bill you've already paid, write: "My Debt of Sin." Cross that out and write this: "CANCELED—FORGIVEN BY JESUS. AMEN!"*

Friday, December 18

Jesus answered, "It is written: 'Worship the Lord your God and serve him only.'" Luke 4:8 (NIV)

When scheduling a get-together with another couple, they suggested Sunday morning. My husband and I didn't want them to think we were inflexible. I was still calculating if we attended the early morning service could we meet them in time when our potential hostess said, "Oh, that's right. Church is part of who you are. So, Sunday morning won't work."

We eventually found another day and time, but I've been musing on the statement, "Church is part of who you are." For our family, church is more than a compartment, one of many, in our lives. Just as Christ isn't a "part" of who we are.

If I'm given the opportunity, I'll tell my friend that Jesus is all of who I am. Church is where we gather with others to celebrate Him, learn about Him, listen to His Word and solid teaching, and enjoy our friendships with others who honor Christ with their lives. Church is not part of us. We're part of it.

But Jesus is our all in all. No service or tradition or activity ranks higher than He does, or even on equal par. He is everything. Is church important to us? Yes. But Jesus deserves and has earned all the importance.

If people know me as a church person rather than a Jesus person, have I been failing to communicate Who has my heart and where my deepest loyalties lie? I honor the institution of His Church. I worship Him alone. —Cynthia Ruchti

Faith Step: *On a sheet of paper, draw a pie chart showing the areas of your life. As you look at it, can you see Jesus? Is He your all?*

SATURDAY, DECEMBER 19

"Are not two sparrows sold for a penny? Yet not one of them will fall to the ground outside your Father's care.... So don't be afraid; you are worth more than many sparrows." Matthew 10:29, 31 (NIV)

SNOW SELDOM GRACES THE YARD of my Alabama home. This week, however, a blanket of bright white covered everything. Dozens of birds swarmed my feeders, in search of food to sustain them above the frozen surface. Chickadees and nuthatches, titmice and towhees, juncos and sparrows.

I focused my binoculars on one of the sparrows. His earth tones didn't stand out in a noticeable way, and his patterns weren't bold or impressive. He was small too—a few inches long and probably no heavier than an ounce. He pecked the icy seed, fluttered to a nearby bush, and then returned for a second helping.

So fragile and insignificant. Yet the tiny creature fascinated me, simply because Jesus mentioned sparrows while teaching His disciples. If the Father cares that much for a sparrow, He certainly cares even more for His children.

One good thing about a winter storm in Alabama is the freeze doesn't last long. The temperatures will rise in a couple of days, and the snow will melt away. My feathery friends can still visit my feeders to enjoy a nutritious snack anytime they wish. I'll be looking for them with my binoculars, especially those little sparrows.
—BECKY ALEXANDER

FAITH STEP: *Fill your bird feeder or set a bowl of seed in your yard. Observe the colors, patterns, and sizes of the feathered friends that fly in to eat. Thank Jesus for caring about the birds and for watching over you.*

Fourth Sunday of Advent, December 20

You shall love the LORD your God with all your heart, with all your soul, and with all your strength. Deuteronomy 6:5 (NKJV)

When I tell my friend Bee "I love you," she usually replies, "I love you more." It's a fun little phrase that parents use with their kids too. Or spouses with each other. Hearing it always makes my day.

Although no one has invented a love-o-meter to measure who loves whom more, Jesus's stepfather, Joseph, should get a huge prize for loving God. I've always admired Joseph for his love and respect for his fiancée, Mary. When Joseph discovered that Mary was expecting a baby, he planned to save her from a scandal and break up with her secretly. As I pondered Joseph's kindness, a thought snuck up on my heart: *Joseph loved God more. Even more than Mary.*

When God told Joseph—through an angel in a dream—that the child in Mary's womb was conceived of the Holy Spirit, Joseph didn't balk. He protected Mary from public shame and wed her right away. Then, setting aside his own desires to consummate the marriage, he kept Mary a virgin until after Jesus was born.

God gave Joseph the monumental task of raising His only Son, Jesus. Of teaching Jesus God's ways. Of showing Jesus by example how to be a man who pleased God. I'd say Joseph did a sterling job of his tough assignment from God. Because loving God the most means obeying Him, even when it's hard. Joseph's reward? A stepson, Jesus, who loved God most. —Jeanette Levellie

Faith Step: *Think of the person you love the most. Then tell God, "I love You more." Pray for the ability to love God more than anyone else.*

Monday, December 21

The LORD will guide you always; he will satisfy your needs in a sun-scorched land and will strengthen your frame. You will be like a well-watered garden, like a spring whose waters never fail. Isaiah 58:11 (NIV)

FOR MANY YEARS, I PRIORITIZED everyone else's needs above my own, tending to my husband, our ten children, and my grandmother with little thought for self-care. It felt selfish to take time for myself. This continued until I reached my fifties. The relentless pace took its toll. Exhausted, I struggled with mood swings and was even unable to keep up with my family on vacation. I recognized I needed a drastic change, and I asked Jesus to give me wisdom.

Immediately, I thought of my friend Amber, who had been in a similar situation and had made effective changes in her life. With Amber's guidance, I began integrating simple, healthy choices into my daily routine. I began drinking more water, finding new ways to move my body several times a week, and pausing in the middle of my day to read a devotional and spend time in Jesus's presence. I also started encouraging others with their health habits, knowing I'd do better if others were looking to me as an example.

Soon, my blood pressure lowered, and my energy increased. I'm able to keep up with my kids, and vacations are a lot more enjoyable.

No matter how it seems, caring for ourselves is not selfish but essential, especially when we can join with friends and Jesus in developing healthy habits. —TRICIA GOYER

FAITH STEP: *In what area of your life do you need to prioritize self-care? Make a habit to take time for spiritual refreshment and follow it up with one simple way to care for your body.*

Tuesday, December 22

Set your minds on things above, not on earthly things. Colossians 3:2 (NIV)

My traditional Christmas tizzy was in full force when my daughter Brooke, who was on crutches from ankle surgery five days earlier, asked me to take her to the mall. The mall? Three days before Christmas? I didn't have time and the mall would be a madhouse, but Brooke needed help. She was usually so busy with her teaching career and social life that we had little time together.

Driving there, I agonized about all the things I still had to do. Horns honked as I ran through a yellow light. "Mom, slow down!" Brooke warned. In the store, we perused racks of hoodies, searching for one that would match her boyfriend's eyes, a seemingly impossible task. Leaving without a purchase, I dashed to my car while Brooke waited at the entrance for me to pick her up.

As I unlocked the door, I noticed in horror a hoodie draped over my arm. I sprinted back, edged past the policeman at the door, and dumped the hoodie on the nearest counter. "I didn't know you were a shoplifter, Mom," Brooke said with a grin.

I felt Jesus whisper, *Breathe, Pat. Slow down. Enjoy your daughter.* I breathed. It felt good! We went to another store, and thank you, Jesus, we found the perfect green hoodie. Then, I asked Brooke if she'd like to get a cup of coffee. As we sat together, we reminisced about Christmases past when she'd read the Christmas story aloud to our family. "I'll do it again this year, Mom," she said. "Right after I tell everyone we almost had to visit you in jail!" —Pat Butler Dyson

Faith Step: *Slow down and savor time with your family, at Christmas and always.*

WEDNESDAY, DECEMBER 23

No one is like you, LORD; you are great, and your name is mighty in power. Jeremiah 10:6 (NIV)

OUR DAUGHTER, ERNESTINE, CHRISTMAS PLANNER extraordinaire, did something a little different this year when we gathered as a family at her home for the holiday. Instead of the cute matching pajamas she usually gets us to wear on Christmas morning, she surprised us with Christmas sweatshirts that reflected each of our personalities or interests.

Ernestine's shirt had "Team Holiday Spirit" emblazoned across it. "Tech the Halls" was on the front of my son-in-law Steve's shirt, and my grandson, Reed, had six nutcrackers standing at attention on his, a nod to his love of *The Nutcracker* ballet. Billiard balls and reindeer danced on my son Fred's shirt. And my husband, Hal, sported a shirt proclaiming "Jesus Is the Reason for the Season," one of his favorite sayings during Christmastime.

When Ernestine presented me with my red sweatshirt, I smiled. She had chosen well. Arranged in the shape of a Christmas tree were various names for Jesus: God, Savior, Immanuel, Lamb of God, King of kings, Light of the World, Wonderful Counselor, Son of the Most High, and Redeemer. How I love the names of Jesus! I thought of a few more—Good Shepherd, High Priest, Bread of Life, Alpha and Omega, Everlasting Father, Prince of Peace.

I'll proudly wear my sweatshirt way past Christmas. After all, the mighty names of Jesus transcend all time and place.
—BARBRANDA LUMPKINS WALLS

FAITH STEP: *Write down some of your favorite names for Jesus. Meditate on what those names mean to you.*

Christmas Eve, Thursday, December 24

Every good and perfect gift is from above, coming down from the Father of the heavenly lights, who does not change like shifting shadows. James 1:17 (NIV)

I DUG INTO MY PILE of brightly wrapped presents and pulled out a familiar favorite—a flat, square package from Hallie. Each Christmas Eve, my niece gives everybody in our family a personalized calendar for the new year. The pages are filled with fun photos of the past twelve months, with handwritten reminders on birthdays and anniversaries. My three-year-old granddaughter sat by me as I flipped from beginning to end. "Look how many birthdays are in December, Chloe. There's Mommy, Mamaw, Sadie, Papaw, and Jennifer." Pointing at the twenty-fifth, I said, "There's a very special birthday on Christmas Day too. Baby..." I paused for her to say Jesus.

"Shark!" she squealed. "Baby Shark, doo, doo, doo, doo, doo, doo. Baby Shark, doo, doo, doo, doo, doo, doo." Chloe sang four verses of the popular preschool song and performed the matching hand motions. I laughed and shook my head.

All the birthdays across Hallie's calendar fade when compared to the One written on December 25. Jesus is the good and perfect gift from above, the baby we celebrate and the long-awaited Savior. On the eve of His birthday, I want to acknowledge His humble entry into our lives and pass that message to the next generation.

So this Christmas Eve, I'll lead Chloe in singing "Happy Birthday" to Jesus instead of listening to "Baby Shark" again. —BECKY ALEXANDER

FAITH STEP: *Whether alone or with others, sing "Happy Birthday" to Jesus, our good and perfect gift.*

Christmas Day, Friday, December 25

The true light that gives light to everyone was coming into the world. John 1:9 (NIV)

IN THE DARKNESS OF THE early morning, I press the remote button and one, two, three Christmas trees light up in my kitchen, living room, and hallway, all visible from where I stand. "Let there be light," I whisper into the quiet glow around me, so calming and serene, pushing back the remainder of night as Christmas Day awakens.

"Let there be light," God spoke in the beginning (Genesis 1:3, NIV) as He placed the sun in the sky, forcing darkness to submit to the light. Thousands of years later, He again gave the world light, as prophesied in Isaiah 9:2 (NIV): "The people living in darkness have seen a great light; on those living in the land of deep darkness a light has dawned." The Father placed His Son on an earthly throne, in a lowly manger, bending the darkness and forcing it to bow to the Light of the World.

As I wait in the silence for my family to awaken, I am thankful for the Christmas lights that bring peace into my home, reminding me of *the* Christmas Light who brought salvation to a dark world. "I am the light of the world. Whoever follows me will never walk in darkness, but will have the light of life" (John 8:12, NIV).

God, I humbly bow in the radiance of your mercy and grace and once again accept the greatest gift you offered the world that first Christmas morning: Your Son, Jesus. —KAREN SARGENT

FAITH STEP: *Carve out a time to sit in the glow of Christmas lights or choose a dimly lit, quiet place. Thank Jesus for His life and for the light He shines in your darkness.*

Saturday, December 26

Rejoice greatly, O daughter of Zion; shout, O daughter of Jerusalem: behold, thy King cometh unto thee. Zechariah 9:9 (KJV)

ONE EVENING DURING A CONVERSATION with members of my Bible study group, we started to chat about various Christmas traditions in our families. A woman from Ghana told us about the origins of Boxing Day, which historically was the day after Christmas, when the wealthy would "box up" gifts to give to their servants. She added that today people exchange presents and celebrate on the beach. Another woman told us that she writes letters from Santa and sends them to her now-grown children. Others talked about the joy of opening one gift as a child on Christmas Eve. I shared how my mother whipped up pancakes as a special breakfast treat on Christmas morning. My husband, Hal, continues the pancake tradition because it means something to me and brings me joy.

There are many other things that bring me joy at Christmastime—the festive gatherings with family and friends, the wonderful music, the good cheer, and the amazing generosity of people. I am also happy to pause to think about how Old Testament scriptures foretelling the coming of Jesus were fulfilled in the New Testament. The prophet Zechariah says to rejoice for the coming of our King, and Luke 2:8–10 recounts how an angel brought the good news of Jesus's birth to shepherds, news that would cause great joy for all people.

I, too, rejoice in Jesus's birth and how His coming brings hope and joy to the world. Nothing tops that for me, not even a delicious stack of pancakes on Christmas morning. —BARBRANDA LUMPKINS WALLS

FAITH STEP: *What are some of your favorite Christmas traditions? Thank Jesus for them along with His coming to save humankind.*

Sunday, December 27

Who then will condemn us? No one—for Christ Jesus died for us and was raised to life for us, and he is sitting in the place of honor at God's right hand, pleading for us. Romans 8:34 (NLT)

ONE OF OUR PASTORS STOPPED me in the church foyer after the Sunday service and asked how I was doing. A family matter weighed on me that day, and I was honest with him about feeling discouraged. He listened, and then he offered to pray for me right there and then. His care and intentionality made a lasting impression. I left our conversation committed to doing the same for others.

My burdens seem lighter when I know others are praying for me, and I assume others feel the same. Nowadays, when someone shares a concern via email, I always try to respond with a written prayer. When I have a face-to-face conversation in which someone expresses worry or fear about a situation, I offer to pray on the spot. I ask permission first because it seems the respectful thing to do, especially if the person seems hurried. No one has turned me down, and everyone thanks me. Who doesn't appreciate a dose of encouragement and hope, right?

Knowing others are praying for me makes me feel supported. Knowing Jesus prays for me does the same but exponentially more. My friend, imagine with me the wonder of His interceding nonstop on our behalf. We might not always have the assurance of others' prayers, but we can be confident of this: Jesus is praying for you and me in this moment, always and forever. Now *there's* a reason for encouragement and hope. —GRACE FOX

FAITH STEP: *Connect with a friend today. Ask her for a prayer request and pray on the spot.*

MONDAY, DECEMBER 28

Mary treasured up all these things and pondered them in her heart. Luke 2:19 (NIV)

MY YOUNGEST SON, ADDISON, TURNED 18 today. We are celebrating him. He has grown into a deep thinker. He's smart, kind, funny, and confident. I remember the night I met Addie for the first time. When the doctor placed him on my chest, I felt the weight of his small frame on mine. I buried my face in his tiny neck, and my heart exploded with love. I pondered who this tiny boy would become. I held him close and cried tears of deep love and joy.

When Mary held Jesus for the first time, her heart must have exploded with love too. The excitement must have been palpable when the shepherds arrived at the stable, straining for a glimpse of her son. Angels had heralded His birth. She must have had some sense of awe as she held the Messiah in her arms. Her child would one day be her Savior. She pondered this infant King. She must have found herself in a place of deep love and joy.

Jesus is still inviting me to ponder who He is this Christmas. He is the infant King born to usher in hope to this broken world. He is God with us. He is my Savior. Christmas is a day to celebrate who He is. And in Him, I find the true meaning of deep love and joy.
—SUSANNA FOTH AUGHTMON

FAITH STEP: *Take time to ponder who Jesus is. If you have a nativity, hold Baby Jesus in your hand. How has He transformed your heart and how you live? Praise Him as He ushers you into a place of deep love and joy.*

Tuesday, December 29

An angel of the Lord appeared to Joseph in a dream. "Get up," he said, "take the child and his mother and escape to Egypt. Stay there until I tell you, for Herod is going to search for the child to kill him." So he got up, took the child and his mother during the night and left for Egypt, where he stayed until the death of Herod. Matthew 2:13–15 (NIV)

RECENTLY, A FRIEND OF MINE revealed that Jesus is doing something surprising in her family's story by leading them to relocate a thousand miles away to another state. This move is a refreshment in many ways after a tough season. But she also mentioned the difficulty of being displaced, which I understood from my own family's experience.

Since I heard her news, I've thought of Mary and Joseph's story many generations ago. When an angel told Joseph in the middle of the night to move their young family to a foreign land for safety, they wasted no time obeying.

At this point in the Bible story, I pause for a deep inhale and slow exhale. The enormity of this move was not a few-sentence recap, as we read it today. This displacement altered their lives at fundamental, daily, personal, legacy-shaping levels.

In His earliest years, Jesus learned to rest in His Father's guidance and care when life shifted in new ways. I'm reminded that He knows how to help us navigate those legs of our journeys too.

Jesus does wondrous new things through redirections.
—ERIN KEELEY MARSHALL

FAITH STEP: *How have you felt Jesus's care during a season of displacement? Ask Him to align your spirit with His to hear and obey when big changes come your way.*

WEDNESDAY, DECEMBER 30

He comforts us whenever we suffer. That is why whenever other people suffer, we are able to comfort them by using the same comfort we have received from God. 2 Corinthians 1:4 (GW)

WHY WAS I SO ANXIOUS about lunch with Nan? As a person rarely at a loss for words, I worried about what I would say to my friend, whose husband, Henry, a cherished companion and Sunday school teacher, had recently died.

I was no stranger to grief, having experienced the death of a young son many years before and an infant grandson recently. But I'd never lost a spouse. I asked Jesus to lead me in what to say to be a comfort to Nan. Nan and I settled into the booth at our favorite Greek restaurant and ordered. She looked beautiful in blue, calm and serene as ever. I marveled at her composure, her ability to talk about everyday things when she was in deep grief. We chatted about our children, who had graduated together; church; and an upcoming trip to Niagara Falls she planned to take. When there was a lull in the conversation, I agonized about what to say next. But as He always does, Jesus came to my rescue.

"How did you and Henry meet?" I asked. Nan's eyes sparkled as she told me the story. From then on, we just talked about Henry. I knew from my own losses how precious it is to mention our beloveds' names, to talk about them. I found out so much about Henry I hadn't known. Nan was comforted by reminiscing about Henry, and I was too. —PAT BUTLER DYSON

FAITH STEP: *Ask Jesus to give you the words to say to someone in grief. He will lead you.*

New Year's Eve, Thursday, December 31

> *No, dear brothers and sisters, I have not achieved it, but I focus on this one thing: Forgetting the past and looking forward to what lies ahead.* Philippians 3:13 (NLT)

THE NEIGHBORS PROBABLY THINK WE'RE nuts. At the stroke of midnight, we charge outside and create the biggest racket we can—banging boisterously on pots and pans with wooden spoons, yelling "Happy New Year!" until we are hoarse. Other than this brief din of noise, the winter night air is still and quiet, with the exception of the *pop! pop! pop!* of firecrackers somewhere off in the distance. Exhilarated by our outburst, my husband and I laugh sheepishly at ourselves as we return to the warmth of our home, satisfied that we've done our part to greet the new year.

Although New Year's Eve is typically a festive occasion, it's also a relief for me. A sort of jubilee passage of time to let go of disappointments, heartaches, grief, and struggles of the past year. Goodbye and good riddance to personal failures or setbacks.

I'm relieved and grateful that, thanks to the loving-kindness of Jesus, I don't have to look back over this past year with regret. In spite of my imperfections and shortcomings, Jesus has accepted me unconditionally. I'm not burdened by a debt of faults and flaws, for I know that Jesus, in His grace, has forgiven me (1 John 1:9–10). Assured of His kindness, compassion, and forgiveness, I, too, can forget the past and look forward to what lies ahead in the new year with Jesus. —CASSANDRA TIERSMA

FAITH STEP: *Before going to bed this last night of the old year, make some kind of joyful noise. Tell Jesus, "Happy New Year!" and thank Him for bringing you through another year.*

About the Authors

BECKY ALEXANDER leads tour groups throughout the U.S. and Canada. Currently, she is on assignment with Road Scholar in the Southeast—Charleston, Savannah, Jekyll Island, St. Augustine, and Nashville. Before her travel adventures, she served as a children's minister for twenty-five years. Now, she invests in kids by volunteering year-round for Operation Christmas Child.

Becky's work has appeared in *Mornings with Jesus*, *Pray a Word a Day*, *Angels on Earth*, and other Guideposts publications. She also enjoys writing devotional books with fellow North Alabama authors. Her favorite is *Coffee and Cookies with God: 31 Devotions for December*. If you visit the world's largest Christmas store in Frankenmuth, Michigan, you'll see it on a shelf!

Send Becky a happy message and find all her happy books at happychairbooks.com. Learn about her life with a prosthetic left arm at onesmileonearm.com.

SUSANNA FOTH AUGHTMON is an author/speaker who loves to use humor, scripture, and personal stories to explore how God's grace and truth intersect with our daily lives. Susanna lives in Idaho with her funny, creative husband, marketer and pastor Scott Aughtmon. She is mom to three fantastic young men, Jack, Will, and Addison, who bring her a whole lot of joy. Susanna likes to connect with her readers through her blog, *Confessions of a Tired Supergirl*, and her *Good Things Newsletter*. You can catch up with her on Facebook and her website, sfaughtmon.com.

JEANNIE BLACKMER is an author who lives in Boulder, Colorado, with her husband, Zane, and their chocolate lab, Ody. Her most recent books include *Talking to Jesus: A Fresh Perspective on Prayer* and *MomSense: A Common-Sense Guide to Confident Mothering*. She's been a freelance writer for more than thirty years and has worked in the publishing industry with a variety of authors on more than twenty-five books, most recently writing content for The MomCo (formerly MOPS International), a global ministry for moms. She's passionate about using written words to inspire hope in women and encourage growth in their relationships with Jesus. She loves chocolate (probably too much), scuba diving, beekeeping, a good inspirational story, her family, and being outside as much as possible. Maintaining a sense of humor has helped save her sanity as she now navigates the fun and challenges of relationships with three very adventurous adult sons, one amazing daughter-in-law, and two grand-dogs. Find out more about Jeannie at jeannieblackmer.com.

ISABELLA CAMPOLATTARO feels supremely blessed to maximize her hard-earned wisdom, faith, and experience to encourage others, particularly struggling seekers and outliers of all kinds. A longtime Guideposts contributor, Isabella has been writing for *Mornings with Jesus* since 2018 and is a contributor to *One-Minute Daily Devotions, Pray a Word a Day, Every Day with Jesus, From the Garden, Daily Guideposts for Recovery, God's Comforting Ways*, and several accounts for the *Witnessing Heaven* series. A ghostwriter, editor, blogger, and speaker, Isabella is the author of *Embracing Life: Letting God Determine Your Destiny*, a Bible study aimed at helping people navigate challenging transitions. Holding an MS in public relations and management, Isabella formerly worked in corporate communications. Raised in Maryland, she lives on Florida's Gulf Coast with her two teenage boys and enjoys travel, Bible study, cooking, her sons' sports, writing, reading, running, arts and culture, all things water and beach, music, and pondering.

PAT BUTLER DYSON writes from her home in Beaumont, on the steamy Gulf Coast of Texas, where she anticipates hurricane season with great trepidation. Jeff, her unfailingly patient husband of forty-three years, is a helpful hardware man, both at the family business and around the house. Parents of five and grandparents of nine, Pat and Jeff enjoy spending time at their hideaway on Galveston Island, where they devour seafood from dawn to dusk. Pat, formerly an English and special education teacher, loves to read, cycle, and hike when she's not attending grandkids' ball games. A contributor to Guideposts publications since 1996, Pat likes to laugh and endeavors to find humor in life. She relishes writing for Guideposts' magazine for caregivers, *Strength & Grace*, and for the website prayerideas.org. This is the sixth year Pat has been privileged to share her heart and adventures with *Mornings with Jesus* readers, who can connect with her on her Facebook page.

GWEN FORD FAULKENBERRY is a mother, teacher, newspaper columnist, and podcaster. She lives in the Ozark Mountains on a family ranch accessible only by a rough dirt road. Gwen figures she is the only Southerner who hates sweet tea, but she loves writing and talking about Jesus. When she's not chasing her kids, teaching, or writing, she bakes artisan bread and takes long walks with Jesus and her bulldog, Mugsy.

GRACE FOX has lived on a sailboat with her husband near Vancouver, British Columbia, since 2018. She's the award-winning author of fifteen books, including *Names of God: Living Unafraid* and *Names of God: Knowing Peace*. She's also a popular speaker at women's retreats and conferences, a devotional blogger, and a member of the First 5 writing team (Proverbs 31 Ministries). She inspires hope, courage, and transformation through God's Word—with a dash of adventure. Grace also codirects International Messengers Canada, a missionary sending agency with a staff of nearly three hundred in thirty countries. She and her husband lead short-term mission teams to Eastern Europe annually. Connect with her to learn more about how you can participate. One of Grace's favorite activities is hosting her marina neighbors for meals or come-and-go coffee times with fresh-baked goodies. Her ultimate favorite is, of course, spending time with her fourteen grandkids. Learn more about her and her resources at gracefox.com and fb.com/gracefox.author. Email her at grace@gracefox.com.

HEIDI GAUL lives in a historic home in Oregon's Willamette Valley. Travel, whether around the block or the world, is her passion, and she thrives on new experiences. An ex-Bible Study Fellowship group leader, she's contributed to numerous Guideposts books, including *Mornings with Jesus* (2019–2026 editions). Her entertaining stories are included in thirteen *Chicken Soup for the Soul* anthologies. She enjoys speaking and mentoring at women's retreats and conferences and leading writers' workshops. She'd love to hear from you at heidigaul.com or on Facebook.

TRICIA GOYER is a celebrated writer, speaker, and cohost of the *Daily Bible Podcast*. Author of eighty books, Tricia has won four Golden Scrolls, two Carols, and a Christian Book Award. In addition to Christy and Gold Medallion nominations, her book sales exceed four million copies. Tricia is a highly sought-after conference speaker, sharing on writing, parenting, and purposeful living. Tricia's most recent work, *Breath of Bones*, is a historical steampunk fantasy coauthored with her son Nathan Goyer. Connect with Tricia at triciagoyer.com

PAMELA TOUSSAINT HOWARD is a native New Yorker who lives and works from her home in Atlanta, Georgia. She developed a love for the written word and the confidence to become a writer and editor from her dad, a newspaper printing plant supervisor. Pamela pursued a degree in journalism from Fordham University and while there won a coveted summer internship at *Essence* magazine. She went on to become the magazine's associate editor and subsequently a trade newspaper reporter, nonprofit media spokesperson, and coauthor of eight published books, including *His Rules* (Waterbrook/Penguin Random House). Also a licensed minister, Pamela enjoys opportunities to teach Bible studies and occasionally on local television. She likes to flip fixer-uppers, work on her next novel, and display a mean slice backhand in her weekly tennis matches. Visit Pamela on Facebook and Instagram.

JEANNIE HUGHES finds inspiration for her writings from personal challenges and her love of Jesus. Her works have appeared in *Guideposts*, *Angels on Earth*, *Strength & Grace*, *The Upper Room*, and *Pray a Word a Day*. She earned a bachelor's degree in journalism, which is when her love of writing began. She shares her life with her husband, Roger, in Hurricane, West Virginia. Jeannie feels blessed to have her daughter and her family close by. She has one son who lives in heaven. She is passionate about her work as a hospice volunteer, where she directs the inspirational card ministry. When not writing, she enjoys walking, buying and selling antiques, and designing handmade jewelry.

GLORIA JOYCE is a happy wife and mother of two daughters who has been homeschooling for fourteen years. She has a degree in human resources management and marketing, and while she has used that experience to train many corporate employees and executives, Gloria says training her children in the aspects of education, life, and our Lord has been her most rewarding position.

A new writer and longtime reader of *Guideposts* magazine, Gloria is one of several winners of the 2022 Guideposts Writers Workshop contest. Residing in Pennsylvania with her family, Gloria hopes to inspire others on their own journey with Jesus, using the little moments of life to bring them greater reward in their relationship with Him. In addition to contributing to *Guideposts* and *Mornings with Jesus,* she is working on her first novel.

JEANETTE LEVELLIE wrote this year's *Mornings with Jesus* devotionals and marveled anew at Jesus's kindness (the theme for 2026), favor, and protection as she traveled to Uganda on a mission trip. The Levellies are now down to three cats, with the sudden loss of Jeanette's beloved Fred (formerly Dr. Phibes). Their others, Pokey, Wally, and Princess Di, love the extra attention Jeanette gives them. Her grandson, Daniel, graduated high school, and her granddaughter, Grace, learned to drive. In addition to gaining a new (to her) car this year, Jeanette published her sixth book, *Shock the Clock*, full of ideas for creatives of any kind to manage their time. When she's not writing, Jeanette works jigsaw puzzles with her husband, Kevin, reads novels that help her escape housework, and watches old black-and-white movies. She still works part-time as a church secretary and loves to lead worship, speak at conferences and churches, and read comments from kind readers. Find Jeanette's hopeful musings at jeanettelevellie.com, Facebook, and X.

ERICKA LOYNES first fell in love with words as a child in her hometown of Chicago, performing speeches under the guidance of her mentor, civil rights activist Mamie Till Mobley, the mother of Emmett Till. Seeing her own mother publish works for a Christian company sparked the idea in young Ericka that she, too, could be a writer. Ericka has written in spaces ranging from college journals to corporate training. She contributed to the book *Blessed Is She: The Transforming Prayer Journeys of 30 African American Women* by Victoria Saunders McAfee and is a coauthor of *The Ashes Have Voices: Stories to Motivate, Inspire and Ignite Healing*. As one of the 2018 Guideposts Writers Workshop contest winners, Ericka is honored to have contributed devotionals to *Mornings with Jesus* and *Walking with Jesus*. Ericka is a director of organizational development and design in the transportation industry and a certified Enneagram coach through the Your Enneagram Coach Certification Network. She enjoys encouraging others through transformational coaching, motivational speaking, and inspirational writing. Ericka lives in Memphis with her husband and young adult son.

ERIN KEELEY MARSHALL has enjoyed writing for Guideposts books for many years and counts those opportunities among her favorite career blessings. Her work spans numerous genres as a writer and an editor, and she is published in both fiction and nonfiction. Visit her at erinkeeleymarshall.com, on Facebook at Erin Keeley Marshall, Author, and on Instagram @erinkeeleymarshall.

DIANNE NEAL MATTHEWS has always loved writing, especially when the topic is Jesus. Since she attended her first writers' conference at age forty-seven, she has written, cowritten, or contributed to twenty-five books. Her five daily devotionals include *The One Year Women of the Bible* and *Designed for Devotion: A 365-Day Journey from Genesis to Revelation* (a Selah Award winner). Dianne has also published hundreds of articles, guest blog posts, newspaper features, stories for compilation books, Bible studies, and one poem. Since 2012, her favorite writing project has been sharing her faith journey with some of her favorite people in the world, the wonderful readers of *Mornings with Jesus*. Dianne and her husband, Richard, have been married since 1974 and live in west Tennessee. When she's not writing, Dianne enjoys volunteering at her church, trying new recipes, reading, soaking up nature, and FaceTiming with her three children and five grandchildren, who all live too far away. She loves to connect with readers through her Facebook author page or diannenealmatthews.com.

CLAIRE MCGARRY is so excited to be contributing to *Mornings with Jesus* again. She is a maker of lists, mistakes, brownies, and soups. Dirty laundry is her nemesis as she tries to focus more on creating a loving home rather than cleaning it. She's the author of *Grace in Tension: Discover Peace with Martha and Mary* and the family Lenten devotionals *Abundant Mercy* and *With Our Savior*. A regular contributor to *Living Faith* and catholicmom.com, her freelance work has appeared in various Guideposts publications, *Chicken Soup for the Soul* books, and numerous devotionals. A former lay missionary and founder of MOSAIC of Faith, she endeavors to fish for more people to bring to Jesus through her speaking engagements, women's groups, and writing. She lives in New Hampshire with her husband and three kids, who always keep her laughing and humble. Eager to connect with you, Claire can be found via her Facebook author page and her blog, shiftingmyperspective.com.

RENEE MITCHELL lives in the Arkansas River Valley. She and her husband of forty-two years, Larry, are blessed with two children and four grandchildren. "They are all my greatest loves!" says Renee. An admirer of Guideposts for years, she has picked up a book or magazine and often been encouraged and uplifted. Renee desires to do the same for others by sharing her life stories. She has been published in *Angels on Earth* and *Guideposts* magazines and is excited to be a part of *Mornings with Jesus* this year. Working from home allows her to enjoy hobbies, including painting, reading, and cooking. Spending time with family around the dinner table and watching her grandkids play baseball are also favorite pastimes.

CYNTHIA RUCHTI and her husband, Bill, are among those who read *Mornings with Jesus* together every morning. She's always blessed by what the other authors contribute and appreciates *Mornings with Jesus* readers who reach out to comment about how God used a devotional to draw them nearer to Jesus, comfort them, or encourage them in their faith walk. She writes for other Guideposts projects, including fiction, and continues to create both fiction and nonfiction stories hemmed in hope. Cynthia and her husband consider the heart of Wisconsin home, among cranberry bogs, dairy farms, and hardwood forests. They live within minutes of all three of their children and their seven much-loved grandchildren. Connect with Cynthia at cynthiaruchti.com.

EMILY E. RYAN began writing devotionals in her late twenties with a bimonthly email newsletter she called *Devos by Emo*. It was a short-lived project sent only to friends and family, but it stirred in her an awareness of Jesus that continues to this day. Now, she constantly sees evidence of His kindness and love in her everyday moments as a minister's wife, mother of four, and junior high English teacher, and she loves sharing those moments in *Mornings with Jesus*. A writer and speaker for more than twenty years, Emily has a knack for encouraging women with practical creativity to ditch guilt and embrace grace. Her latest book, *Guilt-Free Quiet Times*, helps women enjoy and deepen their devotional time with Jesus. Emily and her family live in the great state of Texas, but you can avoid the heat and humidity by visiting her online at emilyeryan.com. She loves hearing how God is working in the lives of her readers, and her virtual door is always open.

KAREN SARGENT says she would never write devotions because she didn't feel qualified, but Jesus had different plans. Nearly ten years later, Karen has written for numerous Guideposts publications and has found her home with *Mornings with Jesus*. She is the award-winning author of *Waiting for Butterflies* and two other novels and leads book launches for Christian authors. Karen and her husband enjoy retirement in a beautiful valley in Southeast Missouri. Visit her at karensargent.com.

CASSANDRA TIERSMA is a self-confessed messy-a.n.i.c. (messy, absentminded, normal-ish, imperfect, creative) woman of faith. Her work's been published in multiple newspapers and Guideposts publications. Her book *Come In, Lord, Please Excuse the Mess!*, a guide for spiritual healing and recovery for messy-a.n.i.c. women who struggle with chronic clutter, was a 2023 SCWC Notable

Book Awards finalist. Cassandra's colorful history as a dance and movement specialist, performance artist, writer, speaker, workshop presenter, and ministry leader has shaped her mission to bless and encourage women in their faith so they can become the full expression of who God created them to be. Cassandra lives with her husband, John, in a small mountain town with the best water on earth, where she teaches exercise and aqua fitness classes, plays autoharp, and serves as women's ministry director at the historic stone chapel that is their church home. Connect with Cassandra via email at cassandra@cassandratiersma.com.

BARBRANDA LUMPKINS WALLS is a writer and editor in northern Virginia, where she fights traffic and gets inspiration daily for connecting God's Word to everyday life. Barbranda served as the writer for the book *My Sunday Best: Pearls of Wisdom, Wit, Grace, and Style* and the lead essayist for the photography book *Soul Sanctuary: Images of the African American Worship Experience*. The former newspaper reporter and magazine editor has written for a number of national publications, including *Guideposts*, *Cooking Light*, and *Washingtonian*. Besides contributing to *Mornings with Jesus*, her devotionals can be found in *Voices* (Our Daily Bread Publishing). Barbranda and her husband, Hal, enjoy spending time with friends and family, especially their adult son and daughter, son-in-law, and beloved grandson. Connect with her on Facebook and Instagram @barbl427.

KRISTEN WEST is a communicator who is passionate about inspiring, encouraging, and challenging others in their walk with Christ. With lighthearted humor and refreshing transparency, her writing highlights what God has done in her life so that others may find that same hope in theirs. Besides debuting in *Mornings with Jesus* this year, she is a contributor to other Guideposts publications, including *Pray a Word a Day* and *Signs & Wonders*. Kristen has authored two devotion-style books, *Inspirational Nuggets from Grace and Glory* and *He's an Everyday God*. A blogger and speaker, Kristen publishes short, weekly devotionals on her website that weave candid stories, biblical application, and scriptural insights together as she invites readers to come alongside her and follow Jesus. She and her husband, Anthony, live in the Northwest Georgia area with the Blue Ridge Mountains right in their backyard. Having embarked on blending a family a couple decades ago, they are now empty nesters who revel in their new honeymoon stage. Kristen loves to travel often, visit small coffee shops frequently, and watch the sunrise every morning. Connect with her at kristen-west.com, on Facebook, or on Instagram.

BRENDA L. YODER is a licensed mental health counselor, elementary school counselor, speaker, former teacher, and author of *Uncomplicated: Simple Secrets for a Compelling Life*; *Fledge: Launching Your Kids Without Losing Your Mind*; and *Balance, Busyness, and Not Doing It All*. She has been featured in several Guideposts devotionals, *Chicken Soup for the Soul* books, and *The Washington Post* and is a contributor to *Every Woman's Bible*. She hosts the

Midlife Moms and *Life Beyond the Picket Fence* podcasts. Brenda twice won the Touchstone Award for teachers. Brenda is a former history teacher and lover of antiques, gardens, front-porch rockers, and her grandkids. She and her husband, Ron, raised four children on their family dairy farm in northern Indiana, where they currently raise Bernese mountain dogs, goats, chickens, and cattle and host an Airbnb. They love camping and visiting their grandchildren and adult children throughout the country. She enjoys gardening, decorating, and having good conversations over coffee. Connect with Brenda on Instagram or at brendayoder.com, where she writes about life, faith, and family beyond the storybook image.

Authors and Subjects Index

A

Abraham, 229
   God's covenant with, 74
   God's sheltering presence and, 83
acceptance, 52, 209
accidents, 99, 160, 314. *See also* auto accidents
Advent, Sundays in, 333, 340, 347, 354
advice, being open to, 229. *See also* guidance *entries*
aging, 209, 312, 316, 324
Alexander, Becky, 31, 35, 45, 67, 99, 129, 156, 187, 210, 227, 255, 274, 288, 313, 334, 341, 353, 358
Alzheimer's disease, 16
angels, 144
answered/unanswered prayers, 102, 130, 206, 210, 281, 282
anxiety/anxiousness, 30, 219, 223, 230, 263
Ash Wednesday, traditions associated with, 49
Aughtmon, Susanna Foth, 10, 38, 65, 84, 97, 121, 136, 157, 197, 230, 244, 279, 305, 343, 362
auto accidents, 3, 144, 283, 304

B

baptism, 298
Barnabas of Antioch, 335
beauty
   finding in people, 124
   in land transformations, 169
   in love of Jesus, 136
   revelation of, 117
Bible, 53
   eternal relevance of, 53
   gifts of, 341
   highlighting/annotating passages in, 211
   as living document, 86
   making sense of verses in, 155
birds
   bringing joy, 119
   eagles, 57
   sparrows, 15, 353
Blackmer, Jeannie, 6, 28, 33, 46, 50, 71, 96, 130, 162, 180, 188, 209, 226, 242, 260, 301, 311, 336
blessing(s), 17, 22, 31, 36, 41, 54, 67, 161, 303
   of daily life, 67, 302
   friends as, 260
   nightly, of children, 181
   pregnancy news, 324
blood, of Jesus, 148, 170
body of Christ, 133, 200, 290, 326, 328

burdens
   accepting help and, 182
   during Christmas season, 338
   encouragement during, 335
   handing over to Jesus, 106, 138, 300
   of recurring guilt, 295

C

Campolattaro, Isabella, 4, 37, 58, 79, 112, 137, 177, 200, 215, 245, 295, 308, 321, 335, 346
cancer
   breast, 274
   pancreatic, 166
   survivors of, 108
caring for others, 35, 41, 99, 118, 187, 231, 353
   intentionality and, 361
   intuitively, 243
   rescue animals, 191
   through the Light, 85
cats, 146, 167, 191, 212, 277
cell phones/smartphones
   in quiet places, 284
   time with Jesus *vs.*, 175
challenges (problems), 22, 41, 124, 222, 282, 342, 349, 365
character traits, of Jesus
   modeling, 239, 284
   reflecting, 212
child of God, 280
   sacred seal of, 307
children. *See also* grandchildren; parent-child relationship
   anxious, gentle approach to, 223
   fatherless, shelter for, 180
   grown, time alone with, 346, 356
   joy in, 298
   learning how to be kind, 317
   letting go of, 183, 336
   lost, 311
   nightly blessing of, 181
Christian faith. *See also* faith/faithfulness
   conflicting conditions and, 210
   inconsistent, 219
   nurturing, 84
   teamwork and, 326
   worship and, 123, 352
Christmas Day, 359
Christmas Eve, 358
Christmas traditions, 338, 339, 343, 357, 360
church attendance, 207, 352
comfort
   Bible providing, 122
   from God, 156
   within groups, 164

   Jesus providing, 52, 64, 259, 314
   offering, 191
communication. *See also* God's Word; words
   changing methods of, 194, 251
   effective, 320
   text *vs.* phone, 253
community, 79, 290
   building, 89, 233, 243
   homeschooling, 254
compassion
   for hungry people, 334
   of Jesus, 112, 156
   for others, 109, 110, 222, 259
   of Jesus, 41, 54, 79
   in strained relationship, 172
complaints/complaining, 152, 154, 350, 360
control (being in charge), 196. *See also* intercession/intervention
   natural/man-made events, 98
   relinquishing, 340
   steps toward, 1, 106
   of time, 261
conversations
   with outsiders/unbelievers, 251
   parent-child, 253
   typed *vs.* phone call, 253
couple's therapy, 318
creativity. *See* God's creation/creativity
cross, 89
   building supporting foundation, 90
   as reminder of Jesus's sacrifice, 91
   symbolism at Easter, 89
crucifixion
   Jesus's sacrifice through, 93
   resurrection and, 94
crying
   for past sins/lost souls, 146
   tears of joy, 146

D

dancing, 153, 165
danger
   highway signs about, 143
   Jesus's protection in, 64, 191, 323
darkness
   overcoming, 30
   in seasons of life, 94, 265
death and dying
   of friend/friend's spouse, 259, 364
   Jesus facing, in Holy Week, 88–95
   Jesus's presence during, 160
   resurrection of Jesus and, 94, 95
debt, 73, 179, 351
decluttering, 139
   donating items and, 328
   physical/emotional, 120

AUTHORS AND SUBJECTS INDEX | 375

dedication, 125, 158
denials, 115, 295
depression, 30, 77
   lifelong pattern, causes of, 266
devotion/devotional time, 151, 258, 355
disappointments, 314
discouragement, 242, 361
displacement, 3, 363
distractions, 125, 249
divine love/power, 2, 14, 282
divine power, 282
divorce, 110, 140, 335
dogs, 56, 118, 191, 260, 323
doubt, 201
Down syndrome, 79
Dyson, Pat Butler, 8, 59, 81, 118, 135, 151, 168, 172, 189, 206, 217, 268, 284, 296, 310, 323, 356, 364

E

Easter Sunday, 95
emotional support, from Jesus, 223, 224, 303
empathy, 41, 251
"empty nesters," 54, 263
encouragement, 7, 113, 137, 156, 158, 194
   from Jesus, 164
   needing/providing, 23, 68, 99, 308, 335
   words of, 228, 285
eternal inheritance/life, 114, 132, 234, 312
exercise
   adding to daily routine, 142
   importance of, 337
   inspiration/motivation for, 17, 82, 240
   physical *vs.* spiritual, 38, 125, 240

F

face of Jesus, seeking, 217, 312, 325
failure
   confession of, 37
   fear of, 120
   feeling like a, 112
   finding Jesus's strength in, 140
   forgiveness for, 115
faith/faithfulness, 20, 49, 133, 234
   in Jesus, 20, 90
   of Jesus, 5, 84, 121
Father's Day, 172
Faulkenberry, Gwen Ford, 30, 78, 116, 140, 222, 316
fear(s)
   as barriers, 64
   facing/fighting, 189
   faith *vs.*, 244
   Jesus calming, 262, 291, 323
   Jesus keeping vigil during, 220
feeling(s)
   angry, 266
   of being unimportant, 242
   like a failure, 112
   reordering, 109
   trustworthiness of, 299
financial struggle, 328
fires/wildfires
   meaningful loss in, 46
   rebuilding after, 6, 50
food and meals, 15, 158, 353
forgetfulness, 204, 252
forgiveness, 210
   from Jesus, 115, 184, 278
   of oneself, 295
   of sins, 10, 43
   in strained relationship, 172
Fox, Grace, 7, 34, 57, 82, 111, 143, 166, 179, 191, 204, 225, 269, 281, 293, 326, 361
freedom, 64
   celebration of, 170
   fragility of, 199
   heaven and, 178
friend(s)
   death of, 259
   encouragement from, 7
   of Jesus, 260
friendship, 160
   development of, 31
   failed, resentment over, 295
   with God, 256
   between infants, 303
   Jesus encouraging, 260, 308
   with nonbeliever, 166
   offering, 129
frustration, 56, 60, 222

G

Gaul, Heidi, 15, 41, 64, 85, 104, 124, 134, 167, 178, 193, 208, 234, 250, 270, 302, 328, 339, 349
genealogy, 280, 287
generosity, 134, 184, 283, 288
gentleness, 124, 223
gift(s), 14, 45, 62, 65, 113, 130, 131, 134, 152, 190, 228, 233, 247, 301, 326, 341, 343
giving thanks, 330
God-given skill/talent, 14, 113, 152, 301, 326
God's creation/creativity, 236, 248, 305, 321
God's love, 80, 266
God's message, 122
   Jesus's delivery of, 51
God's plans, 158, 159, 160
God's truth, 327, 342
God's will, 58
God's Word, 230, 341
   comfort in, 122
   eternal relevance of, 53
   letters in the mail and, 39, 194
   navigating life by, 97
   rebuilding through, 50
   studying, 211
Golden Rule, 111

Good Friday, 93
goodness/good deeds, 65, 121, 162, 206
   cleansing of sins and, 241
   in partnership, with God, 256
   prosthetic elbow repair, 67
   toward paralyzed patient, 123
Goyer, Tricia, 5, 39, 80, 100, 147, 160, 195, 240, 264, 275, 289, 309, 331, 345, 355
grandchildren, 11, 27, 29, 34, 189, 248, 297
grandparents, 32, 84, 100, 197, 227, 303, 319
gratitude, 21, 137
   giving thanks and, 330
   for Jesus's unfailing love, 21
   for kindness, 204
   tiredness diminished by, 317
grief/grieving, 14
guidance, from Jesus, 86, 240, 331

H

habits
   bad, recognizing in self, 235
   life transitions and, 74
   worship, 207
healing, 3, 28, 77, 108
   following fall, 337
   laughter and, 96
   lifestyle changes for, 66
   scripture and, 230
   wisdom through, 226
heaven
   joining Jesus's family in, 197
   living with Jesus in, 177
help
   accepting from others, 182, 283
   asking/praying for, 113, 224, 252, 281, 295, 348
   from Jesus, 29, 189, 210, 230
helping others, 29, 67, 75, 99, 109, 198
   effortful, 123
   international ministry/shelter, 180
   marine rescue, 111
   new ways for, 224
   self-help and, 235
   strangers, 144
   student classwork, 222
holy days and holidays
   Advent Sundays, 333, 340, 347, 354
   Ash Wednesday, 49
   Christmas Day, 359
   Christmas Eve, 358
   Easter Sunday, 95
   Good Friday, 93
   Independence Day, 185
   Juneteenth, 170
   Labor Day, 250
   Lent, 49
   Martin Luther King Jr. Day, 19
   Maundy Thursday, 92
   Memorial Day, 145
   Mother's Day, 130

New Year's Day, 1
New Year's Eve, 365
Palm Sunday, 88
President's Day, 47
Thanksgiving Day, 330
Valentine's Day, 45
Veteran's Day, 315
Holy Spirit, 105, 110, 133, 142, 202, 212, 270, 307, 340
   fruit of the, 255
Holy Week, 88–95
home
   finding in Jesus, 167
   rebuilding after wildfire, 6, 50
   welcoming Jesus into, 92
homeschooling, 147, 149, 264, 309
hope/hopefulness
   finding, 188
   in Jesus, 199, 360
   reminders of, 1
   season of, 265
Howard, Pamela Toussaint, 18, 69, 102, 133, 207, 256, 291, 350
Hughes, Jeannie, 14, 43, 77, 117, 150, 152, 190, 216, 277
humility, 12, 133, 284
hymns and songs, 157, 159, 244, 256, 277, 282, 297. *See also* praise music

I

illness, 3, 189, 348. *See also* cancer
Independence Day, 185
influence/influencer, 103, 327
intentionality
   caring for others and, 239
   kindness and, 285
   relationships and, 239
intercession/intervention, by Jesus, 101, 108, 361
interruptions, embracing, 135
invitations, from Jesus, 62, 201
Israelites, 161, 220

J

jealousy, 12, 266
John (Disciple and Apostle), 187, 217, 318
Joseph (stepfather of Jesus), 354, 363
joy/joyfulness, 10. *See also* rejoicing
   childlike, 298
   crying tears of, 146
   of father-child reunion, 311
   Jesus as first love, 218, 318
Joyce, Gloria, 9, 51, 75, 107, 142, 149, 173, 182, 196, 233, 254, 262, 292, 324, 337
judgment, 109, 271, 284
Juneteenth, 170

K

kindness, 13, 15, 34
   addressing truth with, 232
   community building through, 80
   of Jesus, 36, 65, 78, 100, 131, 143, 191, 365

paying-it-forward, 233
receiving/extending, 35, 54, 68, 99, 111, 129, 158, 182, 227, 231
   as reflection of God's love, 80
   in strained relationship, 172
   toward animals, 191
   treating others with, 233
   words of, 163, 204, 227
"Kindness Week," 313

L

Labor Day, 250
Last Supper, 92
letting go, 36, 113, 183, 229, 328, 336, 365
Levellie, Jeanette, 3, 29, 47, 68, 119, 146, 159, 203, 212, 224, 246, 249, 333, 340, 347, 354
life and living
   Jesus orchestrating, 109, 128, 149, 160, 198, 231, 244, 289, 340
   navigating/misnavigating, 48, 72, 97, 304
   rethinking priorities in, 165
   seasons of, 87, 94, 100, 209, 265
   transformation by Jesus, 116, 169, 176, 269
   walking with Jesus through, 188, 196
lifestyle changes, 66, 355
light/Light, 333
   candlelight, 254
   cell-phone flashlights, 282
   from Christmas trees, 259
   dawn bringing, 286
   Jesus's radiance and, 40, 329, 347, 359
   overcoming darkness through, 30, 85, 293, 333
   purifying, 4
   resurrection of Jesus and, 95
   sunrise/sunset and, 173, 329
limitations, possibilities and, 247
listening/listeners, 71, 138, 168, 335
Living Word, Jesus as, 122
loneliness, 129
love/loving
   actions showing, 44, 76
   affirmation/expression of, 24
   brotherly/neighborly, praying for, 185
   facing situations through lens of, 55
   first, adoration of, 218, 318
   for Jesus, 42, 115, 354
   from Jesus, 2, 27, 46, 76, 84, 93, 127, 136, 303, 327, 331, 343, 365
   keepsakes associated with, 46, 76
   unfailing, 25
Loynes, Ericka, 26, 54, 73, 115, 131, 170, 184, 232, 259, 278

M

Marshall, Erin Keeley, 20, 56, 72, 98, 132, 174, 199, 220, 257, 312, 329, 363
Martin Luther King Jr. Day, 19

Mary (mother of Jesus), 187, 340, 346, 354, 362, 363
Matthews, Dianne Neal, 11, 27, 44, 63, 76, 101, 122, 138, 169, 202, 213, 235, 248, 266, 280, 287, 318, 344
Maundy Thursday, 92
McGarry, Claire, 2, 12, 19, 55, 74, 113, 126, 155, 181, 221, 229, 243, 247, 273, 290, 304, 306, 330
meals. *See* food and meals
Memorial Day, 145
memory/memories, 33, 100
   paired with music, 33, 297
menopause, 312, 324
mental health, activities improving, 234
mentoring/mentorship, 158, 162, 211, 239
mercy and grace, 5, 21, 37, 39, 208, 304
miracles, 33
missionary work, 180, 326, 330
Mitchell, Renee, 52, 109, 164, 228, 300
Mother's Day, 130
mountains, moving through faith, 173
music. *See* hymns and songs; praise music

N

names
   changes to, 74
   for Jesus, 11, 357
Naomi (mother-in-law of Ruth), 312
nativity scene, 333
natural world
   God's creativity and, 236
   lenticular clouds, 70
   as metaphor for life, 87
   solar eclipse, 98
   trees, 83, 84, 102
negativity, 31, 350
   filtering out, 227
neighbors/neighborliness, 35, 54, 233
new/newness, anticipation of, 6, 365
New Year's Day, 1
New Year's Eve, 365
Nicodemus, 108

O

Obed (Jesus's ancestor), 312
obedience, 25, 161, 227, 340, 354
opportunities
   avoiding, 349
   to comfort others, 291
   embracing, 147
   to help neighbor, 293
   thankfulness for, 250
   unlimited, 147, 247
oppression, 180, 199

P

pain
   consolation in Jesus, 9
   emotional, 52, 59, 138. *See also* hurt feelings

AUTHORS AND SUBJECTS INDEX | 377

Palm Sunday, 88
parent-child relationship, 18, 22, 52, 79, 106, 107, 126, 127, 136, 149, 168, 172, 221, 308, 309, 311
   conversations and, 253
   homeschooling and, 264
   praying/worship and, 186
   strengthening, 240
parenthood/parenting
   anticipating, 54
   expectations, 331
   Jesus's love and, 303
   making tough decisions, 264
   priorities in, 186
partnership, with God, 256
passion, 85
Passover feast, 170
patience, 18, 51
   in developing friendship, 166
   enduring, of Jesus, 331
   listening with, 335
Paul (Apostle), 162, 247, 275, 335
paying-it-forward, 233, 288
peace/peacefulness
   examples of, 19, 272
   of God, 276
   Jesus providing, 348
   resilience and, 80
   when praying, 273
perfection, 112, 133
persecution, 94
perseverance, 152, 188
   reward for, 82
personal growth, 39, 188
Peter (Disciple and Apostle), 55, 61, 115, 295
playlists, 17, 157, 214
praise music, 14, 153, 157
   consolation for pain in, 9
   as exercise inspiration, 17
   gospel choir concert, 282
   memories paired with, 214
   off-key singing, remedy for, 277
prayer partners, 7, 335
prayer requests, 7, 242, 335, 361
prayers/praying. *See also* answered/unanswered prayer
   to age gracefully, 209
   breathing focus in, 273
   for brotherly love and affection, 185
   distractions hurting, 249
   for friends, 23
   fulfillment through, 339
   for inspiration, 40
   Jesus's advice on, 86
   for Jesus's help, 281
   learning from early age, 186
   for lost souls, 91
   in manner of texting, 253
   for others, 193, 291, 361
   repetitive, 71
   for self-discipline, 126
   self-evaluation and, 126
   for spirit forgiveness, 104
   through rosary beads, 196
   with votive candles, 254
   to welcome youth ministry group, 183
presence, of Jesus, 273
   during diagnostic procedure, 274
   in time of sorrow, 160
President's Day, 47
pride, succumbing to, 182
problem-solving, 48
   creative, 248
   intermittent issues, 219
   with Jesus's help, 138
   viewed through lens of love, 55
procrastination, 151
Promised Land, 161
promises, of Jesus
   everlasting, 15, 20
   meditating on, 266
   wen facing new situations, 349
prompts, from Jesus, 193, 198, 256, 285, 288, 291, 296
prosthetic joints/limbs, 67, 156
protection, Jesus providing, 64, 191, 323

Q

questions, answering, 115
quiet time, with Jesus, 332, 338

R

reconciliation, 63
redemption, 15, 270, 279, 289
redirection, 363
regret(s), 115, 138, 186
rejoicing, 159, 166
relationship(s). *See also* parent-child relationship
   building, 166, 239
   family trees and, 280
   hurt feelings in, 104, 295
   with Jesus, 62, 78, 103. *See also* trust, in Jesus
   Jesus as first love, 218, 318
   within marriage, 69
   negativity about, 350
relocation, 122, 293, 351, 363
remorse, 295
repentance, 49
repentance of sin, 215
rescue/rescuing
   animals, 191
   by Jesus, 208
   at sea, 111
resentment, 295
rest, in midst of turmoil. *See* calm/calmness; peace/peacefulness; quiet time, with Jesus
resurrection, of Jesus, 94, 95
reunion, father-child, 311
revelations, 117
revenge, seeking, 278
routine(s)
   change in, 147
   hurried, 203

Ruchti, Cynthia, 21, 49, 62, 86, 103, 141, 192, 201, 219, 238, 252, 272, 286, 299, 320, 332, 342, 352
Ryan, Emily E., 13, 48, 88–95, 123, 153, 183, 214, 236, 251, 267, 283, 298, 314

S

sacredness, 297
sacrifice/sacrificial act, of Jesus, 21, 45, 73, 91, 93, 150, 170, 178, 268, 270, 280
sadness, 106, 109, 314
safety
   in Jesus, 138, 183
   of loved ones, lighting candles for, 254
   when driving with Jesus, 225
salvation, 131, 132, 170, 173, 269, 276, 298
Samuel, 195
Sargent, Karen, 25, 42, 61, 87, 108, 120, 144, 161, 185, 211, 218, 237, 253, 271, 285, 303, 319, 359
Saul (king), 195
seasons of life, 87, 94, 100, 209, 265
self-care, 126, 355
self-discipline, 126
self-esteem, lack of, 266
self-evaluation, 235
self-pity, 3
selfishness, 244, 355
senses
   God-given, 33
   touchlessness and, 192
separation anxiety, 223
Sermon on the Mount, 349
shame, cleansing of, 202, 289
sharing, 34
   of confidences, regret over, 138
   goodness and, 121
   of joy, through acts of kindness, 237
   news of God's forgiveness in Jesus, 184
   presence of family, 127
   prompts from Jesus about, 296
sheltering/sustaining, 180
   presence of God/Jesus and, 83
shepherd, Jesus as, 146
Simon Peter. *See* Peter (Disciple and Apostle)
sin(s), 79
   confessing, 43, 241
   crying for past sins, 146
   exposed via text, 271
   forgiveness of, 10, 212, 215, 270, 351
   freedom from, 170
   Jesus as payment for, 268
   removing stain of, 148
   repentance over, 215
   shattered glass metaphor, 270
   spiritual, 43

spiritual cleansing of, 202, 241, 270
spiritual rebirth and, 108
unconfessed, 4
universal nature of, 287
sleeplessness, 230, 286
solitude, need for, 319, 332
sorrow. *See* sadness
soul
  nourishment of, 68, 122, 193
  passion defining/guiding, 85
spiritual cleansing, of sins, 202, 241, 270
spiritual exercise
  benefits of, 38
  distractions and, 125
spiritual rebirth/rejuvenation, 66, 108, 181, 240, 306
steadfastness, 322
  of Jesus, 5, 39, 100
strangers, 118, 144, 168, 198, 288, 325
strength, 17
  of Jesus, 38, 140, 208, 275, 294
  renewal of, 57
stress
  end of school-year, 128
  in homeschooling experience, 264
  Jesus relieving, 56, 263
  nature's seasons and, 265
stubbornness, 229
success, measuring, 161
Sundays
  in Advent, 333, 340, 347, 354
  Easter, 95
  Palm, 88
sunrise/sunset, 173, 286. *See also* dawn
  beauty in, 329
support
  Jesus providing, 56
  offering, to distressed woman, 291
  online fundraising for school trip, 290
surgical recovery
  after mishap during operation, 226
  joyfulness in, 119

T

talking face-to-face
  for important messages, 271
  joy in, 217
"The Tapestry Room" (poem by Corrie ten Boom), 94
teachable moments, 17, 20
teachings, of Jesus, 25, 27
heeding, 143, 227
studying, 234
tears, of joy, 146
temptation
  avoiding, 82, 245
  boundary setting and, 238
texting, 175, 217, 229, 253
  brevity of messages in, 253
  prayer requests via, 242
thankfulness/thanksgiving, 64, 141, 149, 190, 191, 250, 254, 281, 323
Thanksgiving Day, 330
Thomas (Disciple), 201
thoughts
  good. *See* good thoughts
  transformative, 266
  unholy, purging, 205
  on who Jesus is, 362
Tiersma, Cassandra, 17, 40, 60, 70, 114, 148, 163, 176, 205, 241, 258, 276, 322, 351, 365
time alone, 319, 332
  with grown children, 346, 356
time-of-life changes, 312, 324
time with Jesus, 203, 234, 258, 273, 332, 338
  importance of, 306
  journaling Bible and, 211
  smartphone interaction competing with, 175
to-do lists, 23, 57, 109, 125, 175, 274, 276
tolerance, 37
touch/touchlessness, 192, 207
transformation(s)
  in approach to public speaking, 275
  conformation *vs.*, 58
  by Jesus, 116, 169, 176, 289, 325
  of neglected graves, 150
  of unusable land, 169
transition, Jesus filling void during, 221
trees, 83, 84, 102
trust
  in God, 9, 64
  in Jesus, 16, 20, 47, 140, 141, 168, 234, 289, 309, 345
  in one's own feelings, 299
  pledge of, 328
truth, words conveying, 232, 239, 327

U

unconditional love, of Jesus, 266

V

Valentine's Day, 45
Veteran's Day, 315
vigil, keeping, 220
voice, of Jesus, 272, 304, 312

W

walking with Jesus, 25, 88, 90, 246
Walls, Barbranda Lumpkins, 16, 24, 53, 66, 105, 125, 139, 154, 175, 198, 231, 261, 282, 307, 325, 338, 357, 360
weakness, Jesus's power and, 208, 294
well-being, physical *vs.* spiritual, 294
West, Kristen, 23, 32, 110, 127, 171, 194, 239, 294
wickedness, fight against, 180
widows, 31, 179, 180, 206
wisdom, 22, 193, 226
wonder, 177
words, 305, 320, 327, 330
  of encouragement, 228, 285
  of healing, in scripture, 230
  hurtful, 271, 327
  of kindness, 163, 204, 227
  life-giving *vs.* empty, 320
work/working
  in Jesus's name, 250
  workload fatigue, 57
worry(ies), 36, 196, 230. *See also* anxiety/anxiousness
  Jesus's cautions against, 310
  lifelong pattern, causes of, 266
  over diagnostic procedure, 274
  over infection in elderly parent, 348
  release of, 258, 262
worship services, 157, 207
worthiness, 15, 131, 266, 268, 279
wounds
  emotional, 52, 59, 138
  generational, 199
writing. *See* authors/authoring

Y

Yoder, Brenda L., 1, 22, 36, 83, 106, 128, 145, 158, 165, 186, 223, 263, 265, 297, 315, 317, 327, 348
yoga practice, 273

Z

Zacchaeus, 267, 308
Zechariah (prophet), 360

Acknowledgments

Every attempt has been made to credit the sources of copyrighted material used in this book. If any such acknowledgment has been inadvertently omitted or miscredited, receipt of such information would be appreciated.

Scripture quotations marked (AMP) are taken from the *Amplified Bible*. Copyright © 2015 by The Lockman Foundation, La Habra, California. All rights reserved.

Scripture quotations marked (AMPC) are taken from the *Amplified Bible, Classic Edition*. Copyright © 1954, 1958, 1962, 1964, 1965, 1987 by The Lockman Foundation.

Scripture quotations marked (CEB) are taken from the *Common English Bible*. Copyright © 2011 by Common English Bible.

Scripture quotations marked (CEV) are taken from *Holy Bible: Contemporary English Version*. Copyright © 1995 by American Bible Society.

Scripture quotations marked (CSB) are taken from *The Christian Standard Bible*. Copyright © 2017 by Holman Bible Publishers. Used by permission.

Scripture quotations marked (ESV) are taken from the *Holy Bible, English Standard Version*. Copyright © 2001 by Crossway Bibles, a division of Good News Publishers. Used by permission. All rights reserved.

Scripture quotations marked (GNT) are taken from the *Holy Bible, Good News Translation*. Copyright © 1992 by American Bible Society.

Scripture quotations marked (GW) are taken from *God's Word Translation*. Copyright © 1995 by God's Word to the Nations. Used by permission of Baker Publishing Group.

Scripture quotations marked (HCSB) are taken from the *Holman Christian Standard Bible*. Copyright © 1999, 2000, 2002, 2003, 2009 by Holman Bible Publishers, Nashville, Tennessee. All rights reserved.

Scripture quotations marked (KJV) are taken from the *King James Version of the Bible*.

Scripture quotations marked (NOG) are taken from *The Names of God Bible*. Copyright © 2011 by Baker Publishing Group.

Scripture quotations marked (NABRE) are taken from the *New American Bible*, revised edition, © 2010, 1991, 1986, 1970 Confraternity of Christian Doctrine, Inc., Washington, DC. All rights reserved.

Scripture quotations marked (NASB and NASB1995) are taken from the *New American Standard Bible*. Copyright © 1960, 1962, 1963, 1968, 1971, 1972, 1973, 1975, 1977, 1995 by The Lockman Foundation, La Habra, California. Used by permission.

Scripture quotations marked (NCV) are taken from the *New Century Version*. Copyright © 2005 by Thomas Nelson.

Scripture quotations marked (NIV) are taken from *The Holy Bible, New International Version*. Copyright © 1973, 1978, 1984, 2011 by Biblica, Inc. Used by permission of Zondervan. All rights reserved worldwide. zondervan.com

Scripture quotations marked (NKJV) are taken from *The Holy Bible, New King James Version*. Copyright © 1982 by Thomas Nelson.

Scripture quotations marked (NLT) are taken from the *Holy Bible, New Living Translation*. Copyright © 1996, 2004, 2007 by Tyndale House Foundation. Used by permission of Tyndale House Publishers Inc., Carol Stream, Illinois. All rights reserved.

Scripture quotations marked (NRSVUE) are taken from the *New Revised Standard Version, Updated Edition*. Copyright © 2021 by the National Council of Churches of Christ in the United States of America. Used by permission. All rights reserved worldwide.

Scripture quotations marked (TLB) are taken from *The Living Bible*. Copyright © 1971 by Tyndale House Publishers, Inc., Carol Stream, Illinois. All rights reserved.

Scripture quotations marked (WEB) are taken from The World English Bible™.

A NOTE FROM THE EDITORS

We hope you enjoyed *Mornings with Jesus 2026*, published by Guideposts. For over 75 years, Guideposts, a nonprofit organization, has been driven by a vision of a world filled with hope. We aspire to be the voice of a trusted friend, a friend who makes you feel more hopeful and connected.

By making a purchase from Guideposts, you join our community in touching millions of lives, inspiring them to believe that all things are possible through faith, hope, and prayer. Your continued support allows us to provide uplifting resources to those in need. Whether through our communities, websites, apps, or publications, we inspire our audiences, bring them together, and comfort, uplift, entertain, and guide them. Visit us at guideposts.org to learn more.

We would love to hear from you. Write us at Guideposts, P.O. Box 5815, Harlan, Iowa 51593, or call us at (800) 932-2145. Did you love *Mornings with Jesus 2026*? Leave a review for this product on guideposts.org/shop. Your feedback helps others in our community find relevant products.

Find inspiration, find faith, find Guideposts.

Shop our best sellers and favorites at
guideposts.org/shop

Or scan the QR code to go directly to our Shop